Tenement Press 10, MMXXIII
ISBN 978-1-7393851-1-8

I0433867

Last Movies
Stanley Schtinter

Wade more than a dozen pages into *Last Movies* and these
connections start to reveal themselves like constellations on
a cloudless night.
　—Ryan Gilbey, *The Guardian*

In *Last Movies*, artist-curator Stanley Schtinter turns the idea,
that film captures the dead and turns them into ghosts, on its
head. Rather than focus on deceased people onscreen, he finds
out (or, occasionally, makes an informed guess at) what was
the last film that various important twentieth-century political
and cultural figures had watched, bringing together a potted
history of the medium itself.
　—Juliet Jacques, *ArtReview*

A highbrow Wikipedia hole full of fascinating coincidences.
　—Clive Martin, *Plaster Magazine*

All films are haunted, both by the immortal light of the sooner-or-later dead that they curate, and by the filaments of meaning they extrude into unscripted human lives. *Last Movies* is an unexpectedly revealing catalogue of final interchanges between imminent ghosts and counterpart electric spectres on the screen's far side. Profound and riveting, Schtinter's graveyard perspective offers up a rich and startlingly novel view of cinema, angled through cemetery gates before the closing credits.
A remarkable accomplishment.
　—Alan Moore

Very strange, and deeply thought-provoking.
　—Laura Mulvey

Here [is] the endgame of endgames. A commendably perverse demonstration of how it is possible for something to be assimilated, by way of rumour and manipulated history, without being experienced.
　—Iain Sinclair, *Sight and Sound*

A scintillating labyrinth of synchronicities, where Schtinter's meticulous research and encyclopaedic knowledge are as impressive as his intriguing speculations. Essential reading for film buffs, conspiracy theorists and high-end pub quizzers everywhere.
　—John Smith

The more details Schtinter's *Last Movies* uncovers the more mysterious his project becomes. What are we meant to understand from learning that Franz Kafka's last movie was *The Kid* (1921) by Charlie Chaplin? Or that Chaplin started casting it just one week after the death of his son Norman? Or that Norman's tombstone read only 'The Little Mouse'? Or that, after Chaplin himself died in 1977 (his last movie was Kubrick's *Barry Lyndon*), his coffin was dug up from a Lausanne cemetery by two refugees and held to ransom? Perhaps it's the freedom to speculate, the unanswer-ability of those questions, that is its own reward. Boldface names, lurid details, strange connection. Schtinter, always eager to deflate pomposity, likens his project to an "occult version of *OK!* magazine." I myself can't help wondering: what if we were to watch every movie as if it were our last?
　—Sukhdev Sandhu, *Prospect*

And what is a society that values nothing more than survival?
—Giorgio Agamben

Erika Balsom, Killing Time   19–23

(*In order of disappearance*)

Franz Kafka (d.1924),   30–41
The Kid (Charlie Chaplin, 1921), 53m

F.W. Murnau (d.1931)   42–49
Tabu: A Story of the South Seas (F. W. Murnau, 1931), 86m

John Dillinger (d.1934)   50–62
Manhattan Melodrama (W.S. Van Dyke & George Cukor,
1934), 99m

Anne Frank (d.1945)   64–70
The Lighthouse by the Sea (Malcolm St. Clair, 1924), 70m

Charlie Parker (d.1955)   72–76
Stage Show (Dorsey Brothers, 1955, *with* Count Basie,
Kate Smith, & Charlie Manna), 30m

Boris Vian (d.1959)   78–85
I Spit on Your Graves (Michel Gast, 1959), 5m (of 110m)

John F. Kennedy (d.1963)   86–110
From Russia with Love (Terrence Young, 1963), 115m

Lee Harvey Oswald (d.1963)   (*see John F. Kennedy*)
War Is Hell (Burt Topper, 1961), 15m (of 81m)

Pier Paolo Pasolini (d.1975)   112–121
Edipo re / Oedipus Rex (Pier Paolo Pasolini, 1967), 104m

Bernard Herrmann (d.1975)   122–125
God Told Me To (Larry Cohen, 1976), 91m

Phil Ochs (d.1976)   126–134
One Flew Over the Cuckoo's Nest (Milos Forman,
1975), 133m

Charlie Chaplin (d.1977)   (see Franz Kafka)
Barry Lyndon (Stanley Kubrick, 1975), 203m

Elvis Presley (d.1977)   136–156
The Spy Who Loved Me (Lewis Gilbert, 1977), 125m

    INTERMISSION   157–160
    (Bill Drummond)

Ian Curtis (d.1980)   162–172
Cape Fear (J. Lee Thompson, 1962), 106m

Peter Sellers (d.1980)   174–179
Brannigan (Douglas Hickox, 1975), 111m

Rainer Werner Fassbinder (d.1982)   180–195
20,000 Years in Sing Sing (Michael Curtiz, 1932), 99m

George Cukor (d.1983)   196–199
The Graduate (Mike Nichols, 1967), 106m

Olof Palme (d.1986)   200–205
Bröderna Mozart / The Mozart Brothers (Suzanne Osten,
1986), 109m

Sergio Leone (d.1989)   206–210
I Want to Live! (Robert Wise, 1958), 30m (of 120m)

Bruce Chatwin (d.1989)   212–216
Herdsmen of the Sun (Werner Herzog, 1989), 50m

Bette Davis (d.1989)   218–224
Waterloo Bridge (James Whale, 1931), 81m

Kurt Cobain (d.1994)   226–239
The Piano (Jane Campion, 1993), 121m

Heaven's Gate   240–251
(39 crew-members of the 'Angelish-Alien' sect, d.1997)
Secrets & Lies (Mike Leigh, 1996), 142m

Stanley Kubrick (d.1999)   (*see Franz Kafka*)
Eyes Wide Shut, Trailer (Stanley Kubrick, 1999), 59s

Spalding Gray (d.2004)   252–256
Big Fish (Tim Burton, 2003), 125m

Steve Jobs (d.2011)   256–263
Remember the Titans (Boaz Yakin, 2000), 113m

Bob Rafelson (d.2022)   264–273
The Old Man (Jonathan E. Steinberg, 2022), 47–64m,
Episodic

Jean-Luc Godard (d.2022)   274–277
Film annonce du film Drôles de Guerres (1er tournage) /
Announcement of the Film 'Phony Wars' (1st shoot)
(Jean-Luc Godard, 2023), 20m

Nicole Brenez, Last Instants / Drôles de Guerres   279–291
Translated from the French by
Clodagh Kinsella

(An iterative index of sources and works cited.)   293–310
LIBERATION (*grol*) THROUGH HEARING (*thos*)   315
IN THE INTERMEDIATE STATE (*bardo*)
(Acknowledgments & dedications.)   317

Last Movies is a dedication to the absence of choice, to chance. If there is any bias in the cast-list it is a bias coded into the telling of the first century of cinema (that I parasitise); the result, a forensic of the last earthly dance of a star, and the pause they took (if indeed they did) to catch a movie.

    S.S.

*For all of the dead
and the not dead yet
watching*

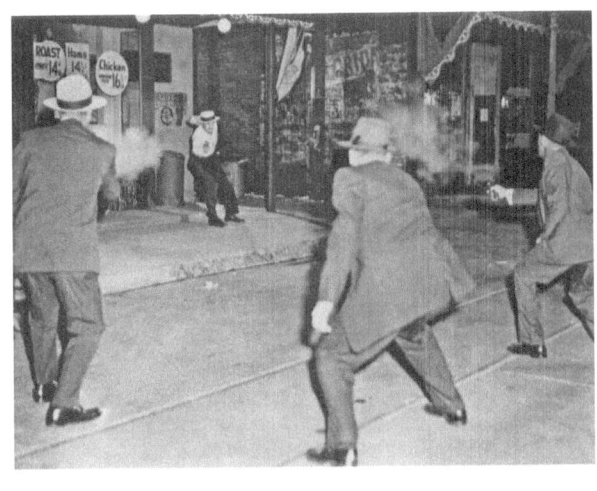

The preceding page shows a re-enactment of the death of John Dillinger, a creative collaboration between Warner Bros. and the Federal Bureau of Investigation, wherein three special agents engage an anonymous actor in a shoot-out (*date unknown*, National Archives and Records Administration, USA).

Erika Balsom, Killing Time

As artist-curator Stanley Schtinter puts it, *Last Movies* allows us to '*see what those who no longer see last saw.*' This marathon screening of the final films watched by famous individuals brings the medium of cinema into contact with the matter of death.* Between the two, there is not the shock of juxtaposition but the bleed of likeness: they curl cosily around one another like the intimate friends they are. There is the cliché, as familiar as it is unverifiable, that when your time is up your whole life flashes before your eyes, like a film experienced in a dilated instant. (Does this mean these last movies are in fact penultimate movies?) And then there are the many evocations of the cinema as a modern memento mori: it is 'death at work' (Cocteau), 'change mummified' (Bazin), 'death twenty-four times a second' (Mulvey). The medium brings us face to face with finitude, not because the stories it tells about death are particularly compelling but because it captures ephemeral traces of life and re-animates them forever after, infusing the petrified past with spectral vitality. In 1929, Jean Epstein ventured that 'death makes its promises via the cinematograph.' Schtinter's epic undertaking yokes these vows to the moment of their fulfilment.

Normally, the flickering screen only quietly whispers vanitas vanitatum. This murmur likely turned into a roar for Bette Davis when, in 1989, aged 81 and sick with cancer, the star watched the last movie of her life, one of her own: James Whale's *Waterloo Bridge* (1931). In it, she has only a small role, sixth billing in the credits. Yet she is nevertheless there, her youthful self is preserved across the decades like an insect in amber. Among Schtinter's selections, Davis's last movie stands out for its apparent deliberateness. It is as if the ailing star sought to at once defeat and welcome death by revisiting one of her earliest on-screen appearances. Of course, it might have been just another professional obligation: Davis was receiving an award from the San Sebastian International Film Festival, where a Whale retrospective was also taking place. She probably had to be there, like it or not. Who knows if she knew it was to be her final visit to the cinema. But wait—*was Davis even at the projection?* It is possible, probable even, but the historical record cannot confirm it.

---

* Balsom's programme notes were first written for Schtinter's programme, 'Towards the Last Movies,' a dry run for the project held at the Batalha Centro de Cinema (Porto, Portugal), day and night, April 29 to April 30, 2023. An unabridged iteration of the project, 'Last Movies,' was premiered across three venues in New York City (NY, USA)—Light Industry, Spectacle, and the Nitehawk—on November 4 through November 5, 2023.

Last movies tend to be like that: they aren't chosen in the way that a last meal would be chosen by a prisoner awaiting execution. And depending on the circumstances, their lastness can throw up some resistance to verification, plunging curator and audience into the pleasures and perils of speculation. Death is a certainty—but the moment of its arrival, for most at least, is anything but. A last movie is just another unremarkable beat in the rhythm of life until the reaper visits. Then a sea-change occurs; retroactively, the movie becomes a crepuscular artefact it had never before been, coloured by the shadow of death's imminent approach, bound forever to the end of an illustrious life. Even though Schtinter includes deaths that were planned (the Heaven's Gate cult) and deaths that were perhaps somewhat anticipated (Bruce Chatwin), his endeavour is a macabre tribute to the curiosity and horror that this radical contingency inspires. As the many hours of the programme pile up, questions might pop into the viewer's mind: is the lastness of these last movies significant in any way or is it a mere fact? Is it but a plausible fiction? What do these films reveal about the lives to which they belong? Perhaps something; likely nothing. Each title sparks a desire for meaning—each last movie is an incitement to discourse, a story to be told—and each equally allows the threat of meaninglessness to run riot.

Last Movies brings together its selections by the force of an external event, one which bears not on the films themselves but on little-known details of their exhibition histories, and then orders them not according to any curatorial vision but by date of disappearance. It abandons all those calcified criteria most frequently used to organise cinema programmes: period, nation, genre, director, star, theme. Nothing internal to these films motivates their inclusion, their 'quality' least of all. Although Schtinter can choose a death to research, the title to be shown is dictated by history. This is all to say that *Last Movies* embraces chance, an avant-garde strategy its orchestrator has been known to marshal in previous undertakings.

And so it should be for a programme about death.

The tenacity of the 'life review' flashback as a trope in fiction films could be attributed to the fact that people who have had near-death experiences claim to have encountered the phenomenon. It is more likely that this convention endures because it satisfies a reassuring fantasy: that life will ultimately attain coherence. The fantasy of that 'last movie' is undone by the reality of Schtinter's *Last Movies*. They are often random and in large part unchosen; they throw significance into crisis and demand acquiescence to externality. They are, in other words, like death itself.

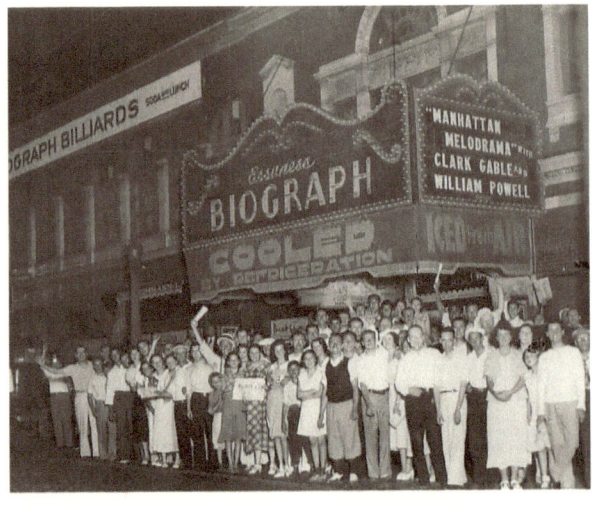

Last Movies

(a book of endings.)

In the morning they throw men to the lions and the bears;
at noon, they throw them to the spectators.
　　—Seneca the Younger

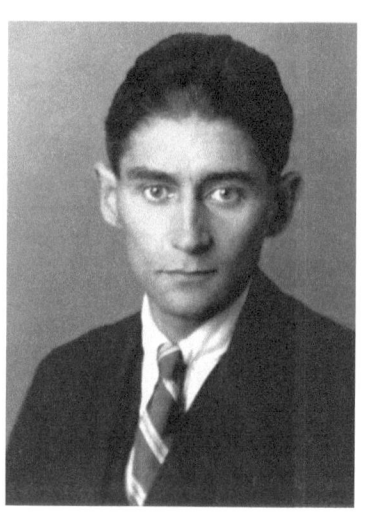

Franz Kafka (d.1924)
The Kid (Charlie Chaplin, 1921), 68m

Charlie Chaplin (d.1977)
Barry Lyndon (Stanley Kubrick, 1975), 203m

Stanley Kubrick (d.1999)
Eyes Wide Shut (Stanley Kubrick, 1999), Trailer, 59s

I think we ought to read only the kind of books that wound or stab us. If the book we're reading doesn't wake us up with a blow to the head, what are we reading for? So that it will make us happy? ...Good Lord, we would be happy precisely if we had no books.
    —Franz Kafka, 1904, in a letter to
    Oskar Pollack

¶ For Kafka, literacy was a mixed blessing. To write down the story is not necessarily to preserve it, but to lose it.

At the picture-palace the writer witnessed a medium pre-literate, a migrant-medium of visionary universalism washing over the dusk-chorus of pirates and gypsies, the spent labourers who built it. Though *close* to the old fire-screen, this pertinacious cinema trapped the ghosts and unified the audience's perception of them (Kafka's death broadly aligning with the death of the silent movie is no accident to the broad historian, says Theodor Adorno in a letter to Walter Benjamin). The trope of distant tribespeople, or fire-men, instinctively resisting the camera in 'first contact' with it—fearing that the snap of the photograph would break or steal some essential part of them—is oft-repeated without vindication. But they were, of course, right. They were *the last*, after all. From man's attempts to influence the hunt to man's insistence on controlling the light, the black magic of the black mirror has smartened and strengthened, tethered as audiences have become to the technologies that in recording experience precisely *remove it.**

If books were 'to wound,' movies for Kafka meant healing reprieve from 'the eternally provisional... the deathly sense of the monotonous passing of the days.' Trips to the kino were filed alongside the coffeehouses and bordellos: demonic certainly, but not that deep. He liked 'Schundfilms'—an early German word for trashy B-movies, and describes knowing screening schedules by heart whether or not he went to see what was on. He devoured the modern pleasure of riding Prague's electric trams, as the billboards and posters advertising the latest releases swept by. Accordingly, his last word on any film is an acknowledgement and not a review (by this time distant from any sociality as the illness that would deny him first of speech and then of life advanced). Illustrating the impoverishment of Berlin in 1923 by the arrival two-years late of *The Kid*, the adolescent coming-of-age for the medium Kafka had witnessed the inception of. 'It has been playing here for months...'

Prague's first permanent cinema was the Blue Pike, established in the city's Old Town in 1907 by Viktor Ponrepo. Performances were advertised on postcards, promising visitors' scenes 'from life and the world of dreams.' Ponrepo would

---

* On Australian television today there is a trigger-warning before any images of dead people are shown on screen, regardless of when they were taken and the circumstances of death; this is because, to the Aboriginal community, such an image is cursed.

perform magic shows in-between movie-reels (which he called 'living photographs'), as bridge between the light-show and planet earth. Ponrepo did it all: programmed and projected the films, stubbed tickets and sold refreshments. But his official mantle was that of 'Versteller,' a Yiddish word combining the German words 'verstellen' (*to masquerade and misplace*), and 'vorstellen' (*to introduce and imagine*), which one journalist bitterly characterised with 'every word a lie' (the audience suspend control without losing agency; the boundary between truth and illusion collapsed by cinema: the most 'dangerous art' forewarned by Plato is gorgeous). In 1986, sixty years after his passing, Ponrepo had an asteroid named after him by a Czech astronomer. Ponrepo 7332. Kafka was gifted his own asteroid one year later: 3412 Kafka.

The cinematic big-bang happened fast: travelling magicians like Ponrepo were forced to enhance their witchcraft with the alchemy of cine-projection. Kafka and his friends were spoilt for choice of where to watch the movies. According to Max Brod—his first friend, celebrant and completist (defying Kafka's death-wish for all of his work to get lost in the fire)—it was the Orient they visited more than any other cinema, and the fierce, severely haunted children's film of 1919, *Daddy-Long-Legs*, which Kafka kept returning to ('for hours at a time he could not be made to talk about anything else but precisely and only about this splendid film'). Kafka himself never directly wrote about it but—in the film—there is a scene redolent of his later, 1922 short story, 'Investigations of a Dog.' A canine on its hind legs is given forever to scale a huge brick-wall, reaching further than the frame's limit. The animal moves with exhausted purpose vaguely in the direction of the camera, never giving in to its natural four-legged-ness. It staggers, spine to the wall—eyes to the skies—proud, drunken, bounce of the ass, three steps forward, two steps back. Kafka in his story conceives a similarly disconnected vignette; a gang of dogs behave in the same way, 'raising their front legs, committing sin and seducing others to the sin of silently regarding them...' Under Brod's direction, Kafka is considered a pained, religious writer but, in his life, he would often read aloud his work to friends as light relief, each of them unable to stay upright, keeled over with laughter. (In certain religious sects to strike a black dog is equivalent to stepping on an onion: punishable by eternal damnation. The dog is the guiding crack of light in the black tunnel of experience: the

accused K in K's most famous *The Trial* is murdered with a
flash of knives at the city's limits before an audience, with the
last words 'Like a dog!')

Daddy-Long-Legs—like *The Kid*—opens with the premise
of a baby abandoned on a heap of rubbish. The child comes of
age fast as 'Rose,' a treehouse-revolutionary liberator of jam for
all of her orphanage comrades. Played by Mary Pickford, Rose
is quite the cardboard-bedfellow for Chaplin's tramp, lifted from
the destitution the Londoner knew so well, and sent to university by an anonymous benefactor she grows to love ('groomed,'
in modern parlance). Chaplin credited no small part of his professional success on commitment to the workhouse aged seven,
because there he was taught to read (at the height of his stardom
he would often dream of a permanent withdrawal to the banks
of some distant river to be alone with his books—sharing with
Kafka a love of Nietzsche). The scale of stardom he was granted
by *The Kid* was unheard of and, like any folk hero worth his salt,
Charlie was hated as much by Adolf Hitler as he was by J. Edgar
Hoover. The character of the Tramp was incompatible with the
submission demanded of the average cinema-goer; his cheerful
resistance a boon for an audience confused and stripped of
agency by reality's merchandised, inflexible direction of travel.
Chaplin got rich embodying the impoverishment of the player
who couldn't (or wouldn't) fall into line, and defined the medium of modernity with it (anarchist by experience rather than
prose, Kafka's favourite book, it stands to mention, was Prince
Kropotkin's memoir).

With Mary Pickford, D.W. Griffith and Douglas Fairbanks,
Chaplin established United Artists in 1919. This put the artists in
charge of their own pictures, giving Chaplin carte blanche when
it came to *The Kid*, improvising the bulk of the shoot in-situ.
He cast for the role of the abandoned child a little over a week
after the death of his infant son, Norman (buried with a tombstone reading only 'The Little Mouse,' Walt Disney in a rare show
of attribution acknowledged the figure of the tramp as Mickey's
basis), and the film is considered his most autobiographical in
the most literal sense; organising rooms on Sunset Boulevard
to mimic his memory of the South London hovels he'd known
as a child. In a test of memory, and bedazzled measure of the
distance he'd come, he accompanied *The Kid* on a tour to London, visiting where he and mother Natalie lived before her insti-
tutionalisation (but eventually refusing to cross the threshold

and go inside). He spent long nights on the streets of East London playing with the vagrants, the pushers, the magicians and the hookers and, in a final reflective punt, met Frank 'The Bomb' Harris to inspect the Death House at Sing Sing prison and meet its inhabitants on his loop back to Los Angeles via New York. It wasn't until 1936 that he'd have the nerve to kill off the Tramp, in what's known as 'the last silent movie,' *Modern Times* (1936). He'd come to regret this decision.

Towards the end of Chaplin's life, long-term friend and producer Jerry Epstein arranged for 16mm film prints of recent releases to be sent to the silent retiree's home in Switzerland. Always a fight fan, Epstein reflected on Chaplin's private 1977 viewing of Sylvester Stallone's breakthrough *Rocky*, muttering under his breath 'excellent... excellent,' as the spools ran out. After *Rocky*, Chaplin received a copy of *Barry Lyndon*—his last movie ('beautiful... beautiful')—which inspired a telegram to Kubrick (13 November 1977).

CONGRATULATIONS AND THANK YOU FOR BARRY LYNDEN STOP WE WERE ALL VERY MOVED BY YOUR BEAUTIFUL FILM AND HATED TO SEND IT BACK BEST WISHES CHARLIE OONA CHAPLIN.

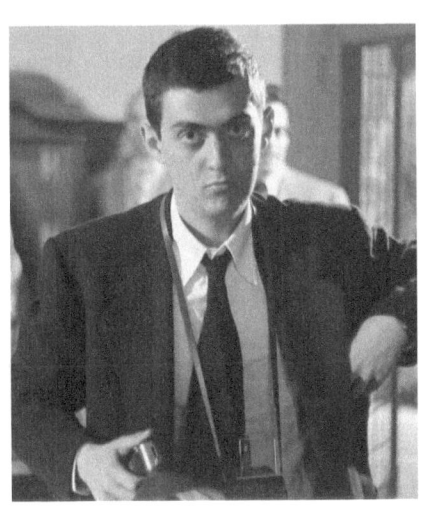

¶ While Stanley Kubrick was making *Barry Lyndon* (1975), the director was already drawing plans for *The Shining*'s Overlook Hotel, and on the back of these drawings he was sketching prototypes for the masked players of the orgiastic ball in *Eyes Wide Shut* (1999). Kubrick completed the commercial trailer for his last film, returned home and suffered a fatal heart attack in his sleep.* He is said to have presented the full film to cast and crew six days before his death, but whether the public got this cut is debated. The literary source of *Eyes Wide Shut* is Arthur Schnitzler's *Dream Story* (1925), which in turn was based on a draft for his play, *The Distant Land* (1908). Kafka, in 1911, recorded in his diary a dream of attending a performance of it: 'The author is somewhere nearby, I can't hold back my poor opinion of the play.' He describes an actor he knows but who is unrecognisable in dream-land, making excited speeches repeating the word 'principum' (a fundamental principle), which he expects to be followed by 'tertium comparationis' (the common ground between two things). *Dream Story*, and the play on which it is based, focusses on a couple grappling with desires outside the societal conventions of their marriage, and the anxieties attached to the ever-increasing number of options available in a modern, bourgeois life. He nearly cheats on her, but doesn't, and she nearly cheats on him, but doesn't. In *The Distant Land* the doctor actually takes part in the famous orgiastic ball, and confesses this truth to his wife on her deathbed (in *Dream Story*, she's only sleeping). In *Eyes Wide Shut* she urgently engages coit; in *The Distant Land*, he's dumped. In Kafka's dream the audience and the players crawl over one another, stage and stalls blur, genders shift and wounds reveal. A paraffin lamp illuminating the theatre blows,

> sparks pour down in a broad gush on the crowded audience that forms a mass as black as earth. Then a gentleman rises up out of this mass, walks on it towards the lamp, apparently wants to fix the lamp, but first looks up at it, remains standing near it for a short while, and, when nothing happens, returns quietly to his place in which he is swallowed up. I take him for myself and bow my face into the darkness.

---

* Long-held lore in the drinking dens of London's Liberated Film underground has κ in-between the cut of film and the cut of life watching *Blight* by John Smith—on the demolition of London housing to make way for a new motorway—and that's what finished him. The director had requested a VHS-copy from *Eyes Wide Shut* composer Jocelyn Pook, as *Blight* was her only original soundtrack credit until Kubrick's employment on the film; in the trailer he uses Chris Isaak's 'Baby Did a Bad Bad Thing.'

Critics of Schnitzler's work enjoyed legitimising their outrage with antisemitic inference. Eastern Europe was a hot-bed for the hatred of Jews, and while its normalisation and increasing severity made some radical and experimental breaks from tradition more likely for artists and patrons, there were many who simply moved away. In the same year as *The Distant Land*, Schnitzler also wrote *The Road to the Open*, and in it one of his protagonists is rapt in the issue, despairing the time he predicts it will take to find a solution: one thousand years. It took thirty. And Kafka knew. Though his work can be read without any kind of Jewish slant or identifiers, after the fact every word emerges to constitute a nightmare before it.

The final film Kafka clearly referenced going to see was on 23 October in 1921. 'Afternoon, Palestine film.' This was *Shivat Zion / Return to Zion*, in a private screening on 22 October at the Lio-Bio cinema in Prague, organised by *Selbstwehr / Self-Defence*, a journal he occasionally wrote for.

Shivat Zion is a feature-length compilation of newsreel footage shot by Yaacov Ben-Dov across 1920; it shows imprisoned Zionists, archeological digs, and a visit from Prime Minister Winston Churchill to Palestine (during this time under British rule). It was produced in part to generate financial support for Jewish settlement in the new-old promised land, and incite more Jews to go there. Kafka studied Hebrew and references often the Talmud, but he couldn't make the Zionist groupthink. Though no opinion of *Shivat Zion* is given in his diary, he is obviously possessed by the images he's seen in the days that follow. He describes dreams of the parched land of Jerusalem, and writes to a friend on its appeal for earth to give reason and purchase to the sand—earth was needed, not lawyers (he being the latter; the former perhaps a reference to the wet clay the hubristic Rabbi uses to form the Golem of Prague, speechless monster-protector of Jews in the pogrom).

Hanns Zischler, the great chronicler of Franz Kafka at the movies, calls Palestine the writer's 'unreachable terrain.' It is unknowable and must remain so, a dream story. The distant land. Cinema. There where the old religion staggers on (hind legs). Kafka often began his sentences 'If...'

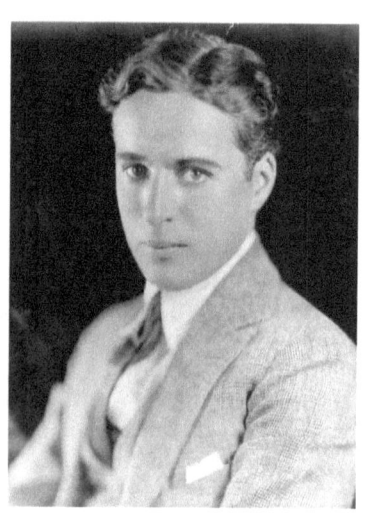

¶ Three months after Chaplin's internment at a small cemetery in Lausanne, his coffin was dug up and held to ransom by
impoverished refugees, Roman Wardas and Gantscho Ganev.
Wardas was the brains ('I decided to hide Charlie Chaplin's body
and solve my problems'); Ganev the braun ('I was not bothered
about lifting the coffin. Death is not so important where I come
from'). The big idea was to hide Charlie's coffin deeper in the
same hole and pretend it had been taken, demanding a ransom
for its safe return. When the night came around and the dig took
several hours, the earth heavy and heavier still with rainfall, they
panicked and carried the coffin to Ganev's estate car. One mile
away from the house Chaplin had called home for twenty-three
years, on the banks of Lake Geneva, they dug a shallow grave
in a cornfield, lowered the coffin into it, and fled. Twenty-seven
phone calls to domicile Chaplin followed asking for $600,000.
The family refused to negotiate, Charlie having prepared instructions during his lifetime that in the case of his abduction no
money was to be paid. Desperate, the two men crawled down to
$250,000, and threatened to hurt the youngest Chaplins, warn-
ing that there'd be just one more phone call. With this the local
police surveilled all 200 public telephone boxes in the area, and
ultimately caught Wardas on the horn, who grassed on Ganev.
The coffin was retrieved and put back in its original plot, topped
off with a few tons of concrete. Oona forgave the grave robbers,
appreciating the slapstick of the stunt, and even reflected on
the site they chose for Charlie's re-burial: that idyllic cornfield
on the bank of the lake, worried that it might have been better
to leave him there.

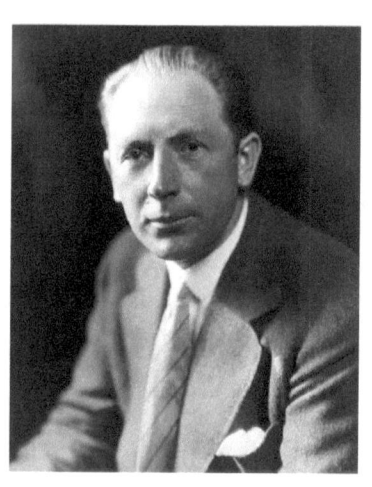

Friedrich Wilhelm Murnau (d.1931)
Tabu: A Story of the South Seas (F.W. Murnau, 1931), 86m

¶ Lotte Eisner described F.W. Murnau's 'generosity' as the asset that kept his Tahitian actors from fleeing the set of his troubled last movie, *Tabu*. The film's cinematographer, Floyd Crosby (who'd go on to shoot presidential favourite *High Noon*, and a score of Roger Corman movies), didn't see it that way, '...he was a very selfish man.'

When the production company committed to funding *Tabu* stopped answering the director's calls for cash, he threw every last dime of the wealth attributed him by previous artistic ventures—*Nosferatu*, *The Last Laugh*, *Sunrise*—to the realisation of the film. Effectively marooned, crew would come to work for the promise of a share in eventual profits; local actors less. Murnau built himself a house with one bedroom on a former burial ground, which tribe elders harshly warned against: taboo! (he built a tiny guesthouse too but a comfortable two-hundred metres away and without toilet facilities: *taboo*). Cameras were affixed to a reef where sacrificial victims had been gifted to the elements. Taboo, taboo! Murnau was a superstitious man, but hurried to innovate against the odds of the production's limitations—and besides felt 'never at home anywhere.' Only when the house burned down did he pause to seek the counsel of a fortune teller.

With the movie wrapped, cut and soon to be premiered, Murnau planned to visit his mother in his native Germany. The teller knew as much, and warned that though he would arrive as planned on April 5, it'd be in a 'different manner' than expected. Having survived a plane crash during the war, Murnau knew the Icarian threat of flight, and now took against travel by road too. He'd 'cheat fate' and go by sea.

Herman Bing, voice of the ringmaster in *Dumbo* (and production chief on several of Murnau's movies), remembered how odd the director's careful route seemed: *via* Panama to get to New York from Los Angeles. Some travel by land was initially necessary to reach the port at San Diego. A motorcycle was asking for it; a train, beneath him; so Murnau would go by car, and—seeking to muddle the reaper—would leave his temporary residence at the Miramar Hotel in Santa Monica for a stop at author William Morris' chateau on the Carmel del Monte. It didn't work. Though he took the boat on which he'd booked his passage, he did so as his pirate-Dracula Nosferatu had before him —in a coffin.

Before leaving Los Angeles, Murnau presented *Tabu* to Paramount. His last screening. The director's autonomy was punished with silent treatment at the private event, but the mountaineers immediately secreted-off a ten-year contract in awe of his silvery pagan love-island, and as a separate matter bought *Tabu* for distribution. Murnau hired a luxury Packard for his travel to the port, as a celebratory extravagance after months of financial brinkmanship. Kenneth Anger's account of Murnau's demise, printed first in *Cahiers du Cinéma* and then in his *Hollywood Babylon*, has him performing oral sex on a fourteen-year-old Filipino valet at the time of the accident. A wagon veers into the lane of the car, presumably at the point this valet, named Eliazar Garcia Stevenson, experiences climax and loses control. The bodies are flung from the Pacific Coast Highway near Rincon Beach. Murnau suffers a fatal head-wound. Stevenson is okay.

Biographer Lotte Eisner heightens the scene by adding fellow travellers to the vehicle: the chauffeur, John Freeland (true), producer Ned Marin (pursued by head-on collisions, his wife and two of their three children would be killed a few years later in a simulacrum accident; Marin is a victim of conflation, he wasn't in the car that day) and Pal, a German sheepdog (true). Eisner laments the 'venomous tongues' wagging, but she also parrots Anger's account of the eleven attendees who made the funeral (inferring Murnau's unpopularity), and the moulding of a Murnau death mask by Greta 'I Want to be Alone' Garbo —the centrepiece of her Manhattan home-office until her own quiet exit (Murnau had two services: the first in Los Angeles was attended by hundreds, the second in Berlin more intimate by choice). The death mask commissioned by Garbo is now in the possession of the Berlin Film Museum.

Tabu's premiere went ahead as planned, one week later on March 18 at the New York Central Park Theatre. Reviews were good, except in *Variety*, with its quip on his burial-mound-bungalow. The film 'is not going to set anything on fire.' Conceived as a collaboration between anthropologist and documentary filmmaker Robert Flaherty (celebrated for *White Shadows in the South Seas*, co-directed with W.S. Van Dyke, see John Dillinger, pp.60–62) as a study of the encroachment of modernity on traditional Polynesian life, the scales were imbalanced by Flaherty's alleged technical ineptitude, and the fact that Murnau ended up paying for it all. In filming the native stars of Bora

Bora, whose on-screen silence pretermits a life-language freed
of words for betrayal and guilt, Murnau, Flaherty and (less so)
Floyd must have known their camera would vampirise this
last paradise, condemning it to the ranks of nearby islands,
characterised by Eisner as 'tourist centres where the white man
has transmitted to the beautiful, careless, childlike inhabitants
his own civilisation, including the Bible, brandy, syphilis, lep-
rosy, and cheap cotton goods.' Following the release of the film,
the serious documentarian Flaherty had little to lose chastising
Murnau for 'Europeanising' the Polynesians. He also accepted
some personal responsibility for the fate of *Tabu*'s virgin protagonist, Reri, who they'd met as a cocktail waitress without
any acting experience, and cast immediately. So infatuated was
she with the white world of total darkness represented by the
makers (her first English words were 'Hooray cinema!') that
she followed them to the States and got a job on Broadway as
a dancer, kicking her legs and crossing her fingers for the drop
of the film and the career ascent that should've but didn't follow.
She married a Polish actor; got divorced; moved to Grunewald
for several months to be close to Murnau's mother, and eventually, eventually gave up. Bruised and broke, back to the island
she went with new words and new meaninglessness.

Murnau's mother attempted to sue the Tanner Motors
Livery Inc., responsible for hiring the car, on the basis that no-
one but the allocated driver should've been behind the wheel.
She tried to sue John Freeland too, but the case was dismissed
'without merit' many months later. Freeland, the designated
chauffeur, stated that he'd stopped for fuel twelve miles out of
Santa Barbara (at the Barnsdall-Rio Grande station, used as a
location in 1981's *The Postman Always Rings Twice*; see Bob Rafelson, pp.264–273). On returning to the vehicle, he found Stevenson in the driver's seat. 'The old man told me to,' he smirked,
and Murnau, the forty-two-year-old—slouched and suggestively
belt-less in the rear, pup on lap—nodded. Freeland protested
but Murnau came in firm. The boy couldn't keep his foot off the
accelerator, Freeland said, 'warning' him to slow down, though
it's unlikely he exceeded 55 miles per hour. The accident happened at five in the afternoon, five miles into Stevenson's alleged
joy-ride, and both police and jury at the subsequent inquest
believed Stevenson's account based on track-marks in the road.
A blind-bend and a lorry veering over the centre-line caused him
to take decisive action. The vehicle had evidently ground to a

halt, surveyed the damage, and driven on. It was, effectively, a
hit and run. Stevenson staggered to the car and pulled a cushion
from it, placing it under the head of Murnau, who lay in a ditch
dying. He made it to the nearest hospital but no further.

Stevenson was at least twenty-eight-years-old at the time
of the accident, and an experienced driver. He was born to a
Mexican mother and an English father. There is no evidence
that Stevenson and Murnau were involved romantically, and
the general charge against the director of closeted homosexuality is false. In Les Hammer's forensic correction of Anger's
endlessly repeated libel of Murnau's end, he supposes Stevenson had an English accent, which 'would've given him cachet
as a valet.' What happened to Stevenson immediately after
the accident isn't clear, but he'd go on to work as a bartender
or doorman at the Cafe Trocadero, the famed Sunset strip nightclub known for its appearance in *A Star is Born* (1937). Outside
of the inquest that followed the crash, and the case brought
against Freeland by Murnau's mother, neither man has com-
mented publicly or granted an interview about exactly what
happened that day. It's fantasy. Cinema. One disproven account
has the beautiful Austrian actress-writer Salka Viertel tailing
Murnau's car (there was no tailing car), descending on her
friend in the shrub. In this story the heap of metal silently pirou-
ettes through the air and kisses hard the ground with its crush
of glass and lick of fire. Like every movie's telling, a tinnitus
din emerges with an earth-quaking bass, chased by the emotional drama of some sugary adagio. Villains flicker out; heroes
escape unscathed. Goddess's plan. The lapping of ocean waves
nearby announces Viertel, whose eyes lock with the eternal
maker (Murnau believed firmly in the talkie as a revolutionary
development of the medium, but when an image of waves can
express the emotions of an actor why bother with synchronised
sound? '...it has come too soon: we had just begun... to exploit
all the possibilities of the camera. And now here are the talkies
and the camera is forgotten while people rack their brains about
how to use the microphone...'). His face, she said (she really
did, but later in the hospital), was drained of all colour. A trickle
of blood from the corner of his mouth. There is the suggestion
of the moon, and the still focus of the warm, evening sun reflected on the car. Through this, off-camera, are the liminal Tahi-
tians; humming and whispering their fragmented lullaby for
the old fire-screen. Fade out.

When Floyd Crosby returned with his wife to the island of filming forty years later, he was met by the rapture of one, old man. 'Sometimes, in Hawaii,' said the man, who'd danced in the movie, '*Tabu* shows. And everyone goes to see grandma and grandpa, and everyone cries because everyone's dead.'

With all of Murnau's savings gone on *Tabu*, the money for the embalming and passage of his body back to Germany had to be raised by friends. Two ships-worth of sailors rejected Murnau as bad-luck cargo, knowing how easily the seas and the skies could take against them, knowing the occult depth of his artistry. When the long brass container with its frosted window onto the waxwork formerly known as F.W.M. finally did arrive at Berlin, it was met by Fritz Lang and Carl Mayer. 'Aloha oe Murnau' went Lang's greeting, as his funeral eulogy ended. At a tomb in the Russian quarter of the Stahnsdorf cemetery, near Berlin, dug specially for F.W. and the rest of the 'Plumpe' family (Murnau took his name from a place he liked to holiday—Plumpe wouldn't do it), down, down he went.

In July 2015, the Plumpe tomb was broken into.* The lid of Murnau's coffin was prized open and, from it, his head taken. On forensic inspection, hard, red deposits were found about the place—the spent wax of candles speculating some ceremonial or ritual significance to the taking of the skull. Cemetery caretaker Olaf Ihlefeldt told the *Washington Post* it could have been 'Satanists' performing 'black magic' or perhaps even 'a photo session or a celebration or whatever in the night.' The whereabouts of the skull remain unknown.

---

* Starting in the 1970s Murnau's crypt has occasionally been entered or damaged. In 2012, at the same cemetery, the sarcophagus of the Austrian-Hungarian farce-master Gustav Kadelburg was broken into, and his coffin smashed. Undisturbed near the entrance lies the grave of Ernst Gennat, the criminologist who inspired the fictional character of Karl Lohrmann in Fritz Lang's *M* (1931) and *The Testament of Dr. Mabuse* (1932). *Dark* (2017) —the German Netflix series about time-travellers having sex—was filmed here and, appropriately enough, a bar called Tick-Tack sits at the cemetery's entrance, covered from floor to ceiling in broken clocks. A downloadable app developed by the cemetery, 'Wo Sie Ruhen' ('Where they rest'), offers a full audio-guide for the venue.

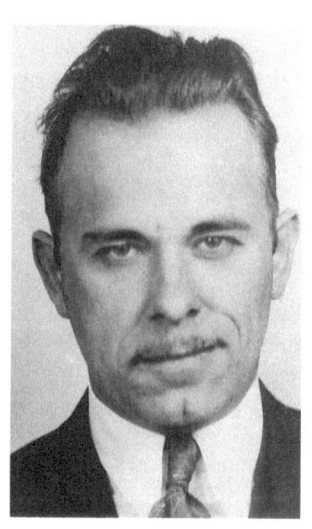

John Dillinger (d.1934)
Manhattan Melodrama (W.S. Van Dyke, George Cukor, 1934), 99m

You gonna kill 'im?!!!
—Gramps, *The Petrified Forest*

¶ Cicero, the Ancient Roman orator, described Ancient Greek writer Herodotus as 'the Father of History.' Until him the written word was poetry, images of song marked in stone. In recording the Greco-Persian wars, the Greek changed the word into something laboured, cold, *fact*. The first document of history. And in this, the first record of scalping:

> He carries the heads of all whom he has slain in the battle to his king; for if he brings a head, he receives a share of the booty taken, but not otherwise. He scalps the head by making a cut around it by the ears, then grasping the scalp and shaking the head off. Then he scrapes out the flesh with the rib of a steer, and kneads the skin with his hands, and having made it supple he keeps it for a hand towel, fastening it to the bridle of the horse which he himself rides, and taking pride in it; for he who has most scalps for hand towels is judged the best man.

Some two-thousand years later, scalping was promoted by the British arriving in America, offering bounties of cloth to indigenous allies for scalps taken from hostile tribes. If the practice already existed in First Nations cultures (tribe representatives since have claimed it was learned and retaliatory), it was in the slice of a salami-sized medallion of skin to be tossed into fires following victorious battles—a ceremony presided over exclusively by clans of intersex shamans—and there was nothing honourable about taking a scalp. On the contrary, this white misconception stems from observations of the Natives surging on the battle fallen. It only takes one Baby Face Nelson,* with their bloodlust and psychopathy, to muddy the waters.

The highest honour in the Native's war-game went to the warrior who would ride weaponless (or with a simple stick) into battle and be the first to touch his opponent. Dead fine, but much better alive. This wasn't about inflicting physical harm, or taking anything from or of the body, but something much more serious: humiliation. Called 'counting coup,' the prod appealed to the theatre of battle, the tragedy and silliness of it all. The Brits didn't get it.

If J. Edgar Hoover (director of the Bureau of Investigation and later the FBI) in Depression-era America had been allowed to peel off his counting-coup nemesis John Dillinger's scalp

---

* Baby Face Nelson (1908–1934): a diminutive Chicago bank robber and late Dillinger ally who reportedly killed for the thrill of it.

for an all-American hand towel, he surely would have done. But his powers limited him to the confiscation of Dillinger's death mask from the morgue, as sanitary, Warholian equivalent of returning to the village with the half-rotted head of the opposition. Dillinger's face hung deprived of vision at the threshold of Hoover's office. The bank-robbing, movie-loving people's hero, John, had been shot from behind with four bullets; one at point-blank range in the back of the neck. Betrayed by a woman in an orange dress that looked red beneath the neon lights of the Biograph Theatre, Chicago, Dillinger was killed leaving the cinema. Those who had filled the auditorium and watched *Manhattan Melodrama* with him fast became a mob, fighting over one-another for a chance to soak their handkerchiefs in his blood.

Dillinger's end was appropriate in its way. Scripted. A nasty conclusion to a messy collaboration. To attempt to control the narrative of Dillinger's fourteen-month crime spree, the young, little-known and hugely ambitious bureaucrat, Hoover, had modelled himself film director; Dillinger his leading man. It was a local Indiana police officer who first fawned over the criminal's innate sense of theatre, and the drooling press seized on this to crown him the Prince of Desperadoes. The fervour was pushed to its extreme by the emergent FBI, dubbing him 'the most brazen killer this nation has ever known.' That Dillinger ever killed is unlikely, with all but one accusation disproven beyond doubt. The Bureau dealt the anarchist the same tried and tested blow as the people of the First Nations. Anyone who won't be scared into conformity will be subjected to a programme of de-humanisation. (It continues.)

It was Dillinger's relative virtue—to say nothing of his fearlessness—that made him so dangerous to the status quo. 'Life is short,' he smirked through the age-old cliche in the creation of his eternal own. 'Take about half of what you hear with a grain of salt, believe half of what's left, and you've got it made.' He luxuriated in the lawmen's production of his image as 'Public Enemy No. 1' and communed: presenting himself as a latter-day Jesse James or Jack Sheppard, through a lookbook of on-screen anti-heroes best performed by Clark Gable (his favourite actor—Rainer Werner Fassbinder's too). Dynamic and relentless propaganda vilifying (heroising) Dillinger trailed the main features of movie houses nationally, foreshadowing the good-evil binary imposed by the papal Hay's Code.* It is an unlikely coincidence that the Code was introduced in the month

Dillinger died, curtailing what could be said and shown on film for decades afterwards. Nor does it feel accidental that the venue of Dillinger's apprehension—his murder—was the cinema. 'He may be sitting amongst you... he may be in your row,' went the police commercial preceding the main feature, with John's Antichrist-sized mugshot projected onscreen. 'Turn to your right, and turn to your left...'

'What's time to me?' Dillinger fed a reporter. 'They took away nine years of my life, and I decided to do some taking of my own when I got out.'

Aged twenty in 1923, in Mooresville, Indiana, Dillinger had fallen in with a local ex-con named Ed Singleton. Desperate for cash, the older man convinced the younger to join him in robbing a grocery store. But there wasn't any money on-site. Singleton panicked; his gun fired. Nobody was harmed but both men were arrested. John's father encouraged him to face the music. Pleading guilty, he was charged with conspiracy to commit a felony and assault with intent to rob. Ten years minimum. Singleton, who'd conceived and led the botched robbery, confessed to nothing and got off with two. The grocery store owner intervened, leading the town's petition for clemency and acquittal, or at least greater leniency in John's term. The state wouldn't budge. Behind bars for the duration of his twenties, Dillinger set about obtaining the only education available. All that he knew outside of the movies he learned in prison. Everyone he knew he met there. And when he finally bounced a free man in 1933, he did so with a gang behind him, a list of banks to rob and *the knowledge*. Commence the spree!... Just as soon as he'd been to apologise to the store-keep of those many moons ago.

Dillinger was gentle in his treatment of bystanders and workers, according to their accounts. 'Honey, this is a holdup,' he told clerk Margaret Good at the bank in Daleville, Indiana, with crossed legs and Tommy gun limp, before vaulting over a six-foot barrier like movie-hero Douglas Fairbanks. He was the 'heart of calm' in his criminal gang too, disliking violence and

---

* Scripts had to be vetted for approval and so did the final films. Without the PCA's 'Seal of Approval' a film could not be distributed through any of the country's major distribution networks, so condemning it to obscurity and / or financial ruin. Example: Michael Curtiz's *Casablanca* (1942) was meant to end with Bogie and Ingrid B in bed together (the Paris affair in the film was allowed because she believed her husband to be dead at the time). In this instance the censors are credited for making the film 'better'... the famous final scene of Bogie letting Ingrid go was a re-write imposed by the Code, as knowing infidelity wasn't an option.

often carrying a wooden replica of a gun, rather than the real thing (again fashioned during a stint in prison: with this boot-polished knock-off he managed to escape through eight locked doors in a later prison break, harming no one). He hadn't the psychotic savagery of Baby Face, nor the adolescent idiocy of Bonnie and Clyde. He looked like a star and he acted like one, but more importantly the public intuited that this was less about personal financial interests, and more about a very public fuck you to the institutions that had betrayed everyone.

'Why should the law have wanted John Dillinger?' a man wrote to an Indianapolis newspaper. 'He wasn't any worse than the bankers and politicians who took poor people's money. Dillinger did not rob poor people. He robbed those who became rich by robbing the poor. I am for Johnnie...' A farmer withdrawing money at the scene of one of the robberies pushed the notes towards Johnnie, who rejected them: advising the man that he was there for the bank's cash, not the people's. The economy had collapsed. Banks were seen to be foreclosing on homes and businesses enthusiastically, setting impossible interest rates to force loans into default. Poverty, inflation, high unemployment and low productivity. It was miserable, and confidence in the future was all but lost. Dillinger refused to take it, and his example inspired hope in people. It also sold. The Hollywood studios, who'd try anything to attract paying audiences to the cinema during the Depression, namely sex and violence, lapped it up. It was this bums-on-seats extremism that helped usher in the Hay's Code. Just as Dillinger's brief career fell at the end of the gangster's powwow in early 1930s America, so *Manhattan Melodrama* arrived just in time to beat the censors. In the movie's blurry twilight-world of dice and romance and upheaval, Dillinger's living legend laughed, leapt, and ultimately refused to die.

Tragically losing his mother aged four, and struggling with the God-fearing, Code-loving dad this condemned him to the care of, Dillinger would've identified with Blackie (a very young Mickey Roonie plays Clark Gable's character as a boy) and Jim from the off. Childhood best friends from Manhattan's East Side, together they are orphaned in a steamship disaster on the Hudson River. Poppa Rosen, a Russian émigré who loses his son in the same disaster, adopts the boys. But no sooner than he does are they orphaned again: out in the street on a soapbox, Leon Trotsky extols the virtues of a Communist Revolution in the States. On Pop it doesn't wash. 'In Russia I starved. I was cold and persecuted ... but here in America there is plenty enough for everyone! So, what we got to fight about, huh?' he calls out, remarking on their shared origin. Another attendee slaps Pop: 'You dirty capitalistic stool pigeon!' The crowd recoils as the Depressed audience likely groaned, and in the ensuing chaos Pop is trampled and killed by police horses. These events set in motion the different courses for the fraternal friends. Jim studies books, Blackie rolls dice. Jim takes against the mob, dedicating himself to the preservation of the law and order the land of the free depends on. 'Maybe ideals have ceased to exist,' he reflects; 'Maybe they're outmoded like oil lamps and horse cars. But they're mine and I'm stuck with them.' Blackie, on the other hand, blames the cops and vows childish revenge—what are they even doing riding around on horses? Wankers! 'I saw it, he didn't do anything and they rode over him!'

Coming to maturity as Clark Gable, he's learned not to take anything too seriously. He's a successful gambler because he doesn't especially care whether he wins or loses. He's bent, but then so is the system, so why play by their rules. Loyalty is sacred—all else? *Go drink a brandy.** Jim (William Powell) probably sees this, but as the self-styled adult in the room understands there's only so far to go with it. His big idea is winning and really winning big. Lawyer, district attorney, governor... President? Jim believes above all else in a system that will sacrifice his brother to uphold its abstractions, fating Blackie to the same electric chair charged Dillinger. 'Class—it's written all over him,' Blackie tells his companion in court, sweating through the disbelief of Jim's attack, as he scribbles away at an electrified self-portrait. It is all daubing: drawing a picture of dread where there should be a flower. For Jim, as for Hoover, the life of Blackie is the possession of the state. For Blackie, as for Dillinger, it is clear that everything possessed outside of love and loyalty is taken in violence. And this is why the state is unbelievable. This is why the only truth, the only authority, is one's own.

---

* In the club scene initiating Jim's gentlemanly theft of Blackie's gal, a prototype for the popular hit, 'Blue Moon,' is sung by Shirley Ross in blackface. 'Oh, Lord, perhaps I'll alter my plan. And overlook if I can. The bad in every man.' The song had been written for a 1934 film titled *Hollywood Party* as 'Prayer (Oh, Lord, Make Me a Movie Star)' (sing it out, it fits the tune), but was rejected. Lorenz Hart, the lyricist, scrambled to re-write it for use in *Manhattan Melodrama*, as 'It's Just That Kind of Play,' but this was rejected too. 'The Bad in Every Man' was the third attempt, reluctantly accepted by the producers, but the song didn't move until it was re-written in 1934 as 'Blue Moon,' becoming one of the best-known ballads of all time.

Dillinger shared his favourite film with President Roose-velt (polls at the time rate the popularity of the men more or less on a par): the 1933 Disney Short, *The Three Little Pigs*, with its infamous refrain: 'Who's Afraid of the Big, Bad Wolf?' The song was adopted as the anthem of the working class: the reality of Depression-era America crushing the once reliable moral les-son of the source fairy-tale. One wise pig slaps down layers of cement with a fart: he works all day to build his house with bricks, whereas the other oinkers, short-distance runners with hastily constructed houses of sticks and straw respectively, sing and dance away theirs. The black time in which Johnnie blazed showed that even if you did work all day every day, forewent the good stuff and used the best bricks, the wolf could take it all away. The point being: it's all a cartoon, all a movie. Make it fun, 'cause wolf or pig, you're gonna get got. Everybody has to eat. Parp.

Watching *Manhattan Melodrama*, Dillinger might have felt gratitude that no individual was so closely bound to his own case. It could also have made him feel lonely. He'd have known the feds were closing in, and known he was probably too hot to keep alive. The dimming of the lights representing the charge of the electric chair at Sing Sing towards the film's end would've been heavy. But Blackie knew and would've buoyed Johnnie's own knowing. Facing fate head-on the character even has the wherewithal to reassure a fellow resident of death's row, whose time is yet to come, as his own number is called: 'Die the way you live, all of a sudden. Don't drag it out. Living like that doesn't mean a thing.' Touché. Blackie is the hero. Neither boy nor man wishes to be Jim. (Dillinger is the hero. Neither boy nor man wishes to be Hoover.) Even if the FBI's plan was to give John a trial, the freedom he represented was too important to languish in prison, or fry in that cruel and embarrassing way. The movie had the class to hide the execution. The state would thrive in its reproduction. Dillinger's own fictionalisation was already well afoot; even in *Manhattan Melodrama* there's the nod of a head to his antics. So why not... Why not if you're already fried (be it dead in Hell, or dead in Mexico) go to the movies with a brash hooker who's almost bound to sell you down the creek—eat pork loin at Chicago's best restaurants —howl to the moon from the highest rooftops—why not, why not. Dillinger had become cinema.

Playwright Robert E. Sherwood had already finished *The Petrified Forest* by the time Dillinger was killed. Its adaptation to film (1936) was the big break for struggling actor Humphrey Bogart, following his appearance opposite Leslie Howard in its original stage version—playing a role based on Dillinger. The drift of an intellectual hobo across America is complicated by the connection he makes with a Bar-B-Q waitress, Bette Davis, and the arrival of Bogie's clan. Every inch of Hump's character was based on footage and photographs of Dillinger. It is impossible to separate the gangster and the actor in the film and in Hump's onward trajectory. His star was sculpted by 'The Last Great Apostle of Rugged Individualism.' (When *The Petrified Forest* was initially slated for adaptation from stage to screen, Howard refused to participate unless Bogie was able to reprise his role. This made him famous, and so grateful was he that the daughter he shared with Lauren Bacall was named Leslie in Howard's honour. By the time Baby Bogie arrived Howard was dead: his flight from Lisbon to Bristol downed by the Nazis. This was a move after the heart of Hoover: Howard was so compelling as poster boy for Britain's campaign against fascism, that the attack was likely orchestrated by Germany's Minister of Propaganda, Goebbels.)

In *High Sierra* (1941), Bogie continues his best impression of Dillinger as 'Roy Earle.' The film namechecks Johnnie as some eternal-elsewhere-other, but every detail down to his prison time and his haircut match up. The only real differences are the apocryphal mountain-top ending, and the girl: a club-footed bundle of fluff, whose ultimate spurning of Bogie rebounds him to his fate of Ida Lupino and her South East London hitchhiker's threat. *High Sierra* was filmed a few times: first with Bogie in a clunky collaboration between John Huston and the writer of its source novel, W.R. Burnett, then as the Western *Colorado Territory* (1949), again directed by Raoul Walsh, and as *I Died a Thousand Times* (Stuart Heisler, 1955). Burnett thought this was the superior version, except for the casting of Shelley Winters and Jack Palance in the roles formerly taken by Ida Lupino and Humphrey Bogart. 'Repulsive people,' Burnett described them: 'Who gives a damn what happens to Shelley Winters? Or Jack Palance for that matter?' And if that was his attitude to Winters and Palance, imagine his take on Marion Cotillard and Johnny Depp in Michael Mann's *Public Enemies* (2009), that unrequited love letter to Burnett and his bank robbers.

In *Public Enemies*, Mann attempts to recreate faithfully Johnnie's final exit: Depp playing Dillinger is seen in the actual

Biograph auditorium, moved by Gable's empowering departure words. Depp leaves from the same door on to the long, long North Lincoln Avenue, with a woman playing Anna Sage (Branka Katic). At that time, the madame Sage was facing deportation to her native Romania on charges of being an 'alien of low moral character.' She believed that turning in Dillinger would grant her the right to remain in the States. FBI agent Melvin Purvis, assigned the case by Hoover (and played by Christian Bale in this film), assured Sage that he would do everything in his powers to halt her deportation in exchange for the betrayal, but ultimately didn't (she was sent back to Romania and swiftly drank herself to death). The plan: Sage would wear a bright orange dress to mark herself out in the crowd. Purvis would stand stage left with a fat cigar. When he saw Sage leaving, he'd light the smoke as confirmation absolute for his agents to act. On exiting the cinema Dillinger immediately sensed danger. He fled to the first corner on the left and made the turn into an alley, but was fired at from behind. The gun Purvis was given by his FBI friends upon leaving the force—after a boastful career of gunning down Dillinger and other men 'like him'—he turned on himself in 1960. Nobody knows what he saw last. He is only ever discussed in the context of the people he killed.

A few doors down from the Biograph Theatre, a nifty barkeep quickly posted signs that said 'Dillinger had his last drink here' and 'Come in and see the famous chair where he sat.' The supposed seat was draped in an elaborate funereal sheet. Each ass was charged for the privilege, plus a premium on all liquor taken. Thousands queued for an opportunity to pass Dillinger's corpse lying-in-state at the morgue. Even the post office did a roaring trade, with corpse-tourists encouraged to send mail home post-marked Dillinger's death-town. On a national level, *Manhattan Melodrama*'s production company, MGM, exploited the murder of Dillinger in a publicity drive for the film decried by its star, Myrna Loy (Dillinger's favourite actress). Her outspoken disgust was so powerful that William Randolph Hearst removed his Cosmopolitan Productions banner from the movie's credits.

Dillinger's body was defiled after death. His brain was removed. Tongue too. Long slits were made down his front and back. The Chicago mortician who embalmed the body sharply criticised the Cook County coroner's physician, denouncing his work as 'unusual pathology.' The thousands whom had queued and many more still showed up for Dillinger's burial. His dad was so freaked out by it all that he had the coffin buried under huge slabs of concrete and scrap metal to deter grave-robbers. At the time of writing, the headstone has been replaced a total of four times due to repeated violations by souvenir seekers, chipping it away to nothing.

Evelyn 'Bettie' Frechette, John's wife and sometime getaway driver—imprisoned at the time of his murder—joined the circus, giving elegant rhapsodies with each Friday re-humanising the monster drawn by Hoover. This angered the FBI. It was meant to be their narrative alone: one of justice and order prevailing. Instead, sympathy with the libertine: crowds would stream into the auditorium for her hard-ass romanticism, pulling at cotton candy and laughing and dreaming as they went. She described her experience of life—even before John—as 'blurred,' and of their first meeting at a dance at the Olympic Lounge in Chicago, she said: 'There was something in those eyes that I will never forget. They were piercing and electric, yet there was an amused carefree twinkle in them too. They met my eyes and held me hypnotised for an instant.' She was played by Michelle Philips opposite Warren Oates' Dillinger in 1973; by Sherilyn Fenn opposite Mark Harmon in 1991, and by Marion Cotillard opposite Johnny Depp in *Public Enemies*.

Public Enemies is notable for touching on her origin as half French, half Native American, and her sympathy with the outlaw as such, unaccepted as she was by white America. Following her sentence of two years and one day in prison for harbouring an outlaw (her hubby!), she toured for five years with the Dillinger family in the *Crime Doesn't Pay* show, and then remarried and returned to the Menominee Indian Reservation, where she was born in 1907 and died in 1969 (in a building that is today a florist). The colonist's scalping-era policy of 'The only good Indian is a dead Indian' had by then shifted to 'The only good Indian is a terminated Indian.' As George Vukelich wrote in 1966's *The Last Menominee*, 'Once we conquered with the cross and the conquistador, then we conquered with the repeating rifle. Now we conquer with bureaucracy: with paperwork, and the broken promise.' The Menominee people had effectively been blackmailed in the mid-1950s, through the federal 'Termination' policy of laws and practices aimed at dismantling tribal sovereignty, and assimilating Native Americans with mainstream American society. This basically meant selling the land from underneath them in exchange for a false people's vote offering $1500 per person. It was dressed up as reparations before the concept really existed, but the small print entirely removed the Menominee's hunting and fishing rights, and all self-managed infrastructure (the tribe had made most of its income through timber, the few remaining there today still do). Without any access to basic resources—by the end of the 60s the Menominee reservation didn't have a general store, never mind a doctor—this forced the community and culture into poverty and despair. Frechette witnessed the Menominee tribe go from being the second wealthiest of all Native tribes in America to practical erasure. It was a story she'd have heard in youth as a fairy-tale, passed down through generations. At the centre of the tribe's land was 'spirit rock,' considered a portal to the invisible world. Here an ancestor of the Menominee once asked God for eternal life, and so angered was God at the selfishness of this request, that he cast him into stone. It was foretold that once this 'spirit rock' had been eroded, so the culture of the Menominee would disappear forever.

Frechette's death in 1969 happened with the flattening of said rock, worn away to nothing. She never regretted being a Dillinger gal—on the contrary, she, like Blackie of Manhattan, found purpose and pride in loyalty.

In 2019, John Dillinger's nephew attempted to exhume his body with an affidavit pronouncing evidence that it may not be his uncle buried there. Wrong eye colour. Wrong ear shape. A heart condition. Opening the coffin would provide an impressive conclusion to a documentary film for the History Channel, and finally put to rest theories supporting the idea that another small-time crook called Jimmy Lawrence was in fact the one killed outside the Biograph. The request was denied.

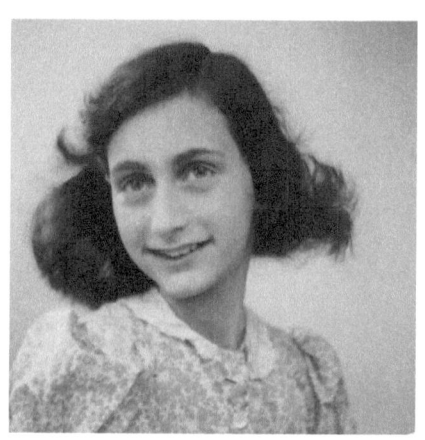

Anne Frank (d.1945)
The Lighthouse by the Sea (Malcolm St. Clair, 1924), 7om

¶ Anne Frank's thirteenth birthday was a big one:
a bouquet of roses, some peonies and a potted plant...
I got a blue blouse, a game, a bottle of grape juice,
a puzzle, a jar of cold cream, 2.50 guilders and a gift
token for two books... A platter of homemade biscuits
(which I made myself), lots of sweets and a strawberry
tart... A puzzle, a darling broach and a terrific book,
Daisy Goes to the Mountain.

There was an autograph book too, which would come to be
used as her famous 'stiff-backed notebook grandly referred to
as a diary,' with a hard cover bound in a red and white checkered
cloth, and a small lock at the spine. Her second entry reads,
This morning I lay in the bath thinking how wonderful it would be if I had a dog like Rin Tin Tin. I'd
call him Rin Tin Tin too, and I'd take him to school
with me, where he could stay in the caretaker's room
or by the bicycle racks when the weather was good.

Biscuits are distributed by Frank to her class and teachers,
and in the afternoon, she has her party, cleaning up with 'two
brooches, a bookmark, and two books... the Rin Tin Tin film
was a big hit with my classmates.'
    When Hitler and the Nazi party took control of Germany in
1934, the Frank family saw the direction of travel and fled. They
quickly became established in their adoptive Amsterdam neighbourhood for a generosity and party-mindedness that peaked
with Anne's thirteenth birthday celebrations in 1942. Her cine-
phile father, Otto, hired a film print of adventure dog Rin Tin
Tin's *The Lighthouse by the Sea* (1924), along with a projector, and
mother Edith issued each audience member their own lavish
gift, and a holy-day-confirmatory slab of her playground-famous
sponge cake. The showing of the movie would have been a significant event for all present, infused with the forbidden energy
of a radical underground happening. Eighteen months prior
the Nazi occupation enforced one of its first major prohibitions
in denying Jewish people access to the cinema. One month later
the rights of Jewish people to attend college were removed; in
March radios were confiscated; on April 1, cafés were to deny
Jewish customers; on September 15 this ruling was extended to
swimming pools, parks, libraries, theatres and museums. Pets
were no longer allowed. On Anne's birthday, Jews were told they

couldn't buy vegetables from non-Jewish shops; bicycles and such vehicles were to be surrendered to the authorities, and participation in sports was banned. Anne makes no reference to any other film or viewing experience in her diary. Within weeks of her birthday on July 6 (on this day Jews are forbidden from making telephone calls and visiting non-Jews) she is forced into hiding with her family.

Rin Tin Tin was a German Shepherd dog from Flirey in North-Eastern France, rescued by an American soldier, Lee Duncan, from a bombed-out kennel in World War I. The two puppies Duncan picked for himself were the most beautiful of a litter of five bald, blind newborns, and he named them Rin Tin Tin and Nanette after lace and leather lucky charms then popular with soldiers (citing two young lovers who had survived the bombing of a Paris railway station early in the conflict). The mother of the pups was part of a pack once supplying the Imperial German Army (for which Otto Frank fought and was stationed nearby). In 'Rinty,' as Duncan came to nickname Tin Tin, he prophesied the making of an international cinema star, inspired by Strongheart, the first canine movie icon, who lived in his own full-sized stucco bungalow in the Hollywood Hills. Believing Rinty and his sister, Nanette, to represent his good fortune in times of war and peace, Duncan snuck his puppies back to the USA. Nanette died shortly after the crossing, but Rinty thrived, subjected to a rigorous training programme. When they weren't practising stunts they were parading up and down the streets of Hollywood's B-movie studios, Duncan knocking on any door and imploring passers-by for Rinty's break. This wasn't unusual. Bit-players at the time were often selected from crowds of the unemployed gathered at the studio gates. Eventually Duncan's walkies paid off: the dog was cast at the last minute in replacement of a disobedient wolf in *The Man from Hell's River* (1922). Warner Brothers were impressed by the performance, and as an infant company considered second rate (or worse) and already on the verge of bankruptcy, played a wild card: *Where the North Begins* (1923) was a script written by Duncan for Rinty as lead. To promote the film Warner's distributed marketing ideas to exhibitors; 'get a crate and inside it put a puppy or a litter of them [and] 'you will be sure to get a crowd.' Another suggested the hiring of 'a man' who would 'walk along the principal streets of the city stopping pedestrians and asking them the question, "Where Does the North Begin?" and upon their answering (or even not answering) he can… tell them it begins at your play-house.' The dog proved the studio's ace and saved the day as only Rin Tin Tin could, which a plucky young advertiser called Darryl F. Zanuck sought to make his own. *The Lighthouse by the Sea* was the second of a dozen scripts written by Zanuck for the dog, the success of which would confirm his status as more than an ad-man, a leading scriptwriter, and then raise his rank to that of film producer, ultimately becoming Warner's studio head by the age of twenty-five (see Rainer Werner Fassbinder, pp.180–195). He credited Rinty for his success but he didn't rate him, and he hated writing.

The global popularity of Rin Tin Tin and Strongheart before him was exploited by Nazi propaganda. Hitler was filmed and photographed dominating his own German Shepherd, Blondi, as Caesar might have been shot with his lions: twisting the origin story of the heroic dog to fit the mythic blueprint of perfect Aryan breeding. (Otto's choice of film might have been quiet resistance, in refusing the appropriation of man's best friend as regime's wolf, gently imparting a subliminal message to the children gathered.)

Conceived by a retired Prussian cavalry captain called Max von Stephanitz, the German Shepherd was a relatively new cre-ation. In 1899, Stephanitz founded a society in Stuttgart to force recognition of the polymorphous sheepdog as German, which was honoured by the English Kennel Club in 1919, and the American Kennel Club in 1927. Stephanitz surveyed his creation in *The German Shepherd Dog in Word and Picture* (1923), writing,

> The German is a real dog-lover, for it is part of his na-ture… to enter into the spirit of the Aryan mysticism, which makes us feel at one, interiorly, with clouds, trees, lake and heath, and with all living creation… This appears in his religious beliefs, for the eagle and the wolf were dedicated to All-Father Wotan, King of Battlefields, Bestower of Victory… his wolves… roam the battlefields, crouch at his feet, and are cared for by the Lord of the World himself… two stones with bason-like hollows were erected to the right and the left of the ancient altars of sacrifice, from which poured the blood of the sacrifice which had been offered in honour of Wotan, so that his wolves could feast on the entrails of slaughtered enemies.

He goes on to say that Jews have always disliked dogs and—although not a 'Nazi'—Stephanitz gives plenty for Hitler and his heavy-petting friends to chew on.

The fierce, wolf-like image of the German Shepherd, and its loyal and intelligent nature, made it an emerging global standard for law enforcement and regime management. Stephanitz located it as such in his myth-making tome, not for political ends but for marketing. It was the breed of dog chosen to 'guard' the concentration camps each of the Frank's would be taken to, with all but Otto perishing. 'If I had to take a new dog,' Hitler is quoted as saying, 'it could only be a sheepdog, preferably a bitch. I would feel like a traitor if I became attached to a dog of any other breed. What extraordinary animals they are—lively, loyal, bold, courageous and handsome!' Facing defeat, Hitler withdrew into the famed exit-bunker with Blondi, wife Eva and her own Alsatian, Wulf. Unconvinced by the cyanide capsules issued by Himmler's ss (Hitler by then considering Himmler a traitor), he insisted they be tested first on Blondi. He was inconsolable at the death of the dog, consuming his own capsules quickly afterwards.

In *The Lighthouse by the Sea*, a Belgian sailor called Albert and his dog (Rinty) are rescued from shipwreck by Flora, the young daughter of a blind lighthouse keeper, whose light has gone out. Albert and dog are then kidnapped by some villains, but Rinty chews through the ropes tying Albert down, freeing him to meet his fate in the making of love with Flora, while the mutt with a mission hordes trash and sets it ablaze to reignite the wrecked light of the house, saving all future voyagers from ruin. Warner Brothers presented screenings exclusively for the blind, with a narrator onstage describing the action and reading aloud the intertitles. Meanwhile, off-screen, Duncan replaced Nanette with Nanette II, and made a stud of Rinty, breeding forty-eight puppies between them. Greta Garbo and Jean Harlow each owned a descendant. When Rinty crossed over in 1932, all major programming in America was interrupted for the announcement, with some media falsely reporting that he died on his own front lawn in the arms of Harlow (they were neighbours). Duncan said he was in his kitchen; an exit-yelp and that was that.

¶ According to the Dutch government, Anne Frank died during a typhus epidemic in March 1945. The previous August an unknown actor ratted out the family to the Gestapo, who were arrested on August 4 in 1944 and stolen away to Auschwitz. There they were split up: Otto and Edith staying put; Anne and sister Margot sent to the Bergen-Belsen concentration camp, losing their lives a short time before its liberation. In Frank's final diary entry on August 1, she reflects on her *self*...

> I'm what a romantic film is to a profound thinker
> —a mere diversion, a comic interlude, something
> that is soon forgotten: not bad, but not particularly
> good either.

Following his liberation from Auschwitz, Otto Frank dedicated his life to the unforgettable goodness of Anne. He returned to the buildings he'd previously rented for his company, Opekta (manufacturing and distributing the jelling agent for jams), which the secret attic annex sat atop. From there he oversaw the publication of Anne's diary—one of the bestselling books of all time, narrowly exceeded in sales by Leo Tolstoy's *War and Peace* (and, uh, Jeffrey Archer's *Kane and Abel*)—and guided through its adaptation for stage and screen. The fate of the building was uncertain until 1957, when a group of prominent Amsterdam citizens came together to buy the property, and founded the Anne Frank House Organisation. Otto was asked if he wanted to have the rooms refurnished during the house's restoration, which he refused: 'No. They took everything out during the war, and I want to keep it that way.' By 1960, it was ready to open to the public. Today, the Anne Frank House is a major tourist attraction, welcoming an annual total footfall narrowly higher than the Heineken Experience and the Sexmuseum; with the zoo, the Rijksmuseum, the Van Gogh Museum and the canal boats the city's only attractions to welcome more visitors. In 2020, the museum initiated a bizarre if well-intentioned Instagram-based project reimagining Frank's written diary if it had instead been recorded with a video camera (and broadcast from the secret annex). The commercial for the series summarises thus...

> Everything about this story is true. The people, the
> events, the location and the story. All of it. Except for
> the camera.

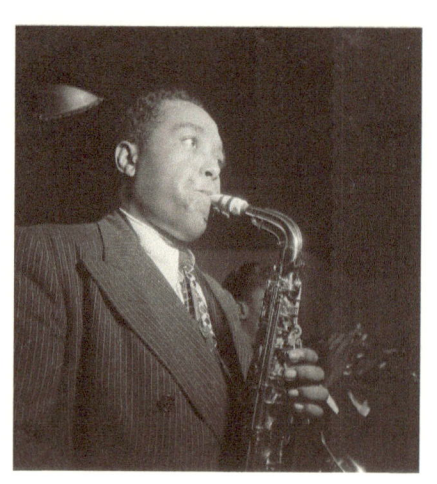

Charlie Parker (d. 1955)
Stage Show (Dorsey Brothers, 1955, *with* Count Basie
and Kate Smith), 30m

¶ Clint Eastwood dramatises Charlie Parker's End in *Bird*,
a film largely based on the account given by his common-law
wife, Chan.

Played by Forest Whittaker, Parker sits on a sofa in a hotel
apartment watching Tommy Dorsey's variety programme, *Stage
Show*, on TV. Two men are juggling bricks before a lively audience, and Parker finds it unbearably funny. In a fit of laughter,
he begins to choke and—a minute later—he's dead. His host,
the jazz patron and disinherited Rothschild, Baroness Pannonica
de Koenigswater, claimed to hear a thunderclap at the precise
moment he passed. The same was said for Beethoven and Mozart. Hotel management apparently asked her to leave with the
deceased, spooked by the tabloid spin of sexual intrigue, casual
racism and enthusiasm for a grisly death. In newspaper reports
at the time, the Baroness is quoted as saying Parker died watching television. Years later she changed her mind in Greenwich
Village impresario Max Gordon's autobiography, 'He was sitting
and listening to a Tommy Dorsey record, 'Just Friends' (Bird
was crazy about Tommy Dorsey),' and further used the opportunity to punish the fancy venue for their cowardice: 'Suddenly
he started spitting blood, jumped up, screamed, and fell at my
feet. I called the house doctor. But the doctor of the fashionable
Stanhope Hotel wouldn't come. He wouldn't attend a black man
dying in a white woman's apartment.' The Baroness' private doctor had come a couple of days prior to Parker's death because
the musician had been coughing up blood. He was prescribed
antibiotics and rest, and asked if he drank much: 'Sometimes I
have a little sherry before dinner' answered Parker (folklore has
him putting away twenty hamburgers and sixteen double whis-
keys before the sherry before the meal).

The problem with the account lifted unwittingly by history
from Eastwood's film, is that the *Stage Show* episode from March
12 was no sooner broadcast than it was lost, and Parker watched
alone. The rights-holder has referenced the segment loaned
for *Bird*'s television choke scene, and it was not from the evening
of Parker's flight. The show did air, and the hours do add up,
but the juggling of bricks? Another night. Count Basie performed,
and so did Kate 'God Bless America' Smith, so it's possible that
the hysterics of Charlie that the Baroness heard were sarcastic
laughter (Smith) or delirious whoop (Count). Incapacitated—
having managed just a sliver of peach and a litre of water in the
preceding 48 hours—he'd been plonked in front of the TV all day.

¶ In the morning he might have caught *Winky Dink, Funny Boners, Kids, Captain Midnight*. Children's programming, no less. At half past midday the 1925 silent film, *Sneezing Beezers*. 'A cab driver helps a deposed king regain his kingdom. After the film, Johnny becomes a king himself by trading his chef cap for a crown. But Johnny learns that being a king is not an easy job.' At one, *What in the World?*—a panel show asking guests to identify unusual museum store-room artefacts—features Vincent Price (when the internet was a man with passion and a little free time on his hands) and the Cubist sculptor Jacques Lipschitz along with exhibits: (A) a Sepik river crocodile, as worshipped by the scari-fication-crazed ghost cult of Papua New Guinea; (B) a limestone two-headed hippopotamus from 1st century Egypt; (C) a Baule mask from the Ivory Coast, produced by men to honour dead female relatives; (D) a chipped Scandinavian spear point from 10–5000 BC; (E) a petrified crocodile head from Costa Rica; (F) an effigy of a hunchbacked human, ceramic (Panama, 14–15C); (G) a tobacco pipe from Borneo. Afterwards, the Harlem Globetrotters played the Washington Generals in a game of basketball. Local infomercials follow to *Stage Show*. If he'd made it through *Stage Show*, he'd have witnessed Mickey Rooney impersonating a TV producer, and a touch of wrestling before *So This Is Hollywood*... 'Stunt girl Queenie Dugan puts her high-stepping skills to good use as she attempts to run away from a berserk man. The merry chase leads through city streets, across rooftops and back again.'

Against all odds, Parker might have risen in a last stand against fate, convention, reality, to disassemble and reconstitute the last post at his last booking that Saturday night in Boston. The alternative was the steeper descent: sofa, Baroness, the co-agulating tin of peaches, and the musical *Connecticut Yankee* on television (followed at 9:30pm by—you guessed it—*Willy*).

Parker found his life's antithesis in Dorothy's legendary cinematic trip: vowing never to return to his hometown of Kan-sas. In the vulnerability of death—death being his favourite topic after bebop, after dreams—he sought the reassurance of Chan: no matter what happened. No Kansas. Though many of Charlie's friends supported Chan's claim to this effect, the intervention of his earlier (legal) wife, in league with the ultimate decision-maker Mother Parker, meant seizure of his coffin from a Harlem funeral parlour and burial in the family's Kansas plot. For all of that trouble, the headstone was engraved with the wrong date of death—March 23 instead of March 12—and its replacement, a bronze plate matching his mother's, was stolen in 1992 (along with hers). In 1994, a new memorial stone was erected at the site, engraved with a tenor saxophone. Parker played alto.

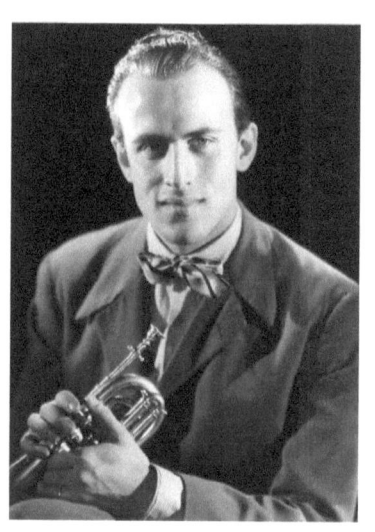

Boris Vian (d.1959)
I Spit on Your Graves (Michel Gast, 1959), 5m (of 110m)

I would be better off earning a living.
But my life, it's mine. I don't need to earn it.
—Boris Vian

¶ 'Is Paris burning?' Hitler famously cabled the occupied city's tubby governor, Dietrich von Choltitz, at Le Meurice hotel. The allies were moving in, and the Führer would sooner see the city in ruins than taken from the Nazis. Choltitz disobeyed, self-styling the 'Saviour of Paris' with his sympathies for the French capital's history and gastronomy, and the belief Hitler had *by then* gone mad. It was more probably a practical issue of how to enact the order. Bridges and buildings were rigged with explosives, but most of the Germans had done a runner. Choltitz knew the game was up; his disobedience self-serving. He was probably drunk. There's no Bordeaux on hangman's row. Better to play sommelier at the hotel bar in those last of last days. Many years later the venue's long-term barman reflected on Choltitz's surprise return in 1956: a pioneer of disaster-tourism, he wandered about as though 'in a daze' (again, drunk), gently demanding to be taken to his former quarters. Perhaps he lunched at the nearby Le Marignan, and bristled when delivered the bill (any bill). Turning right upon exit, back towards Le Meurice, he'd have passed next door the old HQ of the Todt organisation —responsible for building the concentration camps, and organising slave labour—smack next to the occupied kino—no coincidence—and slipped in for a glimpse of the verboten in Anthony Quinn's *Hunchback of Notre Dame*. Nothing is real (says the hangman). Choltitz emerged from war a free man. No charges were ever filed against him. As Hitler cabled, a mere grenade's throw across the Seine, Boris Vian was immolating Horst-Wessel-Lies with his occupation-honed blaze of insatiable jazz cornet, as the various Jean's—Cocteau, Genet, and Sartre —bebop'd in a St. Germain dungeon. Through the throwing of parties Vian had afforded himself the mantle of the Left bank's 'Prince.' Engineer, inventor, actor, critic, choir-master, musician... his literary career too had just begun, with the publication in 1943 of a poem—published under the name of Bison Ravi, or 'Delighted Bison,' one of his twenty-seven known pseudonyms—printed in the clandestine, one-page *Circulaire du Hot Club de France* (a jazz magazine distinguished for intellectualising and politicising jazz music journalism).*

* See, for example, 'I Wouldn't Want to Die' ...*Before having known / The black Mexican dogs / Who sleep without dreaming / The butt-naked monkeys / Gobbling up tropics / The silver spiders in / Webs riddled with bubbles / I wouldn't want to die / Not knowing if the moon / Behind its fake nickel look / Has a sharper side / If the sun is cold / If the four seasons / Are really only four / Not having tried / To wear a dress / On the boulevards* [...]
     et cetera...

His dad, home alone, had just been murdered by burglars.

The scene explodes as though straight from the pages of Chester Himes; the famed writer whose books, along with the films of Michael Curtiz and the music of Charlie Parker, would flood the French market with the end of the censorious occupation.

Americanism was some kind of antidote to the shameful collaboration of the Vichy regime. Through his wife, Michelle, Boris learned English, and together they found a steady source of income translating to French the hard boils of American noir: including Raymond Chandler's *The Big Sleep*, and other titles for Gallimard under the editorship of Sartre. Boris and Michelle, with Jean and wife Simone de Beauvoir, formed a formidable party foursome—Simone in particular rated Boris, finding 'no affectation in his long, white and smooth face, only an extreme gentleness and a kind of stubborn candour'—and Jean gifted him a column in his literary review, *Les Temps Modernes*, called 'Chroniques du menteur' / 'Chronicles of a Liar.' Vian was the titular liar of absurdist dispatches on underground Paris, illustrated as he wished and somewhat at random, with photographs of pin-up girls. He repaid Sartre by characterising him in his first major novel, *L'Écume des jours*, as the world-famous philosopher king 'Jean-Sol Partre,' who shows up to sell-out lectures riding an elephant, and... Michelle rode Jean and it all went to hell.

L'Écume des jours is Vian's best known (and bestselling) literary work, translated as *Froth on the Daydream*, or *Mood Indigo* (and the basis of a film adaptation by Michel Gondry). The central character, Chloé, dies from a water lily growing inside her. The flower must be prevented from blooming at all costs. This might be analogous to the 'weak heart' Vian had been diagnosed with at a young age—and the heart-heavy full blooming beauty of everything he valued and pursued in a short, packed life.

'He was the soldier on the mine,' says Jennifer Walters in her short thesis 'Death and Boris Vian.' Through proximity to war, familial misfortune and especially personal ailment, Vian understood that his time on earth could end at any given moment—as acutely as anyone ever can. In the noir tradition, he's the staggering hunk impossibly delivering on his mission with a deadly wound to the chest. Six foot six. Slightly cross-eyed. Snarling, with a particularly French snarl—Vian believed that as the origins of jazz were found in the self-expression of slaves, only African Americans could really *play* it (except if you were, uh, French)—and sneering, like only the half-dead can sneer. Vian wrote tracts railing against the follies of men, nowhere better expressed than in the creation of a robot that could produce poetry. This he characterised as 'hatred of our species.' 'Why would anyone be impressed by the building of a robotic poet, when last century we already had Victor Hugo?'*

Frustrated by a lack of commercial literary success, Vian decides to write a bestseller. Off he went to a beach somewhere, and returned to Paris little more than two weeks later with a novel, *J'irai cracher sur vos tombes*. He attributed authorship to one 'Vernon Sullivan,' and assigned himself credit for translation. *J'irai...* is, to paraphrase James Ellroy, a French book pretending to be American about a black man pretending to be white by a white man pretending to be black. 'After the lynching of his brother, a black man passing for white seduces and murders a pair of wealthy white girls.' Published late in 1946, the book initially disappeared, but sometime in 1947 it was dug up by one Daniel Parker, leader of a right-wing morality watchdog, who set about getting it banned. Parker got the press involved, and no sooner than he did was the book found at the scene of a murder in a Paris hotel, Sullivan's sections on strangling highlighted by the killer. *J'irai...* was the first book since *Madame Bovary* to be trialled for obscenity in France. Vian maintained that he was only the translator for a good while but—by late 1948—he was forced to admit authorship. The critics hammered him, and so did the courts, charging one hundred thousand francs for the trouble. Around the same time another novel by Vernon Sullivan appeared: the story of a white man who turns to rape and murder, driven mad by the fear that he might actually be black. His given name is Dan Parker.

By the early 1950s, Vian's literary star had waned. His new (and better) better half, a dancer called Ursula Kübler, encouraged him to focus more fully on music. He had loyally tooted at Le Tabou throughout his literary ascent, arranging shows and wining and dining Count Basie, Charlie Parker, Duke Ellington...

---

* Our concept of *the future* has barely changed: aesthetically, it hasn't moved on at all from the excited, teenage comic-book designs of the 1940s. 'The function of the robot will depend on what we put into it.' Alexa; hentai. 'We're adaptable... we can make love, we laugh... oh, I don't doubt that some robots will laugh better; but without doubt not at themselves.' Boris Vian knew.

but now he's focused on writing and touring his own songs —alongside an A&R gig for Barclay's—and artistic direction for Philips.

His 1954 effort, 'Le Déserteur' / 'The Deserter' (recorded and released by Mouloudji) became a French karaoke standard due to its adoption by the student movement of the 1960s, with its full-fat encouragement to live on the dole and give peace a chance. It was banned in France, accused of insulting all soldiers in all places in all times. The song wasn't so much 'anti-military,' Vian would respond, as it was 'violently pro-civilian.' The media continued to characterise Vian as an 'existentialist,' a disparaging label it would use interchangeably with 'troglodyte.' The 'lower depths' of the Paris presided over by Vian were resident to a youth the tabloids defined by 'hatred, jealously, stupidity, and the most vulgar sexuality.' According to Vian, the male troglodytes of the entirely fabricated 'movement' had a shirt done down to the belly button come rain or shine. The lady troglodytes kept pockets filled with tamed white mice, and any use of make-up was strictly prohibited.

It was all a spirit, a world, a scene, a decadence and a rumble that the makers of 1959's *J'irai cracher sur vos tombes* tried to capitalise onscreen for the emergent Beats—latecomers to Vian's Paris though only a smidgeon younger, and only a shade more American.*

For the purpose of this text, I've stayed loyal to Vian's very public exit, and only watched the first ten minutes of the unauthorised film adaptation of *J'irai cracher sur vos tombes*. The copy I used, appropriately dubbed into German for a pirate DVD edition available on Amazon, inappropriately lists Boris as author on the sleeve's artwork. I blotted out his name in tribute. The story goes that Vian attended the film's preview on the morning of June 23 in 1959 at Cinema Marbeuf, Paris, if only to ensure his name had been scrubbed from the titles. The film opens to a man riding a forklift and playing the harmonica, in a tune composed by Alain Goraguer. He's met by actor Christian Marquand's protagonist, Joe Grant, and the camera follows them a little way before the brother is alone, again playing the harmonica, strolling alongside a railway track. A few cars filled with white men show up, and the next thing we know—somehow Joe knows too, even though the white men are still on the scene—he's racing to woodland, his brother hanging from a tree. Joe pulls him down, embraces him, and carries him to his

---

* Vian never went to America.

car. Some say Vian lasted ten minutes. This is unlikely. What I've described is all of five minutes in and it's quite enough. The writer stood up from his cinema seat and shouted: 'These guys are supposed to be American? My ass!' He then fell back, his weak heart finally giving up the ghost.

When Louis Malle—who Vian introduced to Miles Davis, who then went on to score his debut, *Elevator to the Gallows* —was asked by Julia Older if he believed *J'irai...* could have caused his death, the director responded: 'The cinema can kill, just like anything else.'

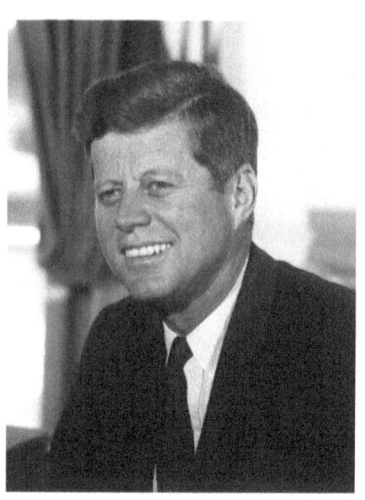

John F. Kennedy (d.1963)
From Russia with Love (Terence Young, 1963), 125m

Lee Harvey Oswald (d.1963)
War is Hell (Burt Topper, 1961), 15m (of 81m)

"Shut your mouth," said the wise old owl
Business is business, and it's a murder most foul
      —Bob Dylan

¶ John F. Kennedy's voracious appetite for books was borne of long hospital stays in his youth (Colitis, Addison's). By 1963, he'd been read the Last Rites many times (Catholic, Irish). He was forty-six; one doctor doubted he would make thirty-one.

In the early days of their courtship Johnnie gifted future wife Jackie *The Raven*, a biography of Sam Houston and the story of the making of Texas; confirming his interest, he'd then given her *Pilgrim's Way*, an embellished autobiography by John Buchan, the Scottish author-politician best known for his spy thrillers (*The 39 Steps* was adapted by Hitchcock), named for the Holy English road established by the assassination of the Martyred Saint, Thomas Becket. *Pilgrim's Way* was the book Kennedy implored anyone who wished to understand him to read. It was referenced as one of the President's favourite titles during National Library Week in 1963. Also listed was *From Russia, with Love*, published 1957, the fifth in writer Ian Fleming's series of James Bond novels. 'Understand me!'

Kennedy proclaimed his love for James Bond whenever he could. First, in a 1961 *LIFE* magazine feature at the height of his political popularity. At that time Bond was nationalist pulp for English public-school boys—he was practically invisible to America—and the President's promotion led to Fleming's first significant sales in the States. United Artists secured the film adaptation rights and rushed *Dr. No* into production owing, in no small part, to Kennedy's adulation of the character.

Kennedy tethered himself to Bond and, in particular, the Bond as embodied by Sean Connery, furnishing his own image with the character's sharp shooting, snazzy dressing, brawny brainy sophisticate. The spy knew anyone ordering a glass of Chianti with a fillet of sole was a villain, and that every hot woman from Sunderland to Siberia would martyr themselves at his elm altar with a bent Hail Mary. Though Fleming was at first distressed by the heft of Connery's card-carrying SNP-member milkman taking the role of his 'refined' (or never-worked-an-honest-day) murderous Tory James, he became so impressed by what the actor did for the character, that he built his Scottish heritage into subsequent books. United Artists' movie adaptations leapt non-sequentially from *Dr. No* to *From Russia with Love* directed by JFK's appreciation; Fleming ventriloquised his gratitude to the President for making him rich with Bond soppily pronouncing 'We need more Kennedys' in the series' next book, *The Spy Who Loved Me* (1962).

Fleming's *Spy* was one of only three books in the possession of Lee Harvey Oswald at the time of his arrest: the others
were Fleming's *Live and Let Die* (Bond is sent from London
to New York to investigate Mr. Big) and *A Study of the USSR and
Communism* by Alfred Rieber and Robert Nelson. Lee actively
sought out the books that Johnnie liked; though frequently accused of being thick, he too loved reading (especially the news),
and even journaled an interest in short story writing, imagining
a possible future for himself as a great literary documentarian
of the contemporary American experience (which may have been
a flicker of consideration as he crouched, cushioned and flank-
ed by book-upon-book, tissue-paper-wrapped or spine turned
inwards, in the room with the view on the sixth floor of the Texas
School Book Depository, from where the shots that killed the
President were fired, be it the books written about him or the
ones he'd write himself in prison).

The film adaptation of *The Spy Who Loved Me* (1977) was
the last movie watched by Elvis Presley (unable to obtain a copy
of his desired film, *Star Wars*), and Kennedy had a fan in Presley.
The singer watched live on television as Lee Harvey Oswald
was escorted towards a city-county jail transfer vehicle, and as
Dallas strip-club owner Jack Ruby stepped out of the crowd to
put a single, fatal bullet in his stomach. The medium's first live
homicide. Why? 'I just had to show the world that a Jew has
guts.' (The weirdo spent the previous night distributing free
sandwiches and soft drinks to police station officers.) Elvis held
court; responded; demanded from his friends there watching
TV with him, be it Jack or be it Lee, that if he, the King, were
to be dealt the same fate as the President, those present must
promise to reach the assailant before the police. A bullet would
be too easy. *Gouge his fucking eyes out.*

Between 1961 and 1963, President Kennedy watched eighty-
one films at the White House cinema: mainly new releases, he
broke in the auditorium with the John Huston and Arthur Miller
collaboration, *The Misfits*, starring Marilyn Monroe and Clark
Gable as capturers of wild horses in their last earthly roles;
thirteen foreign-language productions followed (probably the
dictate of Europhile Jackie) including Federico Fellini's *La Dolce
Vita* (one of the few arty films Johnnie would tolerate), Francois
Truffaut's *Jules et Jim*, Ingmar Bergman's *The Devil's Eye*, the Friedrich Durrenmatt-penned noir *It Happened In Broad Daylight*,
and Alain Resnais' *Last Year at Marienbad* (from which he walked

after twenty minutes); twenty-one internationally-produced movies (eight British, including *Mr. Topaze*; see Peter Sellers, pp.174–179). During these two years, Hollywood studios were transitioning from black and white to colour film, with stock historically expensive dramatically falling in price.

Colour mattered: the advent and accessibility of television meant that film producers had to distinguish their product. At home, 97% of Americans were condemned to a black and white world. Colour was the kino, and the pregnant journey to and fro.

The White House cinema was instituted by Franklin Roosevelt as a part of the President's residential quarters (leading from the West to the East Wing; looking onto a grass flat that Hillary Clinton would spend her First Ladyship stewarding as a sculpture garden). Public knowledge of Presidential viewing habits are entirely credit to Paul Fischer (and backed up in some instances by the diaries of individual Presidents), the one and only White House projectionist from 1953—aged twenty-five—until 1986, his retirement, spooling off titles picked by the three decades' seven US Presidents. Fischer had been a low-ranking Naval officer assigned to Harry Truman's Presidential yacht until someone caught wind of his ability to project 35mm film. Subject to a security review, he was dispatched to Washington and ordered to project whatever and whenever for the then newly-elected President Dwight Eisenhower (favourite movie: *High Noon*). Of his own accord, and to no particular end, Fischer kept meticulous records of the films he screened and the guests invited by the Presidents to watch them, which sat languishing as a stack of green ledgers in his home garage until the turn of the millennium, when a reporter, Irv Letofsky, showed up to prove or disprove their mythical reputation.

On November 11 in 1963, JFK saw *The 5000 Fingers of Dr. T*, an 'American musical about a boy who dreams himself into a fantasy world ruled by a diabolical piano teacher.' A day earlier, on November 10, he watched Nicholas Ray's *55 Days at Peking*, a historical epic about China's Boxer Rebellion starring Charlton Heston and Ava Gardner (one of many starlets with whom he was linked romantically). On November 13, Johnnie had Greta Garbo over for dinner, gifting her an engraved whale tooth and imploring her to stay the night. Garbo made fast work of her *calamares a la bruta* and fled. She knew he had recently shagged her great rival, Marlene Dietrich (sixteen years between her and

Johnnie, she was then sixty years-old) and so had his father, Joseph (which Johnnie *knew*). Prior to becoming a senator, Joseph had been a successful Hollywood producer. It was daddy that had made Johnnie a millionaire ten times over by the time he took office and paid the bribes and the propagandists to get him there. (Meanwhile around a quarter of US citizens earned less than $1500 annually.) Joseph's most coveted affair was with Gloria Swanson, today remembered for her late-career starring role in *Sunset Boulevard*. (*Sunset* is one of Donald Trump's favourite films, and the most repeatedly screened during his tenure as 45th US President; *Finding Dory* was the first he watched in office.) The affair ended when Swanson discovered an expensive gift from Kennedy had been charged to her own account.

It was little wonder Johnnie and Joey had a complicated relationship with sex: when Johnnie aged twelve caught Joey and Gloria mid-coit on the deck of the yacht named after his mother, Joey simply laughed at him (and Johnnie, 'crying, shaking,' unclear about exactly what daddy was doing, jumped overboard to swim to shore). In the early days of Johnnie and Jackie, Joey steered his son's girlfriend away from watching a Ronald Reagan film with the family, so that he could show her a room full of bound dolls, and boast to her about how much Gloria Swanson used to like to bonk with the toys looking on, describing with scientific scrutiny the character of her genitals. Joseph by that time had made the equivalent of $85,000,000.00 from his Hollywood investments (in a 1957 *Fortune* magazine article he was said to have a net worth of between $200–400,000,000.00), including profits from a 'successful' plot to frame a rival cinema-chain owner for rape because he refused to sell to Kennedy something that wasn't for sale. This afforded Johnnie and his siblings the ultra-rare privilege of their own home movie auditorium while growing up. Joey (*laughing*) groomed Johnnie for the country's top role not through his experience in politics, but through the more mercenary practices of shooting film and making stars.

On the morning of November 16, Johnnie travelled from Palm Beach, Florida, to NASA HQ at Cape Canaveral (later renamed Cape Kennedy), where he hung out with Nazi rocket-man Werner von Braun. By the afternoon he was back in Palm Beach taking a swim, and later watched a game of football on TV. In the evening he serenaded his dinner guests with a 'better than usual' rendition of his very favourite tune, 'September Song' by Kurt Weill (former husband of Lotta Lenya who sang a great many of the songs originally composed for and with Bertolt Brecht, and who plays a sabre-toed Rosa Klebb in *From Russia with Love*). On November 17 he watched Tony Richardson's gadabout *Tom Jones* at a private screening in Palm Beach. By contrast with its source material, the film did very little: two earthquakes were blamed on the book's publication in 1749. The film crystallised the 1960s before things really started swinging; giving permission for good guys to sleep about, and even making bad guys of those who didn't. Johnnie would have liked to recognise himself in the titular tom-cat, compensating for a sickly childhood by couching all he desired. True success meant the collapse of fantasy into reality through adventures in sex. The kino was foreplay for the forensic possibilities of real life; the depth and clarity that couldn't be shown on screen (until his head was exploded and all the allusions that made art sacred and sex sexy were exploded with it). Before Johnnie knew Marilyn, he had a poster of her upside down (legs akimbo), pinned to the rear of his hospital door as he recovered from back surgery in 1954. While Jackie complained about the poster, she unwittingly made the problem worse: delivering Johnnie his first encounter with James Bond in Fleming's first book, *Casino Royale*. A fateful, toxic combination. Marilyn, Bond, James... back-brace, bang-bang, smokey-smoke, cortisone, methadone, codeine, change, Demerol, Ritalin, rights, power, powder, meprobamate... and librium, gamma... globulin... the President rose up. The poster was from Marilyn's recent breakout role in *Niagara*, the Technicolor picture by Henry Hathaway that made her a star. It was from this film that Warhol stole the image basis for his infamous Marilyn silkscreens (awarding Jackie the same treatment in the immediate aftermath of Johnnie's assassination); even Fleming references the image in *From Russia, with Love*, titling a chapter 'The Mouth of Marilyn Monroe.' A huge billboard promotes *Niagara* with Marilyn's face; her mouth is a trap-hole a villain attempts to escape through, but who Bond and an ally have sights on. *Tom Jones* may have been John's last movie (it was certainly Tony Richardson's most successful: funds from which he'd use a couple of years later to support the prison break of Soviet spy, George Blake).* There is only Fischer's book-keeping to rely on, and there are errors: according to the projectionist's notes he was showing films for the President's delight all of one week after his death, on November 29.

In the run up to the Texas trip, Kennedy had been on the campaign trail seeking to mend his fractured Democratic Party

and win a second term as President. A brief stopover 'home'
at the Oval Office on November 20 (brother Robert's birthday, for
which a party was held where Gene Kelly and sixty others danced
to the accordion) before jetting off to Texas on the morning of
November 21 would have been an ideal opening to watch *From
Russia with Love*. Fischer records just one guest: Arthur M.
Schlesinger Jr., John's special assistant and 'court historian'
(a screening of the Bond film organised by Schlesinger on the
evening of November 21 when Kennedy was in Fort Worth is
sometimes referenced; this may have happened, but it may also
be misattributed given the chaos of the events that followed.
This was the President's home theatre, after all). Kennedy would
have viewed the movie propped up on pillows from an ortho-
paedic bed set up in the cinema to ease his chronic back pain.
It would have been a touch after midnight and he probably
enjoyed a doobie. During the final two years of his life, regular

---

* Until *Tom Jones*, Tony Richardson's films were shot in a monochrome true
to his locations: Derby, Salford, Nottingham. In the full colour of Dorset,
the director might have seemed to have betrayed something fundamental
to lovers of his realist kitchen sink fare. But two years later, in 1966, the financial success of the film would allow him to fund a prison break (he won
Oscars for best director and best film; netting $17 million at the US box
office alone). George Blake was a British spy convicted of sharing official
secrets with the Soviet Union. He was given forty-two years. The incarcerat-
ed spy once had had the ambition of becoming a Calvinist Priest: in other
words, he had no choice. He was destined to two-time. And if Christianity
prayed for heaven in the afterlife, Communism was minded to make it
on earth. Richardson then was destined to fund his release, persuaded
by a priest, the Reverend John Papworth (former Labour Party councillor).
It was the inhumanity of the sentence's length that inspired Papworth
to help the masterminds of the break: Sean Bourke, an Irishman who'd
served time for trying to blow up a detective (and would later be poisoned
by the KGB), and anti-war campaigners Pat Pottle and Michael Randle (who
eventually went to trial in 1991; the jury exercised their moral judgement,
refused to convict them and set them free of charge). While the inmates
and guards at Wormwood Scrubs were enjoying their monthly movie night,
Blake was able to smash a window near his cell, and escape through a shaft
to the grassy perimeter around the prison wall. Bourke, who had previously
equipped Blake with a walkie-talkie smuggled into the prison so they could
coordinate, threw a rope ladder over the wall and... that was that. After
several weeks shared across London safe-houses, Randle and his wife Anne
hid Blake in their camper van and managed to get him to a checkpoint in
East Germany. He lived the rest of his life on a KGB pension, with a fancy
flat in central Moscow and a summerhouse provided, dying aged 98 in
2020. Alfred Hitchcock spent years developing a film based on Blake's story,
possessing the rights to his memoir and Ronald Kirkbride's novelisation
of the escape, *The Short Night*. Walter Matthau and Catherine Deneuve
were approached to play leads, but these were eventually assigned Sean
Connery and Liv Ullman. The project died with him.

meetings were had with painter Mary Pinchot Meyer—herself a
target of assassination in 1964 (like Johnnie, shot in the back and
the head)—who quoted the President's limit of three spliffs in
any one session. 'No more! Suppose the Russians did something
now.' She was also frequently seeing Timothy 'hero of American
consciousness' Leary at this time. The guru would go on to credit Mary for influencing John's views on nuclear disarmament
(inferring their consumption of LSD). With less familiar guests
the President would sit centrestage in a rocking chair, soberly
(painfully) smoking a cigar. Fischer fails to record 'the bagman'
as Johnnie's guest, but wherever he went—to the pool of Palm
Beach, to Wendy house Meyer or Wendy house Monroe—'the
bagman' was ever present; closer and more constant even than
Jackie, especially as the White House caravan hit the road.

The bagman's job was straightforward. He carried a black,
die cast metal suitcase, with a combination code lock (also
known as 'the black bag' and 'the football'). All he had to do was
carry that case, and remember the code to open it. Inside was
the technology for a telephone line to the Prime Minister in the
UK and the President of France, which could be hastily assembled anywhere with four minutes notice. Also inside were a series of cryptic numbers: the codes to launch a full-scale nuclear
attack, with a literal cartoon-comic book to demonstrate to the
President and his aides in the simplest possible terms how many
million human casualties they could expect from the degrees
of assault they had to select from.

From Russia with Love had premiered in London that
last October. Its adaptation from book to film replaced nemesis SMERSH, the Red Army's real-life counter intelligence unit
(which Bond destroys) with a Russian crime syndicate, lest a
mistaken culture war activate the services of the bagman. The
comma in the title was trashed. Otherwise, it's a straight-up
book-to-movie adaptation: lowest common denominator English spy-thriller fare of haughty cuisine; expensive smoking;
stupid gadgets, car chases, 'semi-rape' and the killing of foreign-
ers and homosexuals. Kennedy had already seen it once, able to
obtain an advance copy screened at the White House on October
23 in the company of his brother Robert, and Ben Bradlee (of the
Washington Post, and Mary Meyer's brother-in-law). 'Kennedy
seemed to enjoy the cool and the sex and the brutality,' Bradlee
reported. 'He seldom sat through an entire film, but he watched
this one to the end.' Jackie held a dinner that same evening,

95

and wore a dress given to her by the King of Jordan. Silk, sequins; as she delivered the roasties she imitated a belly dancer, and the group would have chuckled later in acknowledging the black mirror of the belly dancer in the movie's opening sequence.

The only other films Kennedy is known to have watched twice while in office were the *Guns of Navarone* and *West Side Story*. When *From Russia with Love* released theatrically across the USA in May 1964, it was done with a savvy and macabre marketing ploy: distributor United Artists issued it as a double-bill with Burt Topper's *War is Hell*, the film seen in-part by Lee Harvey Oswald as he hid at Dallas' Texas Theatre, from where he was apprehended shortly after the shooting of the President (initially for the murder of a police officer, J.D. Tippit). This double was a neat riff on LHO's brief abandon to Soviet Russia, and the heat of the Cold War. As the open-topped motorcade passed the Texas Book Depository, and made its way along the grassy knoll of Dealey Plaza, Jackie said to JFK, 'You certainly can't say that the people of Dallas haven't given you a nice welcome,' to which Johnnie responded (his last words), 'No, you certainly can't.' Bang (bang, bang [bang?]).

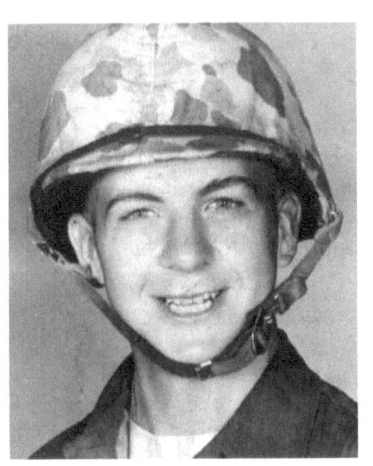

¶ How Lee Harvey Oswald made his way from the Texas School Book Depository to the Texas Theatre is a source of speculation. Perhaps he'd planned to see that afternoon's double-bill, or went on a whim to take advantage of the workday cut short. It was a shoe store employee who noticed an anxious-looking Lee, who had stopped to survey the items in the store window as police cars raced by. Meanwhile, the radio reported the killing of a police officer only streets away. The worker, Johnny Calvin Brewer, then watched Oswald slip into the neighbouring cinema without paying for a ticket. 90 cents to his hourly rate of $1.25. What if he had paid? Unlikely Brewer would have approached the box office and encouraged them to call the police. The manager that day reports selling popcorn to Oswald but it's almost certainly untrue (sneaking into a scantly attended auditorium only to reemerge after eight minutes to announce yourself for the sake of some salty puffs?). From the balcony entrance Oswald could descend stairs to the orchestra, where he sat three seats down, five seats over. The official government report has him browsing the shoes at 1:35pm (before there were any police on the scene), but the cinema workers and Brewer corroborate a time of 1:20pm, meaning that he would have caught the beginning of the double-bill. *War is Hell* opens with a 'dramatic foreword' by Texas' own Audie Murphy, that rare bloom of poverty-stricken forebears who beat his circumstances to become an all-American (rich) golden boy, winning twenty-four combat medals killing 240 people. Replete with an all-American case of PTSD before it had a name (Murphy, like Bond, slept with a loaded gun beneath his pillow), he left the battlefield for Hollywood and turned his military accomplishments into a fairly successful acting career, before a barroom brawl had him on attempted murder charges, and filing for bankruptcy (his final film, *A Time for Dying*, in which he briefly appears as Jesse James, was produced as an attempt to repay a debt he owed to the Las Vegas mafia). Audie would die abruptly at forty-six, the same age as JFK, in a plane crash (he's interred not far from JFK at Arlington National Cemetery; Baynes Barron, star of *War is Hell*, is buried elsewhere, but he was born on the same day and in the same year as JFK).

In the film's foreword, Murphy speaks from what could be any hotel room. It seems that he's dressed himself, in a loose, light, blazer and a skinny tie, and he's strangely hunched, as though accommodating for a stubbornly placed camera, or holding his trousers up, or keeping it all together for the all-important last words struggled through the mortal stomach wound of film noir archetype. The blinds are pulled behind him but with a snick of daylight coming through, willing the booze-soaked undoing of the traumatised veteran in *Apocalypse Now*. 'This then is the story of a man who though carrying the finest in military equipment was not well armed,' says Murphy reflecting on the moral ineptitude of the character at the centre of the film. The frightened sergeant, so goes the synopsis, leads his men to massive slaughter, before feigning gallant emergence as a hero of war. Though the film is considered 'lost' today, we can see about as much as Oswald did. A desert landscape recognisable from American Westerns is cast as South Korea, and two 'baddies' launch bomb after bomb against advancing Yanks who move about the sands shooting, without direction. Most die. The remaining soldiers rest; coldly reflecting on their fallen compatriots, one berates the other for a bad record. Oswald would have winced. It is said that all he could do was shoot. And read, just about. What place for either in Dallas, Texas? There's a cut then in the available copy of the film; a scribble of celluloid chewed up, the minor work burdened by the shock of its unlikely place in history, and a chunk missing to render what remains of the film indecipherable. According to the clock time of the police reports, and citations by the cinema and shoe shop workers, this is just about the point the police would have arrived. The film would have stopped, the house lights brought up.

The feds aborted a raid on a local library when the call came through from the cinema at 1:46pm. By 1:50pm they were in there, cigar-toking and shotgun-wielding. No more than a dozen spectators were in attendance, and cast their eyes to the floor—sucking rather than chewing their popcorn, lest a crunch render them accessory to the unknown crime—as Officer M.N. McDonald made his search up the left aisle, frisking each watcher as he went. He stopped at Oswald and told him to stand up. Oswald did, and cried 'Well, it's all over now,' allegedly punching the officer first and pulling a pistol from his waistband. The gun clicked but failed to fire, and Oswald, beaten by a succession of officers, ceased resistance. 'I protest this police brutality!' He shouted as he was pulled from the exit and into the daylight, from the invisible loser-dom of a vicious twenty-four years, to a fame the size of Pontius Pilate. Bigger. An American Judas. The crowd exited too; fled. But did they re-enter for their money's worth? The second in the double, *Cry of Battle*, at 3pm?*

It's a film Oswald might have identified with more closely; emotionally; principally, describing the plight of a third world country raped and plundered by Imperialist America. In the back of the police car Oswald protested; asked what was going on. 'I don't know why you are treating me like this,' he said. 'The only thing I have done is carry a pistol into a movie.' The cinema manager, or popcornist, immediately reentered the auditorium and replaced the seat still warm from Oswald with an identical other, expecting the authorities to return to take it for evidence (which they did the following day, with the convicted killer's red sitting pretty at the popcornist's apartment; though this, true to form, could have been an elaborate rouse to attempt to later sell one of the standard auditorium seats for the premium of the assassin's sweat).

Though there were many people filming that day only one piece of footage caught the moment Kennedy was shot and shot again. Abraham Zapruder was an exiled Russian Jew to whom America's liberalism was antidote and saviour. In this way the Zapruder movie, a home movie (and a narrative movie) is also a political movie; the dressmaker attended that day out of reverence for Kennedy's politics, and to preserve the moment the President visited his town for his family. By the early hours of November 23, the 8mm format 26-second-long film had sold to Dick Stolley at *LIFE* for $150,000 ($1.5 million-*ish* in today's money), but on the condition the frame displaying the fatal shot be removed from any public exhibition. *LIFE* printed still images from the footage, but it wasn't until 1975 that the film was actually broadcast on television, made possible by that era's violent coverage of the Vietnam War, and the immediate action-replay, the technology for which was developed shortly after Kennedy's killing. What the average viewer could expect and would accept to see on their TV shifted; loosened. A bloody sport. Zapruder had no scruples about making money from his accidental snuff movie, but as he slept on November 22, he had had a nightmare: a billboard in Times Square, New York City, pulsated with the

---

* In Don DeLillo's quasi-fictional account of Oswald's arrest, his 1988 novel *Libra*, *Cry of Battle* is the first picture screened in the double-bill, interrupted by Oswald's apprehension. The film resumes, with the seven male attendees staying put. 'It wasn't just this picture to see to the end. There was a second picture coming up, called *War is Hell*.'

'He had an eerie sense he was being watched for his reaction,' writes DeLillo on Oswald's probable viewing of the movie. 'He felt connected to the events on the screen. It was like secret instructions entering the network of signals and broadcast bands, the whole busy air of transmission.'

words 'See the President's head explode!' (In a later episode of dreams and nightmares, he gifted $35,000.00 of his blood-fortune to the widow of J.D. Tippit.) In the twelve years Zapruder's film remained effectively suppressed, it became an unholy grail of underground movie projections, even performing the role of some kind of genus for an intimate and politically charged film-making sometimes called 'structural' and 'experimental.' The only copies that existed had been made for official analysis, with additional distribution relying on pirating by labs employed to analyse the footage. Copies did get out, with the circumstances surrounding one such screening described in Don DeLillo's elephantine *Underworld*, '...not unlike the showing of a midnight film... The event had a cachet, an edge of special intensity. But if those in attendance felt they were lucky to be here, they also knew a kind of floating fear, a mercury reading out of the sixties, with a distinctly trippy edge.' The recording of the event broke reality; the deadly truth of the black-magic camera was revealed in this readymade of chaos, and Zapruder's movie meant the snuffification of image-kultur. Given first to the loft-radicals —after, to the gore of the emergent *Texas Chainsaw*—and on to the every-man banality of image-consumption today through social media. The last movie; the first. Following its television broadcast, LIFE returned the copyright to Zapruder's family for the gestural fee of $1. In 1999, the United States government approached the family to purchase the original film strip for its National Archives. They asked for $30,000,000.00, arguing that the film should be valued on par with other monumental artworks, specifically Van Gogh's 'Sunflowers,' which had sold for $40,000,000 twelve years earlier. The government bristled, countering with an offer of $1,000,000 and eventually stumping up $16,000,000.

Two months before Zapruder, Kennedy had enacted his own murder in an 8mm home-movie. This is now considered lost, but testimonials from those there on the day describe the shoot: the presidential yacht (the 'Honey Fitz' named for Johnnie's mom in the son's adult purge of dad's callous laughter) docked at Hammersmith Farm in Newport, Rhode Island, where Jackie had grown up. Inspired by James Bond, Johnnie was visited by the muse. Filmed by Naval photographer Robert Knudsen, who often travelled with the first family, the President-Director had his friend Red Fay in a pair of boxer shorts chasing around a bikini-clad Vivian Crespi, the Kennedy's 'house-guest,' ending up writhing around on top of her in the shrub. At some point Kennedy appears to join in and bullets are fired. He is killed, and so is Fay, making ample use of tomato ketchup as Vivien and Jackie step over and beyond the bodies (an alternative recollection of the film has JFK joining the ladies in stepping over Fay [Joey?]). This wasn't the first time Kennedy had steered into creation a film about the death of a politician: *The Manchurian Candidate* was initially blocked from production due to its subject matter involving the murder of a presidential candidate. Only through Kennedy's direct consent to Frank Sinatra, who both starred in and produced the film, was its making possible. Kennedy watched *The Manchurian Candidate* at the White House on August 29 in 1962, accompanied by his brother, Robert, and a handful of others (whose names are not recorded in the projectionist's ledger). It is unknown whether Lee Harvey Oswald ever watched *The Manchurian Candidate* during its cinematic release in Dallas in 1962, but another Sinatra vehicle, *Suddenly*, was broadcast on television shortly before news of the Presidential motorcade's run through Dallas was publicly announced (Forrest V. Sorrels, head of Dallas' Secret Service office, who oversaw the route, had once counted the loot of a captured John Dillinger in Tucson, Arizona). *Suddenly* stars Sinatra as the would-be assassin of a fictional American President, pretending to be an FBI agent in order to enter the building from which he's established the best possible vantage point for the killing shot. (His opponent is the town Sheriff, Sterling Hayden, best known as the Texan playing rodeo with the atomic bomb in Stanley Kubrick's *Dr. Strangelove*, released seven weeks after the killing of JFK.)

Nancy Sinatra, who'd go on to sing the Bond theme 'You Only Live Twice' (intended by producer Cubby Broccoli to be sung by her dad), reflected on her own prevailing memory of Johnnie's death: Frankie cried for days afterwards. The A-lister had been hugely influential in delivering Johnnie to office, an intersection of artistic and political life that was unusual for the time, and which yellow-brick'd the road for literal screen stars to shoot their way to the top job. The Kennedys were more like young celebrities than political institution: Johnnie was the first President to really embrace the camera, and both he and *especially* Jackie were sensitive to the arts ('Art is not a form of propaganda, art is a form of truth,' Johnnie reflected on creative expression in democratic America). There is something candid; an awkwardness and humanity to Johnnie on film that we might assign to an infancy of on-camera media training. It may equally be the tainting of all of the pre-recorded footage in the knowledge of those final, powerless frames. It may more simply be that he was loaded. Frankie is the opposite. Never without a roof on his limo. It's unclear when the two first met, but they'd been friends for years: Pat, the President's sister, was married to fellow Rat Packer, Peter Lawford AKA Dorian Gray (responsible for introducing Marilyn Monroe to Johnnie and Bobbie Kennedy, both of whom would enjoy torrid affairs with the fragile star, and the latter of whom is frequently accused of her murder). At one of the music group's shows in 1960, Frankie bent down from the stage and welcomed Johnnie to Las Vegas, divining him 'the next President of the United States.' A re-worked version of his hit, 'High Hopes'—from Frank Capra's *Hole in the Head*, ahem—became Johnnie's campaign anthem and was released anonymously as a promotional seven-inch single in Virginia and Washington, unmistakably sung by Frank. For stage manager Joey Kennedy, Sinatra's optimistic croon wasn't the opportunity—rather it was what his organised crime ties could do to shape the union vote. These ties would ulti-mately push Sinatra in to an affair with sister Pat as Johnnie's Presidency found its footing, in an attempt to soften the admin-istration's increased pressure on his buddies in the mob. This, and Frank's flagrant mingling with dodgy Italians would see the actor-singer cast out. He was banned from the White House, and responded furiously by excising Peter Lawford from all future Rat-Packing. Sinatra withdrew into fear and conspiracy, ultimate-ly switching sides to support the Republican candidate Kennedy had narrowly beaten to office in 1960: Richard Nixon.

The first film shown at the White House was D.W. Griffith's *Birth of a Nation*, selected by President Woodrow Wilson in 1915. Griffith was there to watch it with him. The event was widely reported and controversial: *Birth of a Nation* revels in the deg-radation of Black Americans, and was considered responsible for a surge in Ku Klux Klan membership. The film travelled first as a roadshow, intentionally failing to meet the scale of public demand: tickets to see it were 'dynamically' priced, with Griffith inflating admission to around $64 per person. This contributed to making the film the highest-grossing picture of all time, until the 1937 Disney picture, *Snow White & the Seven Dwarfs* (watched by Franklin Roosevelt, famous lover of all things animated) which held the record briefly, beaten in 1939 by *Gone with the Wind*. Though exactly what the film grossed is contested, *Deep Throat* would apparently batter this record in 1972; there is no evidence *Deep Throat* was screened at the White House, but Nixon was in office so all bets are off. Nixon's taste in movies is the most adventurous, with a predictable affection for American Westerns offset by a weakness for Robert Altman, Peter Bogdanovich, and British folk horror. As the President was implored to resign over the Watergate break-in—'Deep Throat,' in lieu of the film was the nickname given the informant who first blew the whistle on the Nixon administration's misdeeds—he was whiling away his evenings watching films like *The Collector*, with Terence Stamp starring as 'one of the most cunning, evil characters of modern fiction,' in the story of a young, female art student kidnapped; and Godless works about evil little boys: the far-out *Twisted Nerve* (famed for Bernard Herrmann's whistling theme, recycled in Quentin Tarantino's *Kill Bill* and then by Honda for a 2015 car ad, and slammed for using Down Syndrome to explain murderous tendencies) and further still: *What the Peeper Saw* starring Britt Ekland, Bond girl in *The Man with the Golden Gun* (see Peter Sellers, p.174–179). Nixon repeatedly watched *Patton*, the biopic of the antisemitic warmonger, which reportedly influenced him to retract his commitment to withdraw 150,000 American soldiers from Vietnam, and instead send thousands more to invade Cambodia.

The assassination of Richard Nixon had long been the ambition of a long-forgotten loser called Arthur Bremer. With inspiration derived from Stanley Kubrick's *A Clockwork Orange*, and driven by an appetite for personal fame rather than any political ideology, Bremer dedicated page upon page of a private diary to his plans for Nixon's murder. He eventually decided it would be too difficult and settled instead on the death of Nixon's friend, the pro-Segregationist Governor George Wallace. Wallace was campaigning in the Democratic Presidential primaries when Bremer shot him four times outside a Maryland shopping centre. The governor survived but was permanently crippled by the attack, and his presidential ambitions were ended. Bremer was given a life sentence and his diaries were published, becoming a huge source of inspiration for the Paul Schrader-penned *Taxi Driver*. Another loser called John Hinckley became obsessed with having a 'magical unification' with Jodie Foster's sex-trafficked twelve-year-old character in *Taxi Driver*, and moved to

New Haven, Connecticut when she got into Yale University to, uh, cast the spell. Failing to do so, Hinckley decided he'd kill himself to get her attention, but then revised his plan: instead, he'd kill the President; that old Pioneer player, Ronald Reagan. He failed, but managed to paralyse an agent in the process. Reagan was an appropriate match for Hinkley, famously struggling to distinguish reality from fantasy; Nancy, The First Lady, only let Ron watch the films he starred in on his birthday. One of these, *Murder in the Air* (1940) foresaw the failed 'Star Wars' programme Reagan attempted to implement in 1983, using a long-range laser ray-gun to protect the United States against airborne aggressors.

Gerald Ford (who followed Nixon into the premiership) didn't care about movies but he did like *Home Alone*. In 1975, Ford too was the target of a failed assassination attempt by Lynette 'Squeaky' Fromme, a Manson Family member. It could be said that Kennedy's assassination hailed the beginning of the '60s proper; Martin Luther King's assassination marked the death of the era's possibilities (it *was* a Revolution), and Manson's Tate killings the burial thereof; America 'lost the narrative thread.' Squeaky follows Lee Harvey and the rest of them outside of history and into dreamland. Way ahead of her (end) time, she described her motivation as President Ford's refusal to tackle environmental pollution, and stood barely an arms-length from him when she pulled the trigger. But she'd failed to chamber a round. Ford was fine and Squeaky was put away for thirty-four years. Her pistol eventually found its way to the Gerald R. Ford Presidential Museum, and today, out of dodge, she freely proclaims that she's still in love with Charlie. Lee Harvey's firearms are in the possession of the FBI, hidden under lock and key (estranged wife Marina tried to claim rights to the weapons in order to sell them, having checked out Lee's diary for $20,000 and the photo she took of him with the rifle in question for $5000—a photograph central to Oswald's conviction, as it tied his weapon to his earlier assassination attempt of a far-right General who Oswald believed could become an American Hitler); Jack Ruby's revolver, which he bought for $62.50, was sold at auction in 1991 for $220,000, depreciating in value by 2008 when it was sold again for $200,000.

Jimmy Carter, the farmer of peanuts who chased Ford from the *Casa-blanca* was crazy for *Gone with the Wind*, and movies in general; he screened 480—two to three per week—during his one term in office. Bond titles included *From Russia with Love*, *Man with the Golden Gun*, *Live and Let Die*, *Diamonds are Forever*, *Thunderball*, *Goldfinger*, *The Spy Who Loved Me* (see Elvis Presley, pp.136–156), along with *For a Few Dollars More* and *A Fistful of Dollars* (see Sergio Leone, pp.206–210), *One Flew Over the Cuckoo's Nest* (see Phil Ochs, pp.126–134), *2001: A Space Odyssey* and *Barry Lyndon* (see Stanley Kubrick, pp.30–41; see Charlie Chaplin, pp.30–41), *The Graduate* (see George Cukor, pp.196–199), *The Marriage of Maria Braun* (see Rainer Werner Fassbinder, pp.185–195), and *Patton*. Carter watched more movies starring Humphrey Bogart than any other actor: *The Petrified Forest*, *African Queen*, *The Treasure of the Sierra Madre*, *Maltese Falcon*, *Key Largo*, *The Big Sleep*, et cetera. All the Presidents loved Bogie, and the one cinematic and cultural through-line from day dot is Michael Curtiz's *Casablanca* (meaning 'White House'). It was Johnnie's favourite; Barack Obama's too. Donald Trump is such a big fan of the film that, in 1998, he was involved in a fierce bidding war at Sotheby's for the upright piano used in the Paris flashback scene ('You must remember this...'), losing out to an anonymous Japanese business conglomerate at $154,000.

Lyndon Johnson, who Richard Nixon described as 'an animal' and then as 'a man' (in a tone suggesting the latter the graver of the two), was a Texan known for donning a sombrero and watching *The Searchers*, but he otherwise didn't much care for films. The one that he did project over and over again during his Presidency, was that which he commissioned about himself in the immediate aftermath of Johnnie's killing: a ten-minute short meaning to 'introduce' himself to the American public, voiced by Gregory Peck. This was extended in 1965 to cover his achievements as President, once again narrated by Peck, in a staggeringly boring example of propagandistic movie-making. However vain and insecure, it may have been necessary for Johnson to have crafted these pictures: though he'd been Vice President, this was a role JFK himself described 'a miserable job,' and the less restrained in his administration, 'A pitcher of warm spit.' His celebrity was so non-existent that his home telephone number was listed in the public directory, and Marina Oswald had never heard his name. Even Johnson's codename stank, 'Volunteer' to his wife's 'Victoria,' whereas Johnnie got 'Lancer' and Jackie got 'Lace.' Much later, at Barack Obama's inauguration, writer Harper Lee—who gave Peck his career-defining character in *To Kill a Mockingbird*—recalled a conversation with the actor: he had asked President Johnson if he thought 'we will live to see a Black President.' 'No,' Johnson replied, 'But I wish her well.' In the wake of JFK's assassination, Johnson quickly decided with the FBI's Mr. Big (J. Edgar Hoover) that blame lay squarely with Lee Harvey Oswald and 'the gun that won the West'—the unlikely repeating rifle of Hollywood lore (the particular gun in Oswald's possession was built for Mussolini's fascist troops in 1940; a cheap, surplus rifle obtained in a job-lot by an American mail-order company in 1960). Their motivations for this position and the government's stubborn insistence on it—though Johnson privately doubted a single shooter—have assisted the industry of conspiracy theories around the circumstances of JFK's end. Be it an inside job, or Oswald alone, there is no obvious motive. That Lee was driven to assassinate the President by his Russian wife putting her goddamn foot-down hardly adds up; nor does the idea that Lee had nothing and Johnnie had it all, and that'll do it. Look around. It doesn't.

When Fort Worth culture reporter, Owen Day, found out about Johnnie and Jackie's trip, he used his contacts at the newspaper for precise details of their visit. As an admirer of Kennedy, and on behalf of Fort Worth, he was mortified that Lyndon and his wife, Lady Bird (!), had been booked into the more expensive and luxurious rooms on the 13th floor at the Hotel Texas ($100 per night: Lady Bird had stayed here before; insert your conspiracy). Johnnie and Jackie had a modest suite by comparison, on the 8th ($75 per night: Jackie had never visited Texas), with views of the bus station and a parking lot. Three bedrooms with Delft blue walls; a faux-golden gilded lintel. Sand-coloured corner sofa. Black marble coffee table in four parts. Duff air con. No TV. The last night. Familiar with the sub-Presidential suite, Day hurried to intervene, conceiving each room as a separate gallery for a one-night art exhibition exclusively for the couple. Writer David Lubin characterised Day's actions as an 'act of aesthetic charity,' saving the weary travellers from the faceless 'tedium' of a life lived in lifeless hotel rooms. With the help of banker and society-circle don, Samuel Benton Cantey III, Day obtained paintings and sculptures from different sources, and the project went from conception to completion within five days. The local Republican collector of art, Ruth Carter Johnson, was especially forthcoming, delivering Pablo Picasso's 'Angry Owl' herself by car, seat-belted and destined to sit atop a table beneath a wall-mounted portrait by Monet of his granddaughter. It was a subversive move:

conservatives were broadly rattled by any inclusion anywhere
of artists or anyone else expressing support of that which wasn't
the status quo—mixing such a classic, bourgeois example with
the radical bronze was blasphemy. For this painting and that
sculpture to share the same building, never mind the same
room, was inconceivable; its creator was an active member of
the Communist Party, and recipient of the Stalin Peace Prize.
Jackie might have clocked the affectionate portrait of the child
and admired her as one of her own, or averted her gaze as one
that wasn't to be. This trip to Texas, The First Lady's first time
in the state, was also the first time she'd been seen publicly
in three months, recovering after the stillbirth of a son, Patrick.
And while to Johnnie and his Bible the bird of the night con-
trasting the girl was a symbol of wisdom and knowledge, to
Jackie's cultured reader of Shakespeare it was a bad, bad omen:
the appearance of the owl in Macbeth announces the imminent death of the King. An anagram of Lee Harvey Oswald is:
a shy owl revealed.

Among the exhibits were more divining apparatus: Charles
Marion Russell's 'Lost in a Snowstorm—We are Friends,' de-
picting a group of Indigenous American men guiding a group of
cowboys to safety, is a plea for reflection and correction in a time
of extreme violence and division. Kennedy seemed to represent
this tolerance, and revision, and Fort Worth meant to reassure
him with this painting that so did they, as a city; values anathe-
ma to the pioneer trope of '*good Indian = dead Indian*' that their
anti-neighbour, Dallas, proudly purveyed. 'In my book a pioneer
is a man who turned all the grass upside down, strung bob-wire
over the dust that was left, poisoned the water, cut down the
trees, killed the Indian who owned the land and called it prog-
ress,' Russell is quoted as saying, and it's a sentiment located
surprisingly close in time to the Dallas of Kennedy's visit. Only
twenty years earlier the population of the town had been less
than 300,000. In 1963 this had grown to well over 1.6 million, with
hustlers piling in to attempt to exploit the discovery of the East
Texas oil pool—and, where necessary, take the law into their own
hands. Dallas alone witnessed more murders each month than
all of England; by November 22 in 1963 it had already experienced
110 killings (72% by gunfire; there was no requirement for firearms registration, nor firearms control of any kind). Kennedy's
name was booed in classrooms; it is said the children of Texas
were the only Americans to cheer upon news of his assassination.

Jewish stores were daubed in swastikas. Billboards screamed bloody murder and housewives spat at their politicians. Burn! Kill! Glory to God! Which Kennedy do *you* hate the most? The madness was presided over, engulfed and encouraged by the *Dallas News*, which described Washington D.C. at the time as a city inhabited by 'an unknown number of subversives, perverts, and miscellaneous security risks,' with a President who followed the 'atheistic, godless line... the communist line.' The *News* shared its headquarters on the same plaza as the Texas School Book Depository, the sniper's nest, named Dealey after the newspaper founder's father.

Kennedy had repeatedly expressed his wish not to go to Texas, and particularly Dallas, and his reservations were shared by the Democratic National Committeeman, Byron Skelton, with a hunch that the President would never be made aware of. In letters to the Attorney General, and the right-hand man of Lyndon Johnson, Skelton expressed his growing 'uneasiness' about Dallas and the President's scheduled stop there. The atmosphere was charged and inflammatory, and he believed 'a nut' could act in accord with this violent energy. The letters were taken seriously but failed to have the desired effect of changing Johnnie's itinerary. Skelton went so far as to fly to Washington to appear in person to Jerry Bruno at the National Committee. 'Regardless of previous commitments,' he pleaded, 'it should be avoided.' Senator William Fulbright of Arkansas (bordering Texas) shared the same view, and Evangelist Billy Graham claimed to have experienced a bloody foreboding forewarned by God himself. For Johnnie, Texas was a critical voting base. Part of the reason he'd installed Lyndon Johnson as his Vice President—the two had run against each other for the top job in 1960—was for his stake as a Texas boy. Kennedy had beaten Nixon by only 46,233 votes in Johnson's home State, and this was before he really started making sounds about the Southern-unspeakable of Civil Rights. Ever unpopular with the ultra-conservative voters of the South, Segregationists believed he'd gone way too far in announcing the Civil Rights bill; others, including Oswald, thought that he hadn't gone nearly far enough. Though this was a long way from entering law; even reaching congress, the bill broadly committed to the end of segregation / discrimination in public spaces on the basis of race. It was eventually passed under Lyndon Johnson's administration in 1964. The killing of Johnnie changed everything.

For security reasons, the photographer tasked with documenting the Hotel Texas exhibition, Byron Scott of the Bell Helicopter Company (a friend of journalist Day and, curiously enough, a work colleague of Michael Paine [Bell], the partner of whom, Ruth, was sheltering Marina Oswald having left Lee at the time of Kennedy's assassination), was not allowed into the private quarters of Johnnie and Jackie before they stayed. Scott was able to enter the suite late in the morning they left. It was clear then that the couple had slept in separate bedrooms: Johnnie in the one that had been curated for Jackie, and vice versa. Johnnie's room was windowless, next to the hall of the hotel. He slept his last night nested beneath a painting by Vincent Van Gogh, the bright, reverential 'Road with Peasant Shouldering a Spade,' Jackie slept aware of the rain and underneath the pride of Texas in Thomas Eakins' 'Swimming' (a charged pastoral scene of six hunks mucking about in a rocky pond), opposite Marsden Hartley's 'Sombrero with Gloves.' Maybe this was why Johnnie avoided the room, haunted by hats as he was; maybe he was chivalrous, giving Jackie the view of the parking lot. Over breakfast that morning in the hotel's Grand Ballroom (bacon, eggs, hash brown; a Catholic Fish Friday abandoned for this special occasion) Johnnie would be gifted a wide-brimmed cowboy hat by Fort Worth representatives. This was immediately secreted away, knowing it'd make a goofy front-page headline for Saturday's papers if he wore it. A popular accusation of the time was that Kennedy had single-handedly destroyed the hat as manly fashion staple, having failed to wear one at his inauguration. In fact, men were polled in the early '60s about their motivations to lose the hat, and cited the two World Wars: helmets, itchy felt. Never again. Only upon leaving the hotel room did Jackie stumble on the modest catalogue assembled as reference for the one-night show, and so notice the work around her and Johnnie. Having arrived late the night before they'd mistaken it for reproduction dirt. 'I don't want to leave!' She appealed, clawing at an air suddenly thick with the human divine, dreamily spiralling away from it for the Hellish motorcade of thirty miles per hour, and twenty thousand windows (four minutes *if that* were spent aware of the sixteen artworks around them).

The last telephone conversation Johnnie ever had was thanking Ruth for Picasso's 'Angry Owl.' Its position in the room that night made it appear to be watching over his door.

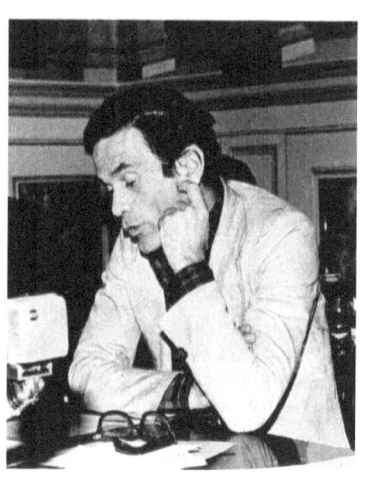

Pier Paolo Pasolini (d.1975)
Edipo re / Oedipus Rex (Pier Paolo Pasolini, 1967), 104m

¶ On October 27 in 1975, Pier Paolo Pasolini travelled to Stockholm accompanied by Ninetto Davoli, player of Angelo in *Oedipus Rex*, and the son in *Uccelacci e uccellini*. (Davoli was often described as the love of Pier Paolo's life; both men stood at 5 foot 5 and 3/4 inches and were apparently always on time.) Pasolini (the self-described 'Artist-Communist-Mystic-Inquisitor') was invited by Anna-Lena 'No Nonsense' Wibom, then director at the city's Svenska Filminstitutet, and Lucia 'Fine-Boned' Pallavicini, chief of the Italian Cultural Institute in Sweden. Davoli tagged along. A four-day trip, Pasolini would attend a reading of his own poetry—a Swedish translation of *Gramsci's Ashes* was scheduled for publication to coincide with his visit—and, following a screening of his films, participate in an audience Q&A. There, while answering a question about his more recent newspaper articles, which railed against abortion and compulsory high school education, Pasolini flatly stated that he expected to be murdered. No follow-up was made by the assembled crowd, no more questions.

¶ *Oedipus Rex*, a sinking sand cinema of ravishing portent, is both a faithful adaptation of Sophocles' story of mother-fucking father-killing, and an autobiography of (Pier Paolo's) infantile self-disgust. It screened last in a double-bill with *Uccellacci e uccellini* (*Hawks and Sparrows*, or, literally 'Birds of Prey and Little Birds'). Pasolini declared *Uccellacci e uccellini* to be his favourite of his own films, if only because it was the one that disappointed him the least. It remains the lowest grossing film (by far) in the catalogue of its star, Totò the clown, then one of Italy's most famous people. Totò was so loved that at the time of his own death, just over a year after filming *Uccellacci e uccellini*, he was afforded three funerals: the first in Rome, his adopted home, the second in Napoli, the city of his birth, and the third (beyond consent and with an empty casket), specific to Napoli's Rione Sanità quarter of his childhood, at the order of the Camorra. Scenes in *Uccellacci e uccellini* needed to be reshot frequently, as the proselytising crow along the road of life, starring alongside Totó (and which he ultimately kills and eats), kept trying to claw at his eyes. Totó learns the language of the birds and he teaches them how to love each other but not, or so it seems, the 'other' (a converted hawk kills a converted sparrow, for there is ideology, but then there is nature). To overcome the passion of the crow, its cage was eventually placed behind the camera, focusing the bird's attention away from the gelatinous peepers of Totó (who had been practically blind for the last decade, once ignoring a gnarly eye infection to continue working). His penultimate film role remains uncredited, as a man at a funeral in *The Head of the Family* (1968).

After the event, Pasolini asked Wibom for a tour of Stockholm's sex clubs. She was keen to oblige, possessing a free pass to any of the city's cinemas. Davoli didn't join them; what he did instead is unknown, possibly having rowed with Pasolini. First, they visited the Lido; a porno kino. It is unclear if and what they watched, as no screening records exist.* They continued with haste to the Chat Noir (still operating at the time of writing; see Olof Palme's future 'Last Movie' site, on Tunnelgatan, only metres away, pp.200–205), a 'much more elegant' strip club, witnessing a man and a woman onstage in coit. Pasolini complained that this was 'appalling, worse than *Salò*'—his final film, wrapped several weeks prior but not released until after his death—and Wibom went home to husband and child, leaving

---

* For good measure, any programme following this publication, 'Last Movies' might chase Pasolini's *Oedipus Rex* with a flash of Scandinavianal *circa* '75.

Pasolini there in the company of two anonymous Frenchmen. On the afternoon of the next day, October 30, the poet's polemicist was back at the Filminstitutet to talk to reporters in the morning, and students in the afternoon (seafood was taken for lunch, during which Pasolini was angered by Davoli's admiration of long legs passing by, women he celebrated as cavalle, horses). He told the students that 'young people have become ugly,' and spoke about sex and power in *Salò* ('set in 1945 because the end of the war marks the beginning of our own time, when eroticism is perverted into commerce'). Afterwards, shopping: he bought a navy, pinstriped suit. There was then a farewell dinner attended by members of the Swedish Academy. How exactly that went is unclear (what they ate is unclear), but they'd very recently awarded the Nobel Prize in Literature to Italian poet Eugenio Montale, who Pasolini publicly respected but personally loathed. He expressed his view that the prize should have instead been awarded to Sandro Penna, the self-proclaimed 'non-homosexual pederast poet.' On Halloween morning, October 31, Ninetto flew back to Rome, with Pasolini stopping for half the day in Paris, dubbing *Salò*, and completing an interview ('To scandalise is a right. To be scandalised is a pleasure'), before following home. 'Did you like Stockholm?' His mother asked. 'Yes, mama, but we could never live there.'

November 1. Saturday. With Ninetto, his wife and two sons, Pasolini ate dinner at Al Pommidoro ('The Tomato'—its patriarch known for his big, red nose, and an excellent gunshot: hunting bunnies and boar by day for sale by night), in the working-class neighbourhood of San Lorenzo.

The group discussed a new film project Pasolini was preparing, which he wished Ninetto to star in, and football. He ate steak and potatoes; they had homemade sausages and a little fruit. The restaurant was not well stocked, set to close for the rest of the weekend in honour of the dead. They left separately —the actor and company in a white BMW; the director in his silver Alfa Romeo 2000GT (which his cousin had washed and his mother had shined earlier that day), license plate G69996. Pasolini drove straight to Rome's Central Station (at this time in Italy there were no speed limits!), and would've ground to the crawl of a tigress seeking pudding, this being a popular meeting point for hustlers—particularly in the bars next to the Moderno and Modernetta porno kinos (that night screening the lost delights, *Porno West* and *My Flesh Burns with Desire*, although PPP didn't

116

go in). There was Antonio Nori's bar, the Grand'Italia, and Pasolini was also known as a regular at the Dey and the Indipendenza, but this night he picked the Gambrinus (named after the mythical Flemish King who is said to have invented beer)... and there was Giuseppe Pelosi, 'Pino.' Seventeen, dark eyes (bulging eyes, for which the press would dub him 'the frog'), long, curly hair, and dressed in tight, pocket-less trousers, with 'strong legs,' Pino described himself as a reluctant prostitute, down on his luck but 'no faggot,' who was effectively victim to Pasolini's perversions; his nature, the hawk and the sparrow, as his eventual defence would have it. Witnesses that night say otherwise: that it was he, who, without prompt, enthusiastically approached the Alfa Romeo, and instigated the engagement.

The couple stopped at a restaurant known to Pasolini, looking out over the river: the Al Biondo Tevere (fellow filmmaker, Communist, and smoker of 120 cigarettes per day, Luchino Visconti, shot Anna Magnani in *Bellissima* around the time of Pino's birth, on its patio). Pier Paolo bought Pino dinner: spaghetti with oil and garlic, and roasted chicken to chase. Both drank beer. With the boy full-up, the two continued to Idroscalo, a spot known to Pasolini for having previously played football there, in Ostia, where the river meets the sea ('where Dante had souls depart for Hades,' writes Barth David Schwartz). Pino has Pier Paolo switching off the engine, removing his glasses, and undoing the boy's trousers, pants, bending over the gear stick and the handbrake, and gently easing his mouth onto his penis. In his first interview with police, Pino says that he didn't ejaculate. In subsequent interviews he describes Pier Paolo completing the job. No semen was found in or on Pasolini's body, though a handkerchief under the driver's seat did contain traces of cum. Pino then has it that he leaves the car; for a cigarette, or to pee, or because Pier Paolo ordered him to. It seems to depend on his mood, or whoever's paying for recall. The area is unpopulated, without any formal roads or lighting. And the moon is almost new, barely even a slither, so only the stars can be relied on for light. A lap of sea, muted by the stretch of a playing field, likely the only sound but the shuffling of the two men: rustle of nylon, creak of leather boots, wheeze and gulp. Pino has Pier Paolo sneaking up behind him, and going for the ass with a plank of wood. He also has it that a john would know, unless explicitly okayed with the hooker in advance, that this kind of play was unacceptable. Pasolini was an advanced hunter, knowing.

Nino was *the man*, Pier Paolo *the woman*, and the roles were not interchangeable. Take a blow job, *un pompino*? Fine. A little bit of pocket money for the ladies, the movies, sherbet. Take it up the ass? Be it cock, or be it plank: *Sodomia? impossibile!* '...he picked up a stick, the kind that are used in gardens, and he tried to stick it up my ass, or at least he pushed it against my ass without even having lowered my pants.' Pino has it that Pier Paolo had left his specs in the car, but nevertheless launched at him with a force and precision police reports struggled with (that is: Pino, apprehended almost immediately after the killing, showed no signs of struggle... a scratch on the nose and a laceration around the hairline is all the police reported; no bruises, swelling, nothing; similarly he described falling into the wet dirt, with this powerlessness as his provocation to lash out—but wasn't at all muddied). Taking control of the situation, Pino describes belting Pasolini in the groin, the head, the chest. He describes grabbing his hair and kicking him in the face, and then, dashing into the Alfa Romeo, switching on the lights and making off for Rome. Pino doesn't remember whether he passed over the body of Pier Paolo, but some analysts believe he did so at least twice. It was the early hours of Sunday, November 2. *Ognissanti.* The day of the dead.

¶ A November 3 headline in *Corriere della sera* read, 'Pasolini killed where he would have shot the film of his own death.' Brutal and humiliating full-colour photographs of scene and autopsy were debuted by the newspaper *L'espresso*, in a feature titled 'Massacre of a Poet,' which immediately sold-out. Pino confessed and was imprisoned for Pasolini's murder, but withdrew the confession in 2005, accusing three unnamed Sicilian men (and that he had admitted to the murder under duress, and for fear of his family's safety—in fact, one level of the initial court judgement finding him guilty of the murder, did acknowledge that he couldn't have acted alone). Pasolini's body showed signs consistent with a group attack: some holding him down, others beating him with a crowbar, where Pino had cited a rotten piece of wood (bloodied evidence destroyed by the insistence of the press that locals should hold it for photo opportunities in the hours following the death). The problem with Pino's ever shifting story is that, released after eight years in prison, he'd have been chomping at the bit for any kind of work, income, revisionary limelight, and these dramatic edits would have been fodder enough for a country still rapt—his retraction of 2005, for example, came by no coincidence at the time PPP's memorial was erected in Ostia (a time of renewed focus on the late writer-director). Pino himself attributed the right moment to the death of his parents. Without them around, no retaliation that bothered him could be made by those actually responsible for Pasolini's killing. It is, in any case, now generally considered a politically motivated murder, planned and collectively executed. It remains unsolved. Pino died in 2017 and nobody wants to know what he saw last. Ninetto continues; does what he can: in Abel Ferrara's dramatisation of Pasolini's last twenty-four hours, he stars alongside a younger, fictional self, in a bad dream of the last movie discussed last at Al Pommidoro.

Though the beating rendered him helpless, Pasolini would still have been alive. It was the weight of the car that burst his heart and ended it all. In Barth David Schwartz's *Requiem* —whose meticulous account is the fount of knowledge for the hours leading to Pasolini's death—the writer describes a considerable loss of blood as inducing 'chemical and psychological reactions favourable to hallucinatory experience. What are the hallucinations of a dying poet, the last mind-pictures of a film director?' It may be that that last, unmade film played out: fresh in the mind and complemented by its extrapolation to and through Ninetto. Pasolini might have reflected on his own words, on his own angelic character 'pissing on the heavenly stairs,' and gazing gratefully down on planet earth, '...the End does not exist,' or on *Uccellacci e uccellini*, fresh in his mind from Stockholm, the black bird protagonist ping-ponging to the score of delirious workhorse, Morricone, and certainly his mother, and possibly *Oedipus Rex*, and hopefully not the funeral rite of the fuckers at the Chat Noir, but the shine of polished silver by the stars, and Ninetto, precious Ninetto, and romance, and friendship, and resistance, and flight, and the long road, and the open field, and beefsteak, and the playing field, and soccer, and the lash of the nearby faraway sea as the echo and the tonic of the thud of the boot in the face, and the breast and the stomach and the ass, and the balls and the cock and the moon, where is the moon?

In December 2022, the former Magliana Gang associate Maurizio Abbatino made a statement to Italy's parliamentary anti-mafia commission, declaring that Pasolini's murder was linked to the theft of *Salò*'s final scenes. He had gone to the beach that night to attempt to retrieve the reels of film. Stefano Maccioni, lawyer for the director David Grieco, and screenwriter Giovanni Giovannetti, launched a petition in response to Abbatino's admission, campaigning for the reopening of the case, garnering thousands of supporting signatures. This was a double-header: part of Pino's retraction in 2005 brought to light the involvement of the stolen reels: the seventeen-year-old had apparently proposed he act as mediator, knowing the cans had been taken from a shed in Cinecittà on August 15, 1975. And in 2010, Maccioni had been responsible for the reopening of the case, which led police to discover five 'new' DNA samples on Pasolini's clothes. Unable to put names to this evidence, the investigation was once again shelved in 2015. The anti-mafia commission speaks of 'serious omissions' in the investigations, including 'the failure to hear the witnesses who lived in the barracks in the area and who had heard what happened that night, and who would have given account from the beginning of the evidence that the attack was carried out by numerous people,' and 'the lack, after the omitted confinement of the area where the crime had occurred, of in-depth reports on the serious injuries sustained by Pasolini.'

The report concluded that it was unlikely those responsible for Pasolini's death would ever be punished for the crime, but important that the truth be known. For Maria Antoinetta Macciocchi, a radical journalist writing for *Le Monde* only days after Pier Paolo's murder, the killer was clear: 'Pasolini was assassinated by society in a savage act of self-defense, a society which could not bear his defiance (of sexual, political, and artistic prohibitions), his undisguised equation of commitment and life. The hatred unleashed against him was expressed in the staging of the crime: a public execution at high noon, so that everyone might see and learn.'

Al Pommidoro lost itself in the story of Pasolini's last supper. Following the COVID-19 pandemic of 2020, the restaurant hasn't reopened. The area of San Lorenzo today, once a no-go zone, is now like any other in Rome, Italy; any other in Europe. It's a kind of working class cum tourist trap that confirms the dreadful prophecy Pasolini foretold in Stockholm, of the imminent globalist project of expansion and eclipse: the totalising homogenising and merchandising of place and people. Al Biondo Tevere similarly traded on the last image of Pasolini alive; his last drink; its great matriarch establishing a shrine in his honour, and simultaneously raising prices, answering the questions of stupid tourists: 'So, did he do it... Pino?' 'He was seventeen,' to her credit, was her only answer. She's dead now, but the restaurant continues to trade on the tragedy and the fantasy of that terrible night.

When John Waters recently visited the holy Pasolini murder scene memorial that now stands in Ostia—a full moon crowned by two doves, which ought of course be no moon, with hawk and sparrow in deathly, sexy embrace—he recalled an invitation from New York Film Festival to programme their drive-in cinema.* He showed *Salò*. In days gone by, it was customary in America to honk a car's horn whenever there was 'nudity or gore' in a movie at the drive-in. Waters asked his audience to honk whenever there was *art*.

---

* See John Waters, *Prayer to Pasolini* (Sub Pop, 2021), 17m04.
('*Maybe it's time for worship.*')

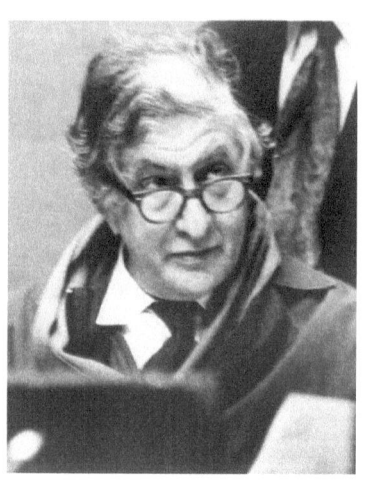

Bernard Herrmann (d.1975)
God Told Me To (Larry Cohen, 1976), 9½m

¶ Bernard Herrmann had a busy schedule planned for 1976.

First up was the Larry Cohen feature *God Told Me To* —a hermaphroditic alien God-head invades the minds of normal people to commit random murder (why? 'God told me to...')—second, Brian De Palma's *Carrie*. Palma had encouraged Martin Scorsese to book Herrmann to score *Taxi Driver* and, as soon as he completed its recording on December 23 in 1975, he went to watch a rough cut of *God Told Me To*. According to Cohen, Herrmann took him to dinner afterwards (why wasn't he taking Herrmann?) and in turn the director escorted the composer back to the Universal Hotel. He died there that night in his sleep.

Cohen tells a story of visiting Herrmann in London at an earlier date, and receiving a telephone call from fellow film composer, Elmer Bernstein. 'Hello, Benny,' says Elmer: 'I'm here in London. How would you like to have lunch?' Benny responded, 'I wouldn't eat with you in Los Angeles. Why would I eat with you here?'

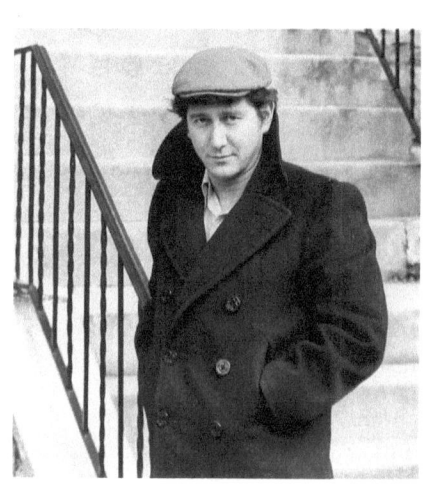

Phil Ochs (d.1976)
One Flew Over the Cuckoo's Nest (Milos Forman, 1975), 133m

That'll be the day, ooh-hoo
—Buddy Holly

¶ 'Though I may look like Phil Ochs and sound like Phil Ochs,' Phil Ochs told his friends, 'I am John Butler Train, killer of Phil Ochs.'

In the time of the assassins, musician Ochs hallucinated into reality his own: a fast-moving free-falling derailing of drinking, drugging, and dropping the song of saving humankind (or America, at least). He'd died once before: in Chicago, 1968, according to the tombstone on his 1969 album cover *Rehearsals for Retirement*, destroyed by the Chicago police riots, the election of Richard Nixon, and the assassinations of Martin Luther King, Jr and Robert F. Kennedy.

Ochs' last-ditch attempt to reconstitute American pop music as an agent for revolutionary socialist change was the 1970 album, *Greatest Hits* (comprised of all original, never-before-released music—Ochs never had a hit). He hoped to reclaim the image of the hero from the right-wing navel-gazing of emergent songsters, overriding the media-spun 'freak' narrative of the so-called left, and reestablishing an organic connection between culture and the working class. If revolutionary art wouldn't cut it, he'd hoax his beloved nation with enormous fun: from a suit of gold and rhinestone belting out the songs of his 1950s rebel forebears; songs of youth a little older now but only truer for it. In his own words—at the New York presentation of *Greatest Hits*, later released partially as live album, *Gunfight at Carnegie Hall* —Ochs told the crowd that after he died in Chicago, God asked him who he'd most like to return as. 'Elvis Presley... if there's any hope for America it lies in a Revolution. And if there's any hope of a Revolution in America, it lies in getting Elvis Presley to become Che Guevara.' Until then, Ochs was known as the acerbic picket line finger picker to Bob Dylan's vaguer (bourgeois) radio blower. ('Dylan despises what I write: he can't accept what I'm doing because it's political, it's therefore bullshit because I'm not writing about myself and my deepest emotions. In other words, he thinks that I could be much more honest with myself.') If he hadn't already lost the crowd with his Merle Haggard cover, and they'd made it through the Buddy Holly medley, an Elvis Presley medley was a rubber-legged step too far. A bomb threat was telephoned in and the show cut short.

A few singles followed, including the rejected soundtrack theme for *Kansas City Bomber* (a Raquel Welch-starring sports drama about contact roller skating), and 'Bwatue,' a Lingala-language collaboration with the Kenyan Pan African Ngembo

Rumba Band, but no more albums. Ochs was inspired by Marxist Salvador Allende's democratic election in Chile in 1970, travelling there and befriending the insurmountable Victor 'La Partida' Jara. He went on to visit Australia and New Zealand, and toured Africa, 'to wash America out of my system—like taking a bath.' In Tanzania, he was violently mugged during a walk along the beach, the assailants strangling him with such severity that his vocal cords were bent, the range of his singing voice permanently limited. Ochs attributed the attack to the CIA, which his friends considered only further confirmation of his faltering grasp on reality (in the years after his death extensive files kept by the American government on the activities and companions of Ochs ['Oakes'] were revealed to exist). In 1973 Allende was the target of a coup: as the palace of the people's power was bombed by the military, he ended his own life with an AK47 gifted by Fidel Castro. Victor Jara, along with many other artists, activists, professors and students, was tortured and executed (another CIA gig: if not enacted by the Americans 'manured' by them, said Christopher Hitchens). This crushed Ochs. The songs wouldn't come, and even if they did: the voice. In '74 and '75 he kept on trying. With indefatigable energy he arranged benefits and actions, and took to writing movie reviews. But the depression ever deepened, and as though the drinking and the drugging couldn't get worse, it did. The end of The Vietnam War in Spring 1975 broadly aligned with the assumption of the Train identity, which involved him carrying a hammer in his belt and living on the streets of New York.

In January 1976, Ochs' sister, Sonny, took him in to her home in Far Rockaway, Queens. John had gone but with him so had much of Phil. He watched television, and just about mustered the energy to play card games with his nephews. Sonny was thrilled when the onset of Spring delivered an unexpected visit from British music producer Andy Wickham, and Phil was sprung from his isolation. A drive to Long Island, a seafood restaurant. He ate it all. And then, in the early days of April, Sonny was able to get Phil out to see a concert by B.B. 'The Thrill is Gone' King, and even to the movies: *One Flew Over the Cuckoo's Nest*. 'The choice... with its insane-asylum setting and its theme about the struggle to maintain individuality in a rigid society, might not have been the best selection, as Sonny herself later admitted.' It isn't known what Ochs thought of the film, but he considered Jack Nicholson (playing Mac) a fine actor, and the all-seeing deaf-pretence of outsider-narrator Chief Bromden, with the voice he couldn't or wouldn't use, he might have associated with his present state (even if only to ward off the traits of Train he shared with the hospital's more broken comrades). Ken Kesey, author of the book on which the film was based, was battling the same big, bad story as Ochs' medicine-music, asking: are individual diagnoses of mental illness really appropriate—even *possible*—when the world doling out those diagnoses is itself so sick? Ochs had to cling to this principle, with the guarantee of his own sectioning in a *Cuckoo*-like hell far worse than Far Rockaway if Train returned.

Kesey wrote *Cuckoo* in 1959 to huge acclaim. Its stage adaptation premiered on Broadway in New York City in 1962, starring Kirk Douglas (in the role that all-time would come to recognise as Jack Nicholson through the movie). Kesey loved it and loved Douglas, the dairy farmer from Oregon a national literary—and now theatrical—sensation, sharing a bill and swilling meds with Spartacus himself. (*Spartacus* was the first film John F. Kennedy watched in office, crossing an American Legion [anti-communist] picket line and in doing so effectively ending Hollywood blacklisting). But the neon's dimmed as Kesey set out home, describing the surreal misery from place to place:

We began to experience the Kennedy assassination... What you saw in the people's faces coming across the country was a grief everybody in the United States felt. It was not so much that we'd lost Kennedy, but we had lost a chance at a real, different, better, hipper, gentler world.

Kesey reconsidered the grounds for *Cuckoo* in his own experiences at first as patient and then as orderly in an Oregon drug testing clinic and asylum (probably as part of MK-Ultra, America's experimental brain-washing drug programme). The obvious solution to the ever-darkening state of play was to insist on colour like never seen before, for all people immediately ever after. Kesey threw his pen at the proverbial prison-master and bought a bus called 'Furthur' (cause that's where they were going!), painting it in the colour scheme that would come to be known as psychedelic. Just as celluloid moved from black and white to colour, so the young minds of America, recently condemned to a monochrome world, could suddenly blow up all preconceptions with a small tab. And so began the 1960s. 'It's been around forever,' said Kesey, 'that you have to move out of a consciousness to be able to see beyond the doorway of the cave. There's nothing new about that. But the fact that there could be a tiny little pill that could give everyone that experience without spending thirty years in a monastery...'

Kesey never saw the film adaptation of *Cuckoo*. He didn't share Ochs' appreciation of Nicholson, describing him as 'too short' for the role of Mac. The attitude, artlessness and miserliness of the producers riled Kesey enough to vow abstention, and that was before the matter of removing narrative duties from Chief Bromden. Nicholson's half-Native subordinate in the film is actually the master of the novel, told from his perspective as the single reliable witness to the chaos. His silence alludes to the voicelessness of the original Americans, the Natives, and the newest Americans, the kids. Through Bromden we understand Mac and the other inmates; the hospital; the country; the moment and the history. The film omits his powerful flashbacks: try keeping a grip on reality when your dad, an alcoholic Chief, has his tribe's lands stolen to build a dam through small-print in the marriage contract to a white woman—mom. Mac brings an individualistic vigour to the impotent clinic: imprisoned for the statutory rape of a fifteen-year-old, he plays dumb figuring hospital time will be easier than prison time. Though he may be wrong about that, he delights in the relative structure of power: using the great matriarch Nurse Ratchet's letter of law to urge his fragile buddies into a twisted mud wrestle of pseudo-revolutionary misogyny. One important scene has Mac attempting to pull up the island of taps at the centre of the communal shower room for his audience of madmen. It doesn't budge an inch. 'At least I tried!' Mac withdraws. At the climax of the film his sentiment of once hopeless resistance is echoed and empowered by the Chief: he lifts the island, water rushing in from the broken pipes like the great flood of revelation. Wading through the bedroom with the chunk of concrete, tiles and steel, he launches it through the shuttered window, and leaps into the freedom of night. 'At least I tried,' is something Ochs said of his activism, and might have thought in his own exit-bathroom: morning, April 9. No island to pull, no night to jump into. A belt. A hook.

Cuckoo wasn't Ochs' last outing. Two more trips from Far Rockaway were taken: into Manhattan to shop for a new guitar on April 5 (returning empty-handed), and back again on April 6 for a dinner of corned beef and pastrami with Jerry Rubin and

Ron Cobb. As Ochs left them on the subway that evening, he performed through the window of the moving train the tying of a slipknot around his neck, and stuck out his tongue. On April 8, he walked along the beach in the company of his by-all-accounts unpleasant mother, Gertrude, expressing to her his gratitude for the happiness of his youth. *Once I was caught playing hooky from school / they found me home in the evening / I confessed I had been to the movie show / When I was a boy in Ohio.* Playing truant, Ochs learned from John Wayne and James Dean the service the non-conformist might perform to challenge and even reform a staid, fearful, contradictory society (Jack Nicholson's inheritance by Ochs' adulthood). Everything, at its core, could be reduced to a fight of good against evil: that the fairness so easily and finally attained in the movies was so hard to come by in reality was un-bearable. In those last days and hours and minutes and seconds of Spring, Sonny has Phil taken over at the piano by the playing and replaying of the greatest hit of *Greatest Hits* that nobody knows, his tribute to James Dean in 'Jim Dean of Indiana'...

He never seemed to find a place
with the flatlands and the farmers
So he had to leave one day
he said to be an actor

...

He played a boy without a home
torn with no tomorrow
Reaching out to touch someone
a stranger in the shadow

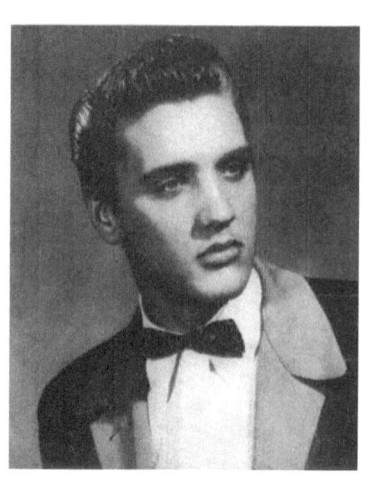

Elvis Presley (d.1977)
The Spy Who Loved Me (Lewis Gilbert, 1977), 125m

¶ Elvis wanted to see *Star Wars* with his twenty-one-year-old girl-friend Ginger Alden, and his nine-year-old daughter Lisa Marie. Unable to get a copy, they chose instead to watch the latest James Bond movie, *The Spy Who Loved Me*. There is some dispute about whether the gang hit the (now demolished) Whitehaven Cinema at 1243 Laudeen Drive, Memphis or the Southbrook 4 Theatre at 1260 East Shelby Drive (closed, though externally the mall that contained the theatre is practically the same, and the auditoriums, though seatless, are all intact). Both theatres were known haunts of Presley, who'd regularly book the floor out-of-hours, and the big E could loan any damn print he wished (except, apparently, *Star Wars*). But of the Whitehaven and the Southbrook 4 only the latter was screening Bond on general release and, as different franchises, the cinemas wouldn't have shared prints. No exceptions, even with Billy 'Club' Stanley and the Memphis Mafia to pull the King's cheese-strings. And that they did, a military-column of gabardine wise-guys with chocolate biscuit lips, pursed behind Private-Hire-Presley, ready and alert to refill his silver platter with ever-more peanut butter fingers. 'He would take Pepsi and put Sweet Tarts in it,' Billy-Club recalls, 'And so when you get finished with it, at the bottom they would be laying there and'd be really soft, so you don't have to really chew on them that much.'

Lisa Marie, born into it and wanting for nothing, wasn't such a pig. Her final photograph with her father was taken by paparazzi at the gates of Graceland on their way back from the film, perched on Ginger's lap with the red and white hazard warning of a popcorn bucket, in daddy's prized 1970 Stutz Black-hawk III. From the mansion to the movies, it was a five-minute drive door-to-door, straight down the line on Elvis Presley Boulevard. Presley would make two more trips out before the big one: visiting his mother's grave (by motorcycle), and then again for a dentist appointment with Lisa Marie (by Blackhawk III). It is likely he watched some *Star Trek* on television in the four days between the last movie and his offski, but we can't say for sure, and anyway his relationship with the box was complicated: 'One night, Elvis and I were watching TV in Lisa's bedroom when a programme came on that Elvis didn't care for. He started making comments about it, then suddenly left the room. He returned with a gun and shot the television.' A cry for help, Ginger. He is known to have kept a Walther PPK—Bond's signature pistol—inscribed with his own name. A whimper.

Today, the excessive airmiles racked up by Presley's unworthy inheritors in song and kultur are frowned upon. But the rightful ritual sacrifice of us coprophagian plebeians resides in the past. The climate—like the physical body—has a memory, and apocalypse now is latent payback for the midnight feast spontaneity of Private-Hire-Presley: jetting out to Denver in search of America's finest bacon and peanut butter loaf, the sandwich known as 'Fool's Gold.' The truth hurts: if anything is more romantic than the end of time, it is that kind of trip for that kind of payoff.

As an adult, Elvis fought the deprivation of his hungry childhood with endless hamburgers, and anything involving peanut butter. His personal cook at Graceland, Ms. Mary Jenkins, describes a particular favourite snack: two slices of pre-toasted bread slathered with peanut butter and topped with sliced banana, deep fried in pure butter. The King was raised on squirrels and possums stolen from the wild woods of Tennessee, with the occasional 'treat' of pig's ears and trotters with greens from the mothers of black friends (a gesture he repaid by stealing their songs). He ate only with his hands; anything difficult, i.e. steak, would have to be cut up for him. According to Jenkins, Elvis told her that only eating brought him joy, but he evidently also liked movies, with a particularly high regard for the more refined of Christmas titles: *It's a Wonderful Life* (Frank Capra, 1946), *Miracle on 34th Street* (George Seaton, 1947), and his favourite, according to wife, Priscilla: *The Way of All Flesh*, Louis King's 1940 remake of Victor Fleming's lost 1927 silent film. In brief, a well-respected banker is travelling with vast sums of his bank's cash, which is stolen from him. Rendered catatonic by the guilt and shame of the theft, he never returns to his family or community, wandering for years and years until... one day, one Christmas, he can't take it anymore. He returns. And peering through the window of the home that was once his own, at a family that was once his own, fully grown, his wife notices and invites him in. She doesn't recognise him. He refuses the invitation, walks away. The End. Such was Elvis' love of the picture that he hoped to remake it himself—casting father, Vernon Presley, as the starved, festive, self-flaggelating vagrant. Analyse that!

In *Casino Royale*, Bond explains 'I take a ridiculous pleasure in what I eat and drink. It comes partly from being a bachelor, but mostly from a habit of taking a lot of trouble over details...

when I'm working, I generally have to eat my meals alone and it makes them more interesting when one takes trouble.'

In *From Russia with Love* (see JFK, pp.86–110), Bond *drank* (Turkish) coffee, ouzo, raki, Kavaklidere (Balkan wine), Chianti Broglio, double vodka martini, vodka and tonic; a pitcher of water, ice water; and *ate eggs* (boiled for three and a third minutes), with two thick slices of whole-wheat toast, a large pat of deep yellow Jersey butter and three squat glass jars containing Tiptoe Little Scarlet (strawberry jam); Cooper's Vintage Oxford Marmalade and Norwegian Heather Honey from Fortnum's; yoghurt... with the consistency of thick cream... green figs; sardines en papillote; a kebab; steak tartare (laced with peppers and chives and bound together with an egg-yolk); ragout; fried eggs with hard brown bread; hors d'oeuvres; tagliatelle verdi, and an escalope.

But Bond, like Presley, didn't always have it so good. In the first novel by Ian Fleming to be adapted to film, *Dr. No*, the writer has the spy condemned to Heinz baked beans with pork, cold and eaten with his hands (a product placement that unfortunately never made it in to the films). 'There were the remains of a fireplace made of lumps of coral and a few scattered cooking pots and empty tins,' wrote Fleming. 'They searched in the debris and unearthed a couple of unopened tins of Heinz pork and beans.' Introduced to America in the 1880s, pork and beans were effectively the first convenience food: rehydrated navy beans packed in tomato sauce, with small chunks of pork, cooked, canned and contained in large pressure cookers to guarantee sterility. Heinz were relatively late to the game with their product, introduced in 1901 and first available for sale at the Fortnum & Mason department store as something sexy. Later in the book, Bond makes up for the horror of the dinner foraged from a Ken Loach climax with a trip to a restaurant in the company of 'Honeychild Rider.' The spy orders lamb cutlets and a salad for himself and, for her, a roast chicken *à l'Anglaise* (a French expression for something cooked 'in the English manner'), with vanilla ice-cream and chocolate sauce for afters. Naturally, she isn't given the opportunity to order for herself. For this, and for his life-times of sins against women, Bond is forced to atone in 2021's *No Time to Die*: starved from food for the film's full course, and finally ritually sacrificed to the Goddess of Kapital as the franchise hammers on its panic-button. Reason: uncertain of the direction of the kultur on which the franchise's continuing success relies, this death presents the option of dividing

Bond (essentially doubling his earnings). Bond A would be (the continuation of) a retroactive film series less accountable to the standards of today's kultur; meanwhile Bond B, present time inheritor of the barcode '007,' could be (under the auspices of 'empowerment') a spinoff re-casting his majesty's service-person for anyone falling outside of Bond's traditional fanbase of young boys, or men who should know better. In other words, protecting the investment (flogging a dead...).

Fleming would have been quietly horrified that an Edinburgh-born ex-milkman (Sean Connery) could be selected to debut Bond on screen. The writer didn't play to class; he couldn't bear to. His big characters were all wealthy. The books, and by extension the films, rely on anything-but-English ethnicity and homosexuality to indicate evil. Ann Charteris, the mother of Fleming's child, Caspar (who shot himself with the spy's signature gun), called James Bond 'cheap pornography.' That the genre persists, and was any success in the first place, is one of those strange and terrible accidents of history... like the Empire it celebrates, like America.

ELVIS PRESLEY FOOD PLAYLIST
(IN ORDER OF DATE RELEASED):

'Shake, Rattle and Roll' (1956)

Well get in that kitchen
Make some noise with the pots and pans

...

I'm like the one-eyed cat peeping in a seafood store

*

'Tutti Frutti' (1956)

In Italian, means 'all fruits.'

In American, means a type of ice cream
containing or flavoured with mixed fruits
and sometimes nuts.

See 'Blueberry Hill.'

*

'Blueberry Hill' (*Loving You*, 1957)

Cover. Bad. Mm, blueberries.

*

'Hot Dog' (*Loving You*, 1957)

Hot dog, baby, baby, hot dog

He's singing about a car but most listeners will think of sausages.
In 1957, the Memphis Draft Board classifies Elvis '1A,' meaning
he's likely to be drafted for military service. He is, later in the
year but—before he goes—he visits Graceland (where he'd live
and die), seeing the place only once, and buying it outright. 90k.
Peanuts! (See 'It's Carnival Time,' p.151) In a televised interview
upon his return from service in Germany, he refuses to answer
any questions about what he ate there.

*

'Let's Have a Party' (*Loving You*, 1957)

Recorded for the first of Elvis' collaborations with veteran
Hollywood film producer Hal Wallis, and his first starring role
as an actor, for which he was paid a paltry $150,000.

The meat is on the stove
The bread is getting hot
Tell me pretty baby
Let's have a party (let's have a party), ooh
Let's have a party (let's have a party)
Send him to the store
Let's buy some more
And let's have a party tonight
We're going to have a party tonight!

*

'Crawfish' (*King Creole*, 1958)

Magnificent call-and-I'll-answer duet between Elvis and Kitty White, through sodden, deserted, Sunday streets:

See I got him, see the size
Stripped and cleaned before your eyes
Sweet meat look
fresh and ready to cook

Kitty White was a popular singer in Los Angeles hotels, and came from a musical family. Her mother, A.C. Bilbrew, wrote 'The Death of Emmett Till' in 1955, which was recorded the same year and released by DooTone Records in January 1956. The song vividly recounts Till's brutal murder—the killing of a fourteen-year-old boy from Chicago who was visiting his uncle in Money, Mississippi—and the innocent charge delivered by the jury in his murderer's trial. The song was hugely popular with DJs in Chicago and LA, and kept the reality of Till's death and the ruling's injustice alive, in a time the mainstream was mounted against any reckoning. Only months later it was the image of the boy's beaten body that motivated Rosa Parks' refusal to give up her seat on the city bus in Montgomery, Alabama. The woman who made the unfounded accusations against Till, Carolyn Bryant Donham, of 'whistling' at her in a grocery store, and so provoking the lynching, is—at the time of writing—alive and unwell, residing in Kentucky with her son and pet Shih Tzu.

Hal Wallis had acquired the rights to Harold Robbin's sprawling novel, *A Stone for Danny Fisher*, about a lower middle class Jewish family who, confronted by the Great Depression, have to rely on the boxing abilities of young son, Danny, to support them. The project was shelved in 1955 following the death of James Dean, the appointed star of the picture, but then resuscitated with Elvis' name attached in 1957. For the new adaptation, Fisher's lifeline would shift naturally from boxing to singing, and the city from New York to New Orleans. *King Creole* was Elvis' favourite of his own titles, as a more serious film that showcased his talents as an actor; talents he hoped to be acknowledged and exploited, considered as on a par with those of Dean, and Marlon Brando.* This is the most 'serious' film he ever played in. *King Creole* was directed by Michael Curtiz, the Hungarian refugee who introduced the world to Spencer Tracy and Bette Davis

---

* They weren't.

through *20,000 Years in Sing Sing* (1932), the film Rainer Werner Fassbinder died watching (see pp.180–195).

Now take Mr. Crawfish in your hand
He's gonna look good in your frying pan
If you fry him crisp or you boil him right
He'll be sweeter than sugar when you take a bite
Crawfish

*

'A Big Hunk O' Love' (1959)

Don't be a stingy little mama
You're 'bout to starve me half to death

...

You're just a natural born beehive
Filled with honey to the top
But I ain't greedy, baby
All I want is all you got

...

I got a rabbit's foot 'round my wrist

*

'A Cane and a High Starched Collar' (*Flaming Star*, 1960)

The song wouldn't be released for another twenty or so years, which really speaks volumes to its quality when everything possible has been squeezed out of product-Elvis. The film may be worth watching, even if only as a money job by Don Siegel (*The Line-Up, Dirty Harry, Escape from Alcatraz*).

Cowboy, cowboy marry me
I'll bake you a cherry pie
Well thank you very kindly mam
But I'm too young to die

...

You sleep all day and spoon all night
And eat your favorite chow
Then why should I get married mam
That's what I'm doing now

*

'Stuck on You' (1960)

You can shake an apple off an apple tree
Shake-a, shake, sugar
But you'll never shake me
Uh-uh-uh
No-sir-ee, uh, uh

*

'Ito Eats' (*Blue Hawaii*, 1961)

Ito is an eating boy
He never get enough from fish and poi
He eat everything he don't care what
He even eat the shell from the coconut
Eat, Ito eat all the night and the day
Eat, Ito eat all the night and the day

'Can't Help Falling in Love' was debuted in the same film,
and this (not 'Ito Eats') was the last song Elvis performed live
(Market Square Arena, Indianapolis, June 26 in 1977).

*

'Song of the Shrimp' (*Girls! Girls! Girls!*, 1962)

I saw three shrimp in the water, two were old and gray
I swam a little bit closer and .. I heard the third one say...
Goodbye mama shrimp, papa shake my hand
Here come the shrimper for to take me to Louisian'

Elvis is known to have hated seafood, but for the Hal Wallis
films that turned his autonomous shaking pelvis into a factory-
farmed shellfish (see 'Do the Clam,' p.153), he sang plenty about
the life of the salty fine. This song is propaganda for the prawn
trade, suggesting youngsters actively pursue the nets of fisher-
men, seeking the tired hands of Creole workers so that they can
be skinned, stirred through a glut of mayonnaise, and pressed
between two cancerous slices of service-station bread.

*

'Thanks to the Rolling Sea' (*Girls! Girls! Girls!*, 1962)

Another one for Hal Wallis, who'd already bagged *I am a Fugitive
from a Chain Gang*, *Angels with Dirty Faces* (and *The Angels Wash
Their Faces*), *The Amazing Dr. Clitterhouse* (with Edward G. Robinson and Humphrey Bogart, with a screenplay by John Huston
—wapow!), *They Drive by Night* (Bogart and Ida Lupino—to pair
with her *The Hitchhiker*), *High Sierra* (wapow, wapow!), *Mildred
Pierce*, *The Maltese Falcon*, *Casablanca*, *Wild is the Wind*, *True
Grit*. Endless. Boss-man Wallis knew that film didn't have to be
compromised to sell, but sometimes went ahead and made the
service-station sandwich anyway. These Elvis vehicles eventually
netted The King an advance of a million dollars per movie, and
also entitled him to half of all profits. 'Thanks to the Rolling
Sea' is the highlight to the soundtrack from *Girls! Girls! Girls!*
—a beat-heavy and mercifully brief paean to Amphitrite, with its
ghoulish factory-fishermen chorus: *Thanks to the rolling (rolling,
rolling) sea, Thanks to the rolling sea (Abalone steaks and tuna fish
cakes, Taste so heavenly, We know who we owe it to, Thanks...)*

*

'We're Coming in Loaded' (*Girls! Girls! Girls!*, 1962)

We gottem packed to the water-line
Some got away but the catch was fine
Never saw such big ones, m'man oh man,
We're comin' in loaded just as fast as we can
Well, well, well, well, well
Oh well now yeah!

*

'Because of Love' (*Girls! Girls! Girls!*, 1962)

Because of love, I'm the happiest guy
And life is sweet as cherry cream pie

Note the deliriously sexy quivering of E's voice at 'cherry cream pie'
—nowhere else in his oeuvre is it quite so hot.

*

'Vino Dinero y Amor' (*Fun in Acapulco*, 1963)

I like to drink wine

*

'It's Carnival Time' (*Roustabout*, 1964)

Popcorn, peanuts and cotton candy
Pink lemonade that's dan-dan-dandy

If 'cherry cream pie' had The King quivering, with 'Peanuts' he explodes. Barbara '*Double Indemnity*' Stanwyck is the great matriarch presiding over the carnival at the centre of *Roustabout*, yet another Hal Wallis production (dragging the smart and sultry stars of noir down into the Technicolor hell-scape with him), which features a young, uncredited Richard Kiel in the role of 'Strongman.' Kiel would go on to star as Jaws in *The Spy Who Loved Me* along with *Moonraker*: the only Bond henchman to survive a film. The character was so popular (or perhaps so frightening) that children wrote to Bond's producers in their droves to request he be converted into a good guy. Weirdly, he was, in as much as he 'came out' and died hard for James.

Roger Moore, Bond in *The Spy Who Loved Me* and a few other titles this deathly project has forced me to look at, was asked in 2007 about whether he liked Elvis' music (a question he dodged), and was told it was the last movie he saw. 'I hope it wasn't a contributing factor!' Moore responded.

*

'Hard Knocks' (*Roustabout*, 1964)

Some kids born with a silver spoon
I guess that I was born a little too soon

...

I walked a million miles I bet
Tired and hungry and cold and wet

*

'It's a Wonderful World' (*Roustabout*, 1964)

Pretty as pink lemonade, it's a wonderful world

*

'Poison Ivy League' (*Roustabout*, 1964)

The ra-ra boys have lots of plans in view
They're gonna have panty raids
And make their own lemonade
They'll live it up just like the big boys do

A tuneless, virginal, proto–'Working Class Hero.'

(See 'Polk Salad Annie,' p.155)

*

'Wolf Call' (*Girl Happy*, 1965)

What a cutie pie I see

...

Lips of honey that's for me

The kind of ass-shaking and dog-barking that'd see a guy and a gal arrested in cacotopia *à présent*.

Devour!

*

'Do the Clam' (*Girl Happy*, 1965)

More shellfish propaganda. Was 'The Clam' ever a thing?
Unlikely, but let's bring it back anyway. And while we're at it:
perukes. Let's bring back perukes (see Charlie Chaplin,
Barry Lyndon, pp.30–41).

Do the clam, do the clam
Grab your barefoot baby by the hand
Turn and tease, hug and squeeze
Dig right in and do the clam
Dig right in and do the clam

*

'Old MacDonald' (*Double Trouble*, 1967)

'Those damn fools got me singing Old MacDonald on the back
of a truck with a bunch of animals. Man, it's a joke and the
joke is on me.' So said Elvis, says Priscilla. Fair. The record that
accompanied the film bombed by Elvis's standards, and this
hot-on-the-hooves of the hugely popular 'How Great Thou Art,'
which had bagged him a Grammy Award for 'Best Sacred
Performance.'

Well, Old Macdonald had a farm, ee-i-ee-i-o
And on that farm he had some cows, ee-i-ee-i-o
With a moo, moo here, a moo, moo there
Cattle everywhere
And when those cows got out of line
Hamburger, medium rare

*

'He's Your Uncle, Not Your Dad' (*Speedway*, 1968)

The food is lousy up the river

    *

'Have a Happy' (*Change of Habit*, 1969)

Google says 93% of people like this film. Rotten Tomatoes say
10% of critics share the same view. 'Dr. John Carpenter (Elvis
Presley) takes the job of running a health centre in a low-income
district. He enlists three women to help out who—unbeknownst
to him—are actually nuns in street clothes.' 'Have a Happy' is
a dreadful, dreadful song.

It takes you to wishing wells
To ice cream and carousels
And yet this magic key won't unlock a thing

    *

'Polk Salad Annie' (1970)

Live in Las Vegas, video on YouTube. In case of any doubt: watch
this. Master. Shaman. Working boy. Duende! And it's a song
about an almost inedible weed.

Down there we have a plant that grows out in the woods, and the fields
And it looks somethin' like a turnip green
Everybody calls it polk salad
Now that's polk salad
Used to know a girl lived down there and she'd go out in the
  evenings and
Pick her a mess of it
Carry it home and cook it for supper
Because that's about all they had to eat
But they did all right

...

All her brothers were fit for
Was stealin' watermelons out of my truck patch
Polk salad Annie, the gators got your granny

...

Sock a little polk salad to me, you know I need a real mess of it
(chick-a-boom)
Sock a little polk salad, you know I need a real (chick-a-boom)
Ching-ching-ching-ching-a-ling (chick-a-boom)

  *

'Promised Land' (1975)

Chuck Berry.

A-workin' on a T-bone steak à la carte, flyin' over to the Golden State

  *

'Jambalaya' (1975)

Hank Williams track, performed live in Louisiana by Elvis.
Never got a studio recording.

Settle down far from town, get me a pirogue
And I'll catch all the fish in the bayou
Swap my mon to buy Yvonne what she need-o
Son of a gun, we'll have big fun on the bayou.
Jambalaya and a crawfish pie and fillet gumbo
'Cause tonight I'm gonna see my ma cher amio
Pick guitar, fill fruit jar and be gay-o
Son of a gun, we'll have big fun on the bayou

*

'Green Green Grass of Home' (1975)

Hair of gold and lips like cherries

*

INTERMISSION

A missive to the author...

I have just read your email for the second time and in between those two readings read your attachments and listened to Tony Joe White's version of 'Polk Salad Annie' and Phil Ochs 'When I'm Gone.' At a tangent I also listened to Dave Van Ronk's 'Hang Me, Oh Hang Me.' I think I was confusing which one was the inspiration for *Inside Llewyn Davis*. And then learnt the chords to 'Hang Me' because I was not sure of one of the chords without looking it up on Google.

The missing chord in my head turned out to be a B-flat-7th.

Also had to double check all the food references—as it happens, I had already made my youngest son peanut butter on toast with sliced banana on top for his breakfast. As in, one of Elvis's favourites according to what you wrote and what I read.

Moving on...

I have little interest in James Bond, and what little interest that I have is only in a negative sense. As in I hate James Bond for all the obvious reasons—fast cars, licence to kill, and Bond Girls.

As for *One Flew Over the Cuckoo's Nest*, this is something else altogether. In 1972, as in my late teens, along with Kerouac, Kesey was my great liberator. After reading *On the Road*, I quit art school and hit the road. After reading *Cuckoo*, I read all Kesey's books that I could find. And once they had all been read, I had to take things to the next level so...

In 1973, I got a job in a mental hospital. I was a ward orderly (nursing assistant) on the ward where patients were sent to die. My job was to feed those that could not feed themselves. Dress those that could not dress or undress themselves. Wipe the arses of those that could not wipe their own arses. And of course, lay them out when they had died before the relatives arrived. The matron on the ward, who I loved, was Nurse Ratched with a West Indian twist of humour.

And while working in the mental hospital, I read *Fear and Loathing*. I then read all the other books I could find by Hunter S. Thompson. And I loved the illustrations by Ralph Steadman.

Then perchance...

In 1975, I had to interpret drawings by Ralph Steadman to build a stage set for a stage production of *Cuckoo* at the Everyman Theatre, Liverpool. Then in-between the play being performed and Elvis going to watch *The Spy Who Loved Me*, the film version of *Cuckoo* came out. And I recognised the actor playing the lead from *Easy Rider*.

Then while lying on a beach in Brittany in 1977, while eating a sandwich made from a freshly baked baguette with brie cheese, I read the words ELVIS MORTE on the front cover of a French tabloid that one of the other people on the beach was reading. I was wearing a Bretton striped top that I had just bought. And as it happens, yesterday I was sent a photo of me wearing that top in 1981 in Italy at a concert that Echo & The Bunnymen were supposed to be playing, promoted by the local mafia to raise money for the local fascist party. The gig never happened. And I no longer have the top, but I still have the same fingers that I am using to type this email to you.

My grandfather died of a heart attack at the age of seventy-four while mowing the lawn. I turn seventy-four in 2027. I have issues with mowing lawns. I used to like doing it, but as I have got closer to the age of seventy-four, I seem to resist doing it.

Films, as in movies, as in the pictures, have never been a big influence on my life, it has always been books or plays or live music.

Bill Drummond, 2023

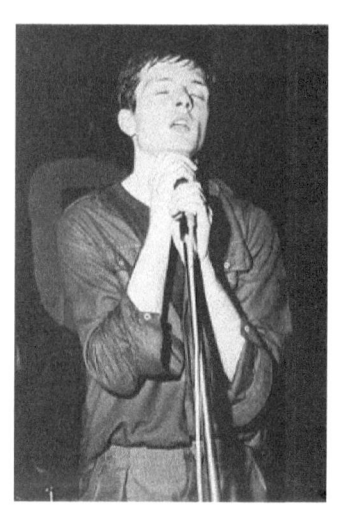

Ian Curtis (d.1980)
Stroszek (Werner Herzog, 1977), 108m;
Cape Fear (J. Lee Thompson, 1962), 106m

I wish I were a Warhol silk screen
Hanging on the wall
Or little Joe or maybe Lou
I'd love to be them all
All New York City's broken hearts
And secrets would be mine
I'd put you on a movie reel
And that would be just fine*

* St. Valentine's Day poem from Ian to Debbie, 1973.

¶ The handsome actor in his mid-twenties asks, 'Ever stolen a car before, lad?' He's wearing a slouchy beanie hat, and a corduroy jacket over an Adidas track-top. Can't remember his trousers, shoes. Pocket ratchet and a touch of magic, he prizes open the door of a BMW M3, and encourages me in with the glint of his to-Hollywood smile. Hyde Park, Leeds. It's early in the morning of a cold, Autumn Sunday, say 5 or 6am, and I don't remember how we became separated from the party. Nor do I remember driving, but the speed and the music I can still feel, and the 'woohoo' of the scrape and the briefly sobering thud. His then-girlfriend would chastise him on our return, but only lightly, for the journey rendered sacred offerings of Marlboro and Oranjeboom. A short while later, I heard he'd left her, enclosing a mysterious powder with a brief explanatory note. 'Met someone else.' The woman who was cast as temptation in the movie's love affair, performing the ruin of the marriage in the true story of his big screen debut, took him for real. The reader, left behind, powered through the substance, ran a deep bath, and did her darndest to end it all (without success; she lives today and lives well). Later in the morning of the joyride, I'd woken on a brown carpet to the dry hump of the mansion's heavy lease-holder, an aspiring music photographer. She'd rented the place with money left to her by her recently deceased father, and filled it with nothing but a handful of the right records, a circular bed, and drugs. She murmured in an affected, American accent: 'Honey, are you old enough to do intercourse?' I wasn't.

Regardless of interests, class, background or ambition, and even age (once in to the teens), up North you get fucked-up with the same commitment and routine you're supposed to assign family and work. More commitment, actually, because the rain falls and the sun doesn't come and all work is shit and most relationships are too. The point of the night out is to pass out. And you start early. It's this oblivion in place and practice that Joy Division—by all accounts unintentionally—so deftly and peerlessly articulate in their music. Their North is still *The North*. You either escape or you don't. The actor escaped. He was working in a crisp factory when he landed his role as Ian Curtis, 'the main player' in Joy Division's biopic, *Control* (he'd earlier played The Fall's Mark E. Smith in the Michael Winterbottom film, *24 Hour Party People*, shot by the master Robby Müller, but his scenes were omitted from the final cut. Neil Norman of the NME once remarked on the difference between the bands:

'Unlike The Fall, who make me want to go out and kick a cat, Joy Division convince me I could spit in the face of God'). The actress he'd abandon Leeds and his partner for was playing the part of the beautiful Belgian music journalist accused of having an affair with Ian by Deborah Curtis (it is often suggested that the singer's indecision and guilt about the affair contributed to his suicide, but the accused denies their relationship being anything other than platonic). The actor and the actress are still together, blessed with a child and living in Berlin. By the time the Curtis film came out I was eighteen—and so a touch beyond the Joy Division I'd previously played truant devouring—but there was some kind of vertigo about it... Things joining up, the barriers between the humdrum and the fantastic thinning.

Curtis' death is depicted in both *Control*, the film biopic directed by Anton Corbijn and based on Deborah's book, *Touching from a Distance*, and in *24 Hour Party People*, an account of the Manchester music community formed around Factory Records. In *Control*, Ian writes a suicide note to Deborah. In this (real) letter he wrote that it is 'nearing dawn.' He can hear birds singing. He also writes that he wants to try again (Curtis had received divorce papers from Deborah a day earlier). In the film, on the turntable, Iggy Pop's *The Idiot* hits its matrix and Curtis tearfully acknowledges the laundry cord. Cut to black. In *24 Hour Party People*, Curtis sits alone in his living room watching Werner Herzog's *Stroszek* on television (this is also shown playing in the background in *Control*, but not at the time he dies). His expressionless face cuts to shoes swaying in the air, as the infamous 'exit' chicken at the end of Herzog's film dances on the screen behind him. *24 Hour Party People* bears a lot of responsibility for the widely held belief that Curtis strung himself up right after watching, or as he watched, *Stroszek*. As confirmed in principle by Deborah's writing and backed up by Tony Wilson, *Stroszek* was his big plan on the night he died. It's echoed too by the words scratched into the runout groove of Joy Division's posthumously released album, *Still*...

(A) THE CHICKEN WON'T STOP, and,
(B) THE CHICKEN STOPS HERE.

¶ In Herzog's film a musician (Stroszek, AKA Bruno S.) escapes the no-hope industrial shit-hole (see Manchester; see Leeds) of Berlin, Germany, for the promise of the American Dream. When he gets there, he finds a caged chicken forced to dance for coins, and not much else. His car is kaput, his girlfriend is gone, his house has been repossessed. The final shots are seen by the character in a penny arcade at a truck-stop: a chicken on a turntable beside a toy piano; a duck; a toy drum and a rabbit on a toy fire engine; and then again, the chicken, to a blues harmonica soundtrack. On a police radio, we hear an officer report: 'We can't stop the dancing chicken...' Stroszek takes a rifle and ascends toward a hilltop on a cable car. He doesn't make it far, the camera tracking up and over his seat to a featureless tip. Gunshot. The cable car feels analogous to David Graeber's 'escalator' notion of the American Dream: in the post-war years, if you got on the elevator and you worked hard, complying to the religion's laws and logic, you could more or less count on ascending some way. The top? Unlikely, but certainly higher. Today, you have to get onto the escalator just to survive. But to get ahead? No, the chicken dances just as hard but the escalator has stopped.

Peter Hook, the bassist in Joy Division, recalls dropping Ian home on the night of the movie; in the hours leading to his death, having danced on the car seats together 'properly shouting, whooping, hollering, "Yeah, America!"', anticipating their departure the following day to Mundus Novus on tour, co-headlining with Cabaret Voltaire.* Others report the singer telling them he'd 'rather die' than travel to America to tour: exhausted; fearful of flying; on medication to treat the ever-worsening epilepsy that compounded the misery he already felt; and with the mother of his child constantly worried about their finances. In hindsight, Hook wonders if Curtis had it all planned out, and that his excitement was an act. Either way, it is inevitable to draw a connection between the musician's suicide, and the musician's suicide that closes Herzog's 115-minute indictment of the kultur in tight and tightening embrace of the group, ascending the ranks of its pantheon as they were. The caged chicken presaging the death-drive has been described by Herzog as a 'great metaphor,' but for what exactly he isn't sure. Critic Roger Ebert, in his original review of *Stroszek*, delivers his theory: 'A force we cannot comprehend puts some money in the slot, and we dance until the money runs out.' This is a peculiarly American reflection, through the prism of capital and Christianity.

---

* *Trivia*—Hook also says Curtis was allergic to 'foam'! Allergic to FOAM?!

For me, it's less metaphor and more a statement of hard fact: dance... for wherever you are and whoever you are and whatever you do, you're fucked.

Joy Division's American debut was set for Hurrah's in New York City, playing three nights—May 21, 22, 23—to answer demand. They'd take a day then to travel west to Toronto, and play The Edge in the evening of May 25. Bookies, Detroit, May 26. Over to Chicago for May 27, playing Tuts. Merlyn's next, Madison, Wisconsin, on May 28. From there to Duffy's in Minneapolis on May 29, the four-hour journey gains less than an hour for a gentle detour to Plainfield. Curtis might have campaigned for it. This tiny, remote village in Waushara County, Wisconsin, is where Herzog filmed and set *Stroszek*. The director first visited the village as the result of a pact with documentarist Errol Morris for a collaborative film on Ed Gein. It was never made. Gein exhumed and stole the bodies of all those that 'circled' his buried mother at Plainfield Cemetery, making lampshades with their skins, masks with their faces, belts with their nipples and bowls with their skulls. His impact on the culture and history of cinema has been enormous, providing the inspiration for *Psycho*; *The Texas Chainsaw Massacre*; *The Silence of the Lambs* (and all the emulations since). He's also the only reason anyone ever goes to Plainfield, to the eternal upset of its few permanent inhabitants. Herzog and Morris decided that they had to know whether Gein also exhumed his mother, and intended with or without consent to dig deep and find out. Morris chickened out and the grave was never opened, but Herzog had already travelled to meet him. His car broke down, and, impressed by the mechanic who fixed it, conceived a role for him, conceived *Stroszek*. There in Plainfield the movie wrote itself.

This macabre diversion for the Joy Division that never made America may yet have proved a little close to home: during the UK tour of the year previous, 1979, drummer Stephen Morris was arrested after playing at Brannigan's club in the red-light district of Leeds, suspected of being 'the Yorkshire Ripper.' This was a case that terrorised Britain from 1975 to 1980, epically mishandled by police. By the time of Morris' arrest, at least eleven women in Leeds, Bradford and Manchester had been murdered, and many more attacked. Peter Hook was questioned too but he'd kept his cool and drawn the quick conclusion that the invariably dodgy areas of the clubs in which the band were playing, were obvious hunting grounds for the killer. Morris, by contrast, panicked. The police flagged the blue transit van the band moved around in (presumably Morris and Hook were the named drivers), and a sequence of killings were timed and placed with their tour dates. It is unknown whether Peter Sutcliffe—professional HGV driver and Gein-alike gravedigger, finally in 1980 apprehended and convicted for the murder of at least 13 women —was a fan of Joy Division (his ex-wife Sonia liked Elvis best: as recently as 2015, she received a figurine by post from Pete, sculpted in his prison ceramics class), but, as the police agreed, the synchronicity of the gigs and the attacks in Bradford, Huddersfield, Leeds and Moss Side feels too unlikely to chalk off as coincidence. Just as Sutcliffe more probably followed Joy Division than didn't, Curtis almost certainly watched *Stroszek*, but was it his last movie?

¶ *Stroszek* began at 9:50pm on BBC2 and was viewed by 0.7 million Britains. Curtis could have switched out ten minutes in for *Match of the Day* at 10pm on BBC1, watched by 8.4 million, with Wales beating England four goals to nil, or *Tales of the Unexpected* on ITV, watched by 6.3 million. May 17's episode of *Tales...* was adapted from Roald Dahl's 'A Fine Son,' a short story first published in *Playboy* magazine (Austrian Klara gives birth to a son, fathered by Alois. She's already had three children but they all died, so she's very worried. Alois isn't really bothered, but she prays to God that the baby will survive, and she prays hard, and he does... revealed at the close of the show to be Adolf Hitler). Following a shift working the bar at a wedding reception, Deborah visited Ian at the house. He mentioned watching *Stroszek*, and they had a nasty row about the future of their relationship. He asked her to drop the divorce. Feeling him getting more and more worked up, she was afraid he might have a seizure and offered to stay the night. She left then, driving to her parents to tell them she'd be staying with him, but returned to be asked by Ian to leave, and not to come back to the house until after 10am the following morning, when he'd have already set off for Manchester. News and weather followed *Stroszek*, on BBC2, while over on ITV until CD ('close down,' cut to black, end of transmission for the day) at 12:30am: Barry Westwood's *Talkabout* (a series of programmes in which members of the public talk about 'important issues'); *Pro-Celebrity Darts*; *Lifeline* (reality TV show that took place in a hospital emergency room. Each episode would follow one or two patients through their process); *The Electric Theatre Show* (cinema news and interviews: unknown which titles were covered on the show transmitted on this date); *Darts World Knockout Cup*; *Vegas* (Michael Mann-produced Robert Urich and Tony Curtis-starring show; included a crossover with the *Charlie's Angels* series for the penultimate episode, with Urich appearing as his character in their programme: see famous quote attributed to J.G. Ballard, stolen from the show, 'Deep assignments run through all of our lives, there are no coincidences'); *Barney Miller* (American sitcom set in a Greenwich Village police station—almost all of which takes place in the squad room, with any action recalled rather than enacted by the players); *The Practice* (short-lived answer to *Coronation Street* set in a GP's practice in fictional suburb of Manchester called Castlehulme); *The Entertainers* (stand-up and sketches from the 'brightest' new comedy stars); and *Fully Licensed for Singing*

and Dancing (with Roy Walker of gameshow, *Catchphrase*). ITV's
packed schedule clashed with *Saturday Night at the Mill* (with
Kenny Ball and his Jazzmen) and Phil Silvers as *Sergeant Bilko* on
BBC1. If Deborah arrived as the credits of *Stroszek* rolled around
10:45pm, Curtis and her could have argued for a good twenty
minutes before International Golf highlights began (the same
0.7 million who watched *Stroszek* apparently also watched this).
The couple had an additional forty-five minutes to really go
at one another before the 'Midnight Movie' started at 11:50pm,
which I'd wager on in a cockfight with *Stroszek* as the true last
movie: *Cape Fear* (3.1 million, dropping by 0.2 million after its
first fifty minutes). All transmission ceased at 1:35am, but Ian
didn't die until dawn. This would give an ample window of time
for him to write a considered letter to Deborah (one that express-
es a wish to die but certainly no intention to commit suicide...
'reality is only a term, based on values and well-worn principles,
whereas the dream goes on forever'); get absolutely blotto on
whiskey, and listen on repeat to Iggy Pop's *The Idiot*—an album
named for Dostoyevsky's novel of the same name about an
epileptic, by an epileptic (Prince Myshkin says of his seizures
that epilepsy is 'The height of harmony and beauty, and gives
an unheard-of and till then undreamed-of feeling of wholeness,
of proportion, of reconciliation, and an ecstatic and prayer-like
union in the highest synthesis of life'). According to 'cultural
engineer' and fellow Mancunian, Genesis Breyer P-Orridge, who
had befriended Curtis in his ascent, a more likely 'last' record
might have been Frank Sinatra's 'Laura,' the title track from
Otto Preminger's film of the same name, or something by his
own band, Throbbing Gristle. While the other members of Joy
Division would be off drinking beer, Curtis would be brooding
in his parents' lounge, holding Frank's record sleeve like 'a holy
relic' ('the laugh that floats on a summer night, that you can
never quite recall'). P-Orridge described many years later having
had the last known conversation with Curtis, speaking on the
telephone in the early hours of May 18, the singer singing back
to P-Orridge the lyrics of his own song, 'Weeping' ('We created
cars to fight for space to be in / We created work to waste our
time / We created love so one can be the victim / We all need,
as a result, we all need love / But don't know what to do with it').
The veracity of this claim has to be disputed, if only for Gen's
long and detailed recall neglecting to reference any conversation
about what they'd watched on telly that night.

In Peter Hook's book-length wandering on what finally broke Ian, he cites Candy the dog as the only detail to set the night apart. While Joy Division had recently been on tour across the UK (to raise funds for their imminent trip to the US), Deborah, lumbered not just with a baby but also with Candy—a border collie belonging to the singer—had arranged for the dog to be 'sent away,' increasingly struggling to control it, and to find the money to feed it. There was talk of a farm in Rochdale, but this was probably code for putting the animal to 'sleep.'

In *Cape Fear*, convicted rapist Cady is freed from jail and pursues the person he blames for his sentence: Sam, the lawyer that happened upon the attack, and so was able to testify against him.* Cady begins to stalk Sam and his family, planning to get even. A father, a mother, a daughter. He won't leave them alone. The presence of Cady crosses a line with his first physical attack: Marilyn, the family dog, is poisoned and killed, though Sam can't prove Cady's responsibility. Everything escalates horribly thereafter with the last violation implicit in the first. Aboard a houseboat in the area of Cape Fear, the two men have it out. Sam ultimately overpowers Cady, who appeals to him to 'finish the job.' He refrains, recalling what the dog-killer described to him as the worst possible punishment: prison again, 'to count the years, the months, the hours.' The inquest into Curtis' death found that he had consumed an extreme amount of alcohol that night and morning. Might he have found a twisted mirror in the lawyer sending off the dog-killer (Deborah) to live the remainder of their life condemned? A precedent existed for drama and derangement under the influence: a half-cut Ian once approached William S. Burroughs at a book signing in Belgium and, unable to afford a copy, asked if we could have one free. 'Fuck off, kid,' said Bill. His answer was to drink even more. The shame of that. The shame of the failing marriage (the horror). The agony of Natalie. The deadening of the drugs. The impossible Belgian. The graft of America. The dancing chicken and the butchered dog, with an interval of international golf highlights. Yup. That'll do it.

---

* The word 'rape' was removed from the script at the command of the film censors, because the source novel, John D. Macdonald's *The Executioners*, casts Cady as a soldier court-martialled for the crime, which would 'adversely' reflect on US military personnel.

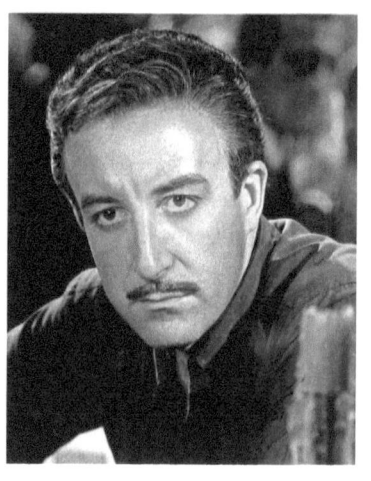

Peter Sellers (d. 1980) in *Brannigan* (Douglas Hickox, 1975), 111m

¶ Divining future London as an entirely surveilled but ultimately lawless playground for the global super rich without principle, passion or point (in a word: *movie*; of the moment: *now*), Douglas Hickox's *Brannigan* has John Wayne as Roman among Pagans, a Chicago cop with blocked arteries, tourist entitlement, and barely the intelligence to form a sentence, leching about the ancient river settlement like the Old Wild West of Hollywood lore.

Holed up at The Dorchester Hotel on Hyde Park in Mayfair, Peter Sellers—an actor and impersonator who frequently claimed to have no identity outside of the characters he played, and believed he was haunted by the long-deceased Victorian music hall comic Dan Lyons guiding his decisions and shaping his fate—watched BBC1's 'Sunday Film' (19:15–21.05), *Brannigan*, on his hotel room's television. Wayne's 'Big Jim' Brannigan is issued orders to extradite a Chicago gangster who has fled to London and taken board at... you guessed it, The Dorchester. The camera floats over Hyde Park before descending on the unremarkable villain departing the hotel for a midday massage, passing the duckies of the Serpentine Lake, and ascending the steps flanking the Institute of Contemporary Arts *en route* to the red lights of Soho.

Sellers was delighted to recognise Roy Scammell, the London stuntman (*From Russia with Love*, *The Spy Who Loved Me*, *Barry Lyndon* and many others) doubling as Wayne, as he'd doubled for Sellers himself in *Casino Royale* (1967). It was Stanley Kubrick's desire that the two actors would face-off in *Dr. Strangelove*, Sellers the titular doctor (and many others) and Wayne Major Kong, but he rejected the part. Stuntmen were a breed Sellers felt a particular affinity with, drawn to the circus and bound to the supernatural, he proudly originated from prizefighting stock: his cousin four times removed was Daniel Mendoza, the famous Sephardic Jewish bare-knuckle boxer of Georgian Whitechapel (he'd sometimes boast ascendance from Lord Nelson too, which was nonsense). After the collision of Dorchester on Dorchester, Sellers might have picked out locations in *Brannigan* as one does when familiar with the filmed city. Impossible leaps in time and space reveal the apparatus of the cine spell. Sellers loved film and ceaselessly recorded his own life, especially the women in it. He was by then suffering from advanced heart disease and knew that death was onto him. He locked himself in his hotel suite of rooms 611 and 612 (the most expensive), as if the reaper might obey the doorhanger authority of client over room service, believing a repeat of Hollywood 1964 was the worst that could happen. Whatever doctors said, and whatever he felt, whatever he knew, Sellers *believed* above all else in a clairvoyant's reading of many years earlier: there'd be four wives, he'd be a household name, and he'd die aged seventy-five. Two out of three ain't bad.

In '64, a massive heart attack had rendered him clinically dead for ninety seconds, which he attributed to poppers-fuelled 'mooey-wooey' with then-wife, 'the landlord's daughter' Britt Ekland (who had an appetite for monsters: she'd later live with boyfriend Rod Stewart in his mortgage-free property, for which he charged her rent). Sellers had first met Ekland at the Dorchester, and might have recalled their peaks and falls amidst the psychic wreckage of present time's broken relationship (he died before his divorce from Lynne Frederick completed, which he intended to finalise during his stay in London, entitling her to his entire £4.5 million estate, and to each of his children just £750. Frederick spent the rest of her days on vodka and cocaine, watching and re-watching her almost ex-husband's movies, dying aged thirty-nine): 'I was in the bath... Burt, Mr. Seller's valet, knocked on my door and invited me to his suite. That was it.' He took her to see his own film, *The Pink Panther*, at the Odeon on Leicester Square, and proposed over the phone two days later. In eleven days, they were married. Sellers' children watched the event on television.

In Roger Lewis' sprawling account of *The Life & Death of Peter Sellers*, he describes the actor watching *Brannigan* the day before he died, and various sources cite Sellers' arrival at the Dorchester on July 21. Brannigan was actually broadcast on BBC1 on July 20, and Sellers didn't eat his last meal until lunchtime on July 22—a double dose of Dover sole with salad—before collapsing into the bright blue hotel carpet (though he didn't stop breathing until July 24, he never regained consciousness).*

Clashing with *Brannigan* on ITV was American dramatic mini-series *Best Sellers*—no connection to Peter—and then *Lady Killers*, a Granada-produced serial series dedicated to murderous women (a second season opened up to take in the murder of women by men too). Sellers might have blinked at the listings, mistaking one following the other as a double-bill tribute to his work (1955's *Ladykillers* stars Sellers in his movie breakthrough

---

* The only meal we are aware of 'Big Jim' eating is a Dover Sole presumed for him by a Sir at the Garrick Club, which he rejects requesting, instead, 'eggs over easy, bacon crisp, and a short stack.'

role opposite Alec Baldwin, Herbert Lom and Cecil Parker, as
a group of Dadaist criminals posing as musicians to rent a room
from which to plan and execute a bank robbery). A dull pang of
disappointment, and back to BBC1 for International Golf Highlights (see Ian Curtis, pp.162–172). Standby. On July 21 he visited
his parents' ashes at Golders Green Crematorium for the first
time ever (he'd join them in his own charred form within days,
selecting Glenn Miller's 'In the Mood' as his funeral exit track).
Back at the hotel, he likely caught some more television (July 21
a stepdown even from the progamming on July 20): cricket, more
cricket, *Olympic Grandstand*, more *Olympic Grandstand*, *Songs
of Praise*, *Billy Two Hats* (western with Gregory Peck), *Oklahoma*
('Oh! What a beautiful morning'... Oh! Witness the camera
through the corn!). *The World We Live In*, *Portrait of an Artist*,
Something Different, *Best Sellers* (repeat), *Against the Wind*,
Doctor, *Bedtime*, *Rainbow*, *Clapperboard*. Close down.

¶ Sellers' final years were spent campaigning the writer Jerzy Kosinski to let him film *Being There*, a novel about a gardener, John 'Chance' Gardener, who gleans all of his experience and motivation from television. With no employment record or right of residence, the death of his master means immediate eviction. Illiterate 'Chance' is an avatar of channel-flicking out in the world for the first time as a fifty-four year old man: relaying back to fellow spectators what television has already told them, or speaking in elliptical gardening terms, and trying to clip anything unpleasant with his remote control. His calm, simplicity and apparent purchase on reality is mistaken for wisdom, and he's thrust into the American political arena. Almost a decade before Sellers died, he had started printing his business cards and stationery with the name 'John C. Gardener.' Learning of this, Kosinski confronted him one day in Malibu. Sellers responded that he, Kosinski, had invaded his life: 'You don't understand. I am John C. Gardener.' Eventually he did understand. After a lifetime of pretending to be other people, in 'Chance' he felt he could finally be Peter. The big reveal in nothing at all. Less than nothing, animated entirely by the projections of others. By changing the television channel, the character changes too, in the moment, but retains nothing, going 'through phases as a garden goes through phases, but as rapidly as he wished, twisting the dial backwards and forwards.' The movie ends with a funeral—not his—and as Chance walks out on a lake of water, 'Life is a state of mind,' are the words that echo down from another place as the picture fades to black.

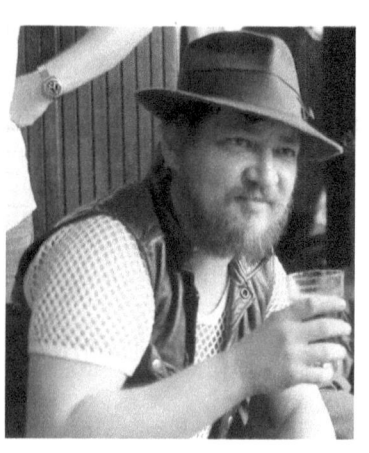

Rainer Werner Fassbinder (d. 1982)
20,000 Years in Sing Sing (Michael Curtiz, 1932), 99m

Death sings a slow song.
—Angel in *Berlin Alexanderplatz*

¶ Udo Kier, or 'Dodo'—the tap-tap of tongue pimped by a teen-age Fassbinder and thrummed by old paying strangers—calls actress Isolde Barth to breathe the news. Dead. The director is dead. Dead as a dodo, dead. And of all days on this day, when the Rolling Stones play Munich.

Fassbinder's room is lit by a postscript of television static. Michael Curtiz's *20,000 Years in Sing Sing* (1932) is the poem that has run out the screen, stilled behind the VHS-player's lip. Before the film's grey announcement of The End, the last light is with Tommy—our knowing protagonist—zapped at the anti-throne of Sing Sing prison's electric chair. George Cukor's *Manhattan Melodrama* (1934), the film watched by John Dillinger before he emerged from the cinema to a panic of police bul-lets, finishes at the same prison in the same way and, by some coincidence, both films also feature an inmate named Blackie: a bit-part escapologist staring confusedly into the mirror in *20,000 Years...* finding his big break in Clark Gable's face two years later as the Blackie of *Manhattan Melodrama*.

Juliane Lorenz, Fassbinder's film editor; aegis [Last Wife] and authority on The End, switches off his television, which usually wakes him up. Nothing. It's a little after 4:30am, she's checked her make-up, and she's got a bag of hot rolls. The two had planned to breakfast together. 'I saw a tiny blue point on his eyelid. And there was a little bit of blood coming out of his nose. I got scared. I shook him.' Nothing. In Fassbinder's hand is a Camel cigarette burned to the butt, ash clinging on. Nude, he is the swollen pharaoh of the New German Cinema buffered by a bed of literary kindling. Pages and pages on 'Rosa L.,' that night's particular curvet towards the film adaptation of Frau Luxemburg's story, the Revolutionary khorovodnitsa who'd be played, so Fass insisted, by Jane Fonda. Half a line of cocaine lies interrupted on the bedside table. Lorenz is pleased to remove it, and proceeds to flush away all of the drugs in the apartment before the medics (and the police) arrive.

At around 1am Fassbinder had his last known conversation with Harry Baer, the 'artistic consultant' ordained by the direc-tor to be 'too beautiful to work in an office,' and one of only five people to have the number to his bright-red bedside telephone. Baer is excited to have found what he believes to be the nightclub venue perfect for shooting another imminent Fassbinder pro-duction, *I'm the Happiness of this World*, about three failed private detectives becoming rock stars. 'Do a deal,' Fassbinder instructs. Baer agrees. 'How are you doing?' He continues. 'I'm watching television, video. In between my reading,' replies Fassbinder, who'd fiddle with a nipple when lost in thought. 'I have a few more things to do.'

The autopsy reports Fassbinder's death around 4am on June 10 in 1982, as a result of 'cerebrovascular accident' (stroke). In 1982, German television ceased transmission around midnight. Lorenz finds his body still warm. There's no reason he would've kept the set running were it not to play his video copy of *20,000 Years...* (The student-movie notion of the director caned and pained and splayed out taking revolutionary notes to static must be resisted.) Rainer's brain most likely failed to make the necessary electrical connections as *Sing Sing*'s anti-hero, Tommy, has his own brain forcibly overloaded with them. Tommy's last request is for a light. The benevolent prison warden reaches down with a trembling hand, steadied by he who stares at death. Exhale. The End.

Or, if not the shared climax of that last cigarette, then Fassbinder's final living moment might have come earlier in the film, with Spencer Tracy's defiant Tommy reassuring Bette Davis' Fay that everything will be—as it won't be—alright. *Remember, Fay? I loved you more than life*. The End.

¶ Or, earlier still, with a bed-bound Fay raising a pistol towards Tommy's would-be fixer, Joe Finn, the flat-arsed lawyer with proclivity for bodged bribes, bad acting, and hospitalising girls. The End.

A cliffhanger!

Or, earlier and earlier *still*: did Fassbinder notice the date of the telegram received by Tommy at Sing Sing? This is the message that sends him on his course to the end of the light: Fay is in a critical condition after an 'automobile accident', unlikely to survive. The warden lets him out for the day. You know the score. The telegram is stamped exactly fifty years to the day, Rainer Werner's last, June 10 1982–June 10 1932. *Snort*. A body forever dying to forget itself is given subliminal permission by Sing Sing's celluloid ghosts. The prisoner evaporates in the plume that's shared through a leak in the picture tube. Fassbinder had become cinema.

Smoking one hundred cigarettes per day, with Weisswürstchen (a Bavarian sausage made of veal) for breakfast, Krautwickel (again Bavarian: cabbage leaf wrapped meatballs simmered in sauce, best made by Dodo, who by The End doubled as a live-in cook) for lunch, and prime rump steak for supper (for all of his adult life: even when there hadn't been money to afford it his faithful ladies would sell their bodies to ensure it), Fassbinder downed the lot with beer, schnapps, and smack, using at least seven or eight grams of cocaine every day to keep his pecker up. To sleep: three Valiums and two Mandrex (banned), a prescription repeated each thirty minutes if sleep didn't come. He'd managed to produce forty-three films by the time of his death aged thirty-seven—many he also wrote, edited and starred in. By comparison, the enigmatic Hungarian director, Mihály Kertés, arrived in Hollywood the same age with sixty-eight pictures to his credit. Working strictly within the confines of the studio system—first Austrian and German, and then American, this prolificacy captivated Fassbinder. Hollywood's conveyer-belt logic of over-production was an ideal he sought to reproduce with his adopted filmmaking-family in Germany. Curtiz was proof he could do it without compromising the output's quality. Even in the Hungarian's lacking titles with leaky scripts and bad actors there is life, brilliance and signature. Where Fass saw anarchy in Kertés, the Warner Brothers saw opportunity. No sooner than one of the 'Brothers' arrived on set in Vienna to witness Kertés work—his last European picture, *Moon of Israel* (a re-telling of

Exodus)—was he told with a Biblical authority to pack up his shadows and his crane shots for America.

Anglicised as Michael Curtiz, Kertés was 'broken into' Hollywood with a second-rate Chicago-based gangster flick. He didn't speak a word of English and he'd never been to Chicago, so he convinced the Los Angeles sheriff to award him a week in county jail for a fast-track course in the kultur. It was another six years before the breakthrough picture, *Sing Sing*, announced Curtiz as a seriuz American director (and blessed audiences with the first advanced roles for Spencer Tracy and Bette Davis), and four years more until *Captain Blood*. With this he raised rank to become Warner's number one director in economy, execution, and critical and audience reception. *Blood* was also the first leading role for a previously unknown extra named Errol Flynn; a favour the deliriously handsome and notoriously warted alcoholic swashbuckler repaid by marrying Curtiz's long-term other woman, Lili Damita (they met aboard the boat from London to Los Angeles in 1934, and it was probably her who sorted out the gig). On the wave of the Captain's success, the studio booked Flynn under Curtiz's directorship again in *The Charge of the Light Brigade* (1936), which did even better at the box office. The title of the film is taken from Lord Tennyson's poem, written rapidly after a British charge on Russian forces in the Crimean War. Due to bad military intelligence and unclear orders, the Brit's light infantry 'trotted' into an open field with swords and no amour, where they were shot and shelled to hell (by an enemy assuming them drunk, so mad was the advance). The film throws in a love triangle and a quest for revenge, which a tickled Curtiz might have met by ordering 125 horses to be trip-wired for the final scene. 'Bring on the empty horses!' He is said to have hurled. Twenty-five of these were killed immediately or later put to sleep due to their injuries. A well-known horsey guy, Flynn summarily smacked the director and tripwires in Hollywood were banned.

In 1980, Fassbinder pens a brief text on Curtiz, 'Anarchist in Hollywood? Unorganised Thoughts on a Seemingly Paradoxical Idea.' He claims to know nothing of Curtiz's personal life or outlook, nor any project trivia. Of 178 films, Fass only namechecks *Casablanca*, reflecting on the old-*ish* German-Jewish couple attempting to reach America via Casablanca in the early years of WWII, and practicing the language as they go: 'What's the watch?'—'Ten watch.'—'Such much?' This literal translation from the German to the English Fass declares to be 'one of the most beautiful pieces of dialogue in the history of film,' but insists there are 'more important things' by a 'cruelly overlooked' Michael Curtiz. His concern is with the worldview he intuits across the filmmaker's wildly varied and excessive output (having watched at the time of writing, he says, about thirty-five titles). These films are charged with moral ambiguity and emotional intelligence, where normality is contemptible and compassion is for the weak. Herein lies the possible anarchy. Through ambivalence in cinema the audience might find greater agency in life. 'I want to give the spectator the emotions along with the possibility of reflecting on and analysing what they are feeling.' Obedience is tyranny. Illegalism is principle. Everybody loves Robin Hood. Fassbinder understood his responsibility as a maker facilitated by the subsidy system of Germany's post-war economic miracle: bite the hand that feeds you. Anything less would mean the single worst fate anyone faces in his films, in the death of the spirit.

Only two films by Fassbinder climax with escape to life and not terror and death: *The Marriage of Maria Braun*, and *Lili Marleen*, both films about women. The men are always doomed. The director whose influence was most profound on Fassbinder was probably Douglas Sirk, whose films, Fass observed, enjoy the rare quality of portraying 'women who think.' The same can be said for *20,000 Years...*, *Casablanca*, and especially *Flamingo Road*—Fass' favourite Curtiz film, and one of his all-time top-ten. Based on the book by Robert Wilder, author of the Sirk-adapted *Written on the Wind*, Joan Crawford stars as Lane, a matured and un-jaded ex-carnival attraction who finds herself anchored in the fictional town of Truro, Florida. Lane falls in love with a Sheriff's deputy, and he with her. The Sheriff, Titus Semple—a carbon copy foreshadowing of Orson Welles' police chief in *Touch of Evil*—is appalled: he has ambitions for the deputy at the Senate, and Lane's class, background and circus association (and in the book on which the film is based: the colour of her skin) is all wrong. The deputy sacrifices their love in pursuit of status. He marries a pain-in-the-arse, and gets endlessly pissed instead of addressing his missteps. Ultimately, he's driven to suicide by his own bullshit. Lane, meanwhile, is pursued by a man she loves less, who has an even higher status. She finds him in the bottles and the bluff and she straightens him out with a Whiskey Sour. Turns out the concerns on class and background were rubbish. None of that matters. He takes her to restaurants; he takes her to the dance. They marry. She's permitted to love again like cinema has tricked us in to thinking isn't really possible. A little love, but isn't it often? Better than without until it isn't and then it's over. Lane knows the score. By the end of *Flamingo Road* she's held in a cell. Bound still by chains aplenty, but freed of others, she is exonerated from the accusation of involvement in her old lover's suicide, and the Sheriff, mercy, is dead. Unlike in *20,000 Years...*, the cell door opens and the light of morning —of living again!— burns brighter than the charge of the chair. Had it been this film Fassbinder watched that night, and had it been Joan's ghost in attendance, perhaps, perhaps, he might have stayed a little longer.

THE FUNERAL OF RAINER WERNER FASSBINDER:
A FEATURE-LENGTH (PRESUMED) PLAYLIST

At the funeral, reports attendee Robert Katz, the assembled
crowd stood before an empty coffin and listened to 'a solid ninety minutes of Fassbinder movie music: Vangelis, Leonard Cohen,
Elvis, The Platters, some hard rock and the theme from Lili Marleen.' Afterwards they went to the Deutsche Eiche, Fassbinder's
favourite bar, to drink beer and eat Weisswürstchen.

Johann Strauss II, Berliner Philharmoniker, 'An der
schönen blauen Donau'
Dean Martin, 'Memories Are Made of This'
Paul Anka, 'You Are My Destiny'
Marlene Dietrich, 'Lili Marleen'
Leonard Cohen, 'Why Don't You Try'
Elvis Presley, 'Santa Lucia'
The Platters, 'Smoke Gets In Your Eyes'
Rocco Granata, 'Buona Notte bambino' [German version]
Leonard Cohen, 'Lover Lover Lover'
The Velvet Underground, 'Candy Says'
Ben E. King, 'Stand by Me'
Glenn Miller, 'In the Mood'
Elvis Presley, 'One Night of Sin'
The Walker Brothers, 'In My Room'
Leonard Cohen, 'Teachers'
The Platters, 'The Great Pretender'
Connie Francis, 'Schöner fremder Mann'
The First Edition, 'Ruby, Don't Take Your Gun to Town'
Kris Kristofferson, 'Me and Bobby McGee'
Leonard Cohen, 'So Long, Marianne'
Elvis Presley, 'Jailhouse Rock'
The Rolling Stones, 'We Love You'
Fleetwood Mac, 'Albatross'
Pearls Before Swine, 'Morning Song'
Roxy Music, 'A Song for Europe'
Kraftwerk, 'Radioactivity'
Glenn Miller, 'Moonlight Serenade'
The Berlin Ramblers, 'High on a Hilltop'

(1h30m)

AFTERPARTY AT THE EICHE:
A FEATURE LENGTH (PRESUMED) PLAYLIST
WITH MUSIC FROM THE FILMS OF RAINER WERNER
FASSBINDER & MICHAEL CURTIZ

Less than two weeks before Fassbinder's death, a customarily
lavish birthday party was held at the Eiche (Oak) Hotel—*his*
place—in the centre of Munich. Guests were treated to lobster
and caviar with new potatoes and champagne. Fassbinder kept
his hat and sunglasses on throughout, and avoided the windows.
Accepting only cash as payment, he was pleased to be handed
on arrival a briefcase for his (theatrical) directorship of *A Street-
car Named Desire* (all of which would be spent on the cocaine
contributing to his death). One bystander suspected the black
handkerchief in his blazer pocket to be a mark of respect for
those passed, but nobody asked. On this day—four years earlier—his lover and star of his films, Armin, had overdosed on
sleeping pills and booze, after Fass made it clear they were together no more. They'd met at the Eiche—Armin cleaning glasses to subsidise his day-job at a slaughterhouse. Fass thought
he looked like James Dean. Heinrich Himmler would've been
proud. A keen breeder of rabbits, Himmler had initiated the
Lebensborn in Nazi Germany, with a view to crossing 'the best
with the best.' Armin was a product of this, meeting his mother
just once and his father never. With the end of the war, he was
condemned to an upbringing with nuns, and somehow later fell
into the hands of an evil doctor who used him as a sex slave for
twelve years. Rainer too felt he had been abandoned as a child,
though he maintained a close relationship with his mother into
adulthood: humiliating her on set for trying to kill him with
'unripe apples.' It was his mother who found Armin in a state of
decomposition at the kitchen table of the apartment they shared
together; an apartment well within eye-shot of the hotel. Their
bedroom had brown velvet walls, dark carpet, large leather bed,
and no natural light. A long narrow mirror ran along all four
walls at the height of a man's erect cock. Fass designed it himself, but he wouldn't go back with Armin's passing. After a stint
staying at the Eiche he'd be gifted a tastefully decorated apartment by an aspirational producer, and that's where he watched
his last movie.

The Eiche today is bigger and stronger than ever, expand-
ing extensively over the past forty years. A sauna with a 300-man

capacity takes up part of the venue, labyrinthine and complex, it is designed around a cat-and-mouse layout. Open non-stop from Friday noon 'til Monday 7am. During the few off-hours, the hotel and sauna offers educational tours to school children of no less than fourteen years (Germany's age of consent), showing off the venue's glory holes, slings, private cabins and 'devices.'

Mario Nascimbene, 'Theme and Main Title' [*Francis of Assisi*]
Anton Karas, 'The Café Mozart Waltz'
Maurice Chevalier, Alessandro Cicognini, 'A Breath of Scandal (i)'
Friedrich Hollaender, Marlene Dietrich, 'Destry Rides Again: The Boys in the Backroom'
Malando, 'Ole Guapa'
Comedian Harmonists, 'Veronika, der Lenz ist da'
Freddy Quinn, 'Unter fremden Sternen'
Georges Moustaki, 'Le métèque'
Ein grosses Bundesblasorchester mit Männerchor, 'In einem Polenstädtchen'
Dalida, 'Am Tag als der Regen kam'
Johnny Horton, 'The Battle of New Orleans'
Karl-Heinz Steinfeld Chor, 'Horch, was kommt von draussen rein'
Sanford Clark, 'Run Boy Run'
Jeanne Moreau, 'Each Man Kills the Thing He Loves'
Gogi Grant and The Ray Heindorf Orchestra, 'Why Was I Born'
Max Steiner, 'Four Wives—Symphony Modern'
The Warner Bros. Studio Orchestra, 'Play It Sam... Play "As Time Goes By"' [*Casablanca*]
Mario Nascimbene, 'Clara's Theme' [*Dressing of Clara*]
Bernard Herrmann, 'The Ruins' [*The Egyptian*]
Bernard Herrmann, 'The Red Sea and Childhood' [*The Egyptian*]
John Ashley, 'The Hangman'
Peer Raben, 'Sailor's Accordion'
Gogi Grant & The Ray Heindorf Orchestra, 'Speak to Me of Love'
Alessandro Cicognini Orchestra, 'Courtly Humour / Olympia'
Benny Goodman, 'Misson to Moscow'
Michael Curtiz, Theme [*The Comancheros*]
Gogi Grant & The Ray Heindorf Orchestra, 'On the Sunnyside of the Street'
Elvis Presley, 'Trouble'
Peer Raben, 'Each Man Kills the Thing He Loves'
Nino Rota, 'Amarcord'
Jeanne Moreau, 'Men Are at Peace'

Mario Nascimbene, 'Death of Francis'
The Warner Bros. Studio Orchestra, 'As Time Goes By' [*Casablanca*]
Alessandro Cicognini Orchestra, 'Austrian Dream Waltz / Finale'

(1h30m)

FIRST DAY IN THE WORLD
(OR, DAWN CHORUS, MONDAY MORNING):
CLASSICAL MUSIC + THE SADDEST SONGS
IN THE WORLD (FROM THE FILMS OF RAINER
WERNER FASSBINDER)

Suicide, 'Frankie Teardrop'
Giuseppe Verdi, Luciano Pavarotti, ' La traviata / Act 1:
Un dì felice, eterea'
Robert Schumann, Vladimir Horowitz,
'Kinderszenen, Op.15: No.1, Von fremden Ländern und Menschen'
Domenico Modugno, 'Amara terra mia'
Leonard Cohen, 'Bird on the Wire'
Louis Spoor, Margaret Baker, '6 Deutsche Lieder, Op.103:
No.4, Wiegenlied'
Max Bruch, 'Violin Concerto No.1 in G Minor, Op.26: 1. Prelude.
Allegro moderato'
Wolfgang Amadeus Mozart, 'Symphony No. 33 In B-Flat Major,
K. 319: 1. Allegro assai'
Georges Moustaki, 'Rue des Fosses Saint-Jacques'
Heino, 'Kein schöner Land'
Leonard Cohen, 'Suzanne,' 'Winter Lady,' 'Chelsea Hotel #2,'
& 'Sisters of Mercy'
Peer Raben, David Ambach, 'The Tears of the Lady'
Rudi Schuricke, 'Capri-Fischer'
Heino, 'Am Brunnen vor dem Tore'
Gustav Mahler, Wiener Philharmoniker, 'Symphony No. 5
In C Sharp Minor: IV. Adagietto. Sehr langsam'
Juventino Rosas, First Separate Exemplary Orchestra of USSR
Defence Ministry, 'Over the Waves'

(1h30m)

ADDENDUM—Fassbinder watching Curtiz' *20,000 Years...* depends on his ability to record VHS tapes from the television. At this time there was not a commercially available copy of *20,000 Years in Sing Sing*, and the film did not screen on television on the night he died. It did screen a couple of weeks earlier on May 28 at 11:05pm, on ZDF. Fassbinder may have watched Renoir's final film, *The Woman on the Beach*, the night before he died. It screened at 9:50pm, again, on ZDF. Renoir's final film was radically reworked after an unsuccessful preview. The director's original is now lost, but Jacques Rivette called it 'pure cinema.'

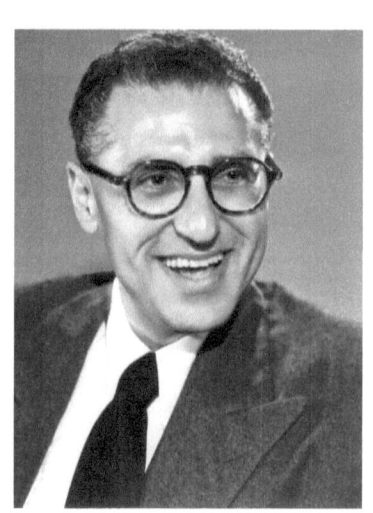

George Cukor (d.1983)
The Graduate (Mike Nichols, 1967), 106m

¶ On January 23 in 1983, George Cukor—director, producer, and *maître'd* of Hollywood's gay subculture—requested the evening's dinner be served on his Beverly Hills household's finest china. This was unusual. His friends, Tucker Fleming and Harris Woods, had the sense that it was 'an exceptional evening, almost a formal good-bye.'

Cukor ate little and retired for a nap at 7:30pm. Fleming and Woods kissed him on the forehead and bid farewell. When he woke, Cukor decided he'd like to watch a movie: Mike Nichols' *The Graduate* was chosen, and the screening facilitated by an almost graduate, the young student Robin Thorne, employed to care for George. 'I was surprised that he had never seen it before,' reported Thorne, 'He thought Dustin Hoffman's performance was excellent but that the film dragged in some places' (directionless Dustin graduates from college and is inexplicably taken up by an older woman, whose affections he reciprocates and ultimately repays by pursuing her daughter). The credits rolled and Cukor gasped. He was having a heart attack. Thorne realised, and helped the director to the floor, administering CPR. Paramedics attended immediately and took him to Cedars-Sinai Hospital, but with the arrival of January 24 he was dead.

(For further remarks on George Cukor, see pp. 50–62, 106, 183, 223.)

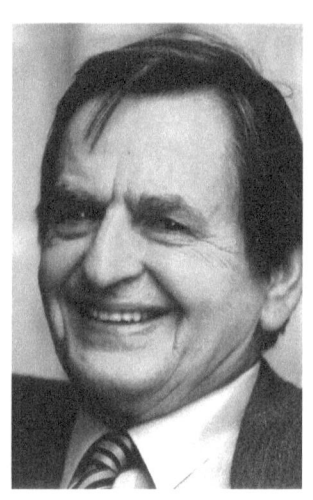

Olof Palme (d. 1986)
Bröderna Mozart / The Mozart Brothers (Suzanne Osten, 1986), 109m

¶ Between the Monet and the Matisse credited to Elmyr de Hory (the glaucous star of Orson Welles' *F for Fake*) at Vienna's Museum of Art Forgeries, is Operation Bernhard's five-pound note. Considered to be the finest forgery of all time, Bernhard was a German WWII initiative that gathered dozens of master forgers at Sachsenhausen concentration camp, creating hundreds of millions of pounds to flood and cripple the British economy. Initially the plan was to rain the money down on British soil from the sky, but a more clandestine distribution method was chosen, giving inflated sums to informants and spies (some unbeknownst). The British authorities later downplayed the scheme's success: the money circulated for years during the war, and continued even after it ended, finally requiring the complete withdrawal and re-design of all notes including and above the denomination of five. The creative team behind the stunt were transferred to Austria's own Mauthausen concentration camp—unique in its focus on imprisoning the intelligentsia and working them to death—in the months leading to allied 'victory,' but in an unusually happy ending for the time, the order to murder the prisoners was delayed by an 'overly precise interpretation.' The forgers were saved by bureaucracy.

Also notable at the museum are the small studies by Rembrandt via Eric Hebborn. No forger of the previous century is believed to have infiltrated as widely as Hebborn, a disgruntled Royal Academy graduate and working class queer who sought to prod, shame and break the pomposity and guarantee of the market-driven 'expert.' Hebborn went so far as to 'time bomb' some of his painted work: applying a glycerine layer beneath the paint's surface so professional cleaning would cause a destructive chemical reaction. The publication of Hebborn's *Art Forger's Handbook* represented a period of openness in the daub's erstwhile secret life, discussing with candour his time-travelling, truth-beating master-unworks. More memoir than how-to, his tome and his chat threatened to undermine some very healthy investments belonging to some very dubious people, and the man who declared the world as a thing that 'wants to be cheated' was found with blunt instrument head wounds on a street one night near his home in Rome. His killer remains at large. What did he last see? Nobody knows.

CM von Hausswolff—my museum company—is in Vienna convening *freq_out 12*, a summoning of sound art's temple masters (this particular edition included JG Thirlwell,

Hans-Joachim Roedelius and Peter Rehberg). Hausswolff and I had agreed to meet at the sewer popularised by Carol Reed's *The Third Man*, but eventually choose the Museum of Art Forgeries in tribute to it. (Vienna's booming underground tourist trade is also a sham: Orson Welles actually refused to enter the sewer for fear of rats and faeces. The whole structure had to be re-created in London.) 'Did you watch the film?' Hausswolff grins. He doesn't mean *The Third Man*. And yes, I did. Nameless, and without credits, a faded VHS transfer hummed and stuttered, initially uncertain of itself (or, perhaps, its viewer). The lens struggled for focus, and zoomed, also reluctantly, into an ancient and abused French map; a swirl, a scribble and a scratch denoting the steepest climbs of modern-day Iran. 'This film describes a journey to the remote Alamut area situated in the Alburz Mountains in the North of Persia [Iran].'

Hausswolff explains:

With a friend of mine, Erik Pauser, we picked twelve spots around the world that were difficult to go to. Iran was one of them. It was clear we had to get to Alamut, we just didn't know how. We had a magazine: a radio magazine, which of course didn't have any copies, yet, but we had the letterhead... so we wrote an introduction letter to the Iranian embassy in Stockholm, and we said we would like to send these cultural journalists to Iran to cover the post-revolutionary Iranian culture. And soon we had our visas. So we went.

The year was 1986. Alamut was the mountain fortress of Hassan-i Sabbah, a character whose contemporary cultural kudos stems largely from the fabulist exposition of him by William S. Burroughs and Brion Gysin. In the eleventh century, Sabbah ruled great swathes of Persia without an army, instead employing hashishin (the Islamic sect formally known as the Nizari Ismailis), from which we take the English word 'assassin' (we take 'alcohol' from them too). Sabbah would select his hashishin by identifying the empire's most able young men, inviting them one-by-one up to the fortress of Alamut, and knocking them out with the greatest hash (and opium and mushrooms and other loveliness). Men would wake and find themselves in Sabbah's 'garden of earthly delights.' Wine, women. They believed that Sabbah had shown them God; the promise of paradise, and possessed, as or like a prophet, immortality. They would henceforth on Sabbah's word go off to hashashinate trash-talking leaders of any far-flung opposition (or simply leap, on command, from the highest peak at Alamut, knowing exactly where they were going for having gone before). The best-known account of Sabbah and his Hashashins is Vladimir Bartol's *Alamut* (1938), which witnessed a huge spike in sales after the attack on the Twin Towers in New York City in 2001, as Americans scrambled to unpick the logic of their new, vivid enemy, with an entirely fabricated action-adventure novel about an ancient Persian emperor.

> With the reputation of Hassan i-Sabbah, we also thought it quite amazing that... when we came back to the hotel from Alamut, we discovered someone had assassinated our prime minister in Sweden. Olof Palme. Shot him down in the street. Still they haven't caught the assassin. I remember, we looked at each other and we said... 'Jesus, did we do something here?' Because sometimes very strange things happen when you do things. I mean, other things can happen, as this [Alamut] was of course for us a very, very special place.

Palme, leader of the Social Democratic Party, had been the Prime Minister of Sweden since October 1982. He was in his second term. On Friday February 28, the day of Olof's death, his wife Lisbeth had called their son, Mårten, around 5pm, to ask if he and his partner would like to go to the cinema. They were way ahead of her, having already booked two tickets at the Grand Cinema, Stockholm, to see Suzanne Osten's *Bröderna Mozart / The Mozart Brothers*, a Swedish comedy about people 'who work in theatre; who live for the theatre; who think of nothing but the theatre.' Director Suzanne Osten had earlier contacted Palme, requesting that he star as the theatre director in the film. Perhaps this connection had pushed Mårten to book *Bröderna Mozart* over the cinema's other offering that night, Lasse Hallström's *Mitt liv som hund / My Life as a Dog*, though whether or not he knew is unclear. Olof called his son at 6:30pm to discuss the plan, and finally confirmed it around 8pm. (Police later searched Palme's apartment, as well as Lisbeth and Mårten's workplaces, for wire-bugging devices or traces of any such equipment, but found nothing.)

At 8:30pm the Palme's left their apartment (without any security escort) to catch the metro at station Gamla Stan. The couple left the train at Rådmansgtan, and walked to the Grand Cinema. There they were greeted by Mårten and his girlfriend around 9pm. By this time, tickets for the screening were almost sold-out. Recognising Palme, the clerk wanted him to have the best seats, and assigned he and Lisbeth the director's, middle (for a charge).

With the film finished, the couples re-joined at the cinema's exit, talking briefly before continuing on their separate ways at 11:15pm. It isn't clear what Olof thought of the film. He and Lisbeth walked south on the west side of Sveavägen, towards the northern entrance of the Hötorget metro station. At Adolf Fredrik Church they crossed Sveavägen and continued on the street's east side. The couple stopped for a moment to look at something in a shop window, before continuing past the arts supply store, Dekorima (later Kreatima, now Urban Deli), to Tunnelgatan.

At 11:21pm, someone appeared behind the couple and shot Olof Palme at point-blank range in the back of his head, then firing a second, altogether less certain shot at Lisbeth, who survived. The assassin then jogged down Tunnelgatan street, up the steps to Malmskillnadsgatan, and continued down David Bagares gata, where they were last seen. Palme was pronounced dead shortly after midnight. The motive of the killer is still unknown: they have never been captured.

Tunnelgatan was later renamed Olof Palme gate.

Exactly seven months earlier, on June 28 in 1985, Andrei Tarkovsky filmed a dream sequence for *The Sacrifice*, which sees a crowd of people fleeing an apocalyptic attack in the exact spot Palme was shot. Palme and Tarkovsky had met a couple of times, primarily as Tarkovsky appealed to statesmen to help secure the escape of his son from the USSR. A few months later, in the same year, he too would be dead. Cancer. The producer of *The Sacrifice*, Anna-Lena Wibom, had a decade before, in 1975, hosted Pier Paolo Pasolini in Stockholm, organising the screening that would be his last movie (his own! *Oedipus Rex*, see pp.112–121). Suzanne Osten's next effort, *The Guardian Angel* (1990), takes place in an unknown country in an uncertain time, and focusses on the assassination of a government minister.

I haven't seen it.

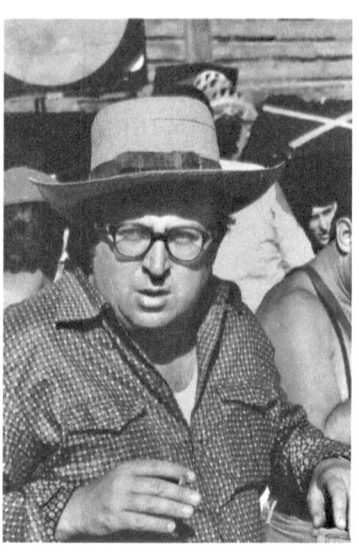

Sergio Leone (d.1989)
I Want to Live! (Robert Wise, 1958), 15m (of 120m)

¶ The joke of dying during a film with this title would not be lost on even the most Italian of Italian film directors.

In the early hours of Sunday April 30 in 1989, Sergio Leone and wife Carla were together in bed, at home in Rome on Via Nepal, watching television. About fifteen minutes into *I Want to Live!* Barbara Graham (Susan Hayward) is calling bluff and making losers as the only woman at a card table. 'I'm out!' Cries one of the players, throwing down his hand as Leone leant his head on Carla's shoulder, uttering words to the same effect: 'I'm sorry, I don't feel very well.' In the time it took for a thrown dice to settle on a number, he was gone. It wasn't a heart attack like the obituaries claimed; the organ simply stopped.

I Want to Live! is an account of the *real* life of Barbara Graham, a prostitute and petty criminal who was framed for murder (probably)—forced into confession—and ultimately sent to a California gas chamber. To ensure its accuracy in the film, director Robert Wise attended an execution at San Quentin prison. Almost the whole final third of the movie's run-time is handed over to Graham's demise, and is delivered with a clinical precision. Wise does not glare back at the individuals staring in to the glass canister containing a bound and blindfolded Graham as her hand shakes to a stop; rather, he takes aim at the system that can preside over and instruct such an action. The script by Nelson Gidding was based on Graham's own letters, and on Ed Montgomery's articles about the case, a journalist who had 'first crucified Barbara Graham in print and then attempted to undo what he had done.' Critics praised Wise's film for the very quality Leone's would at first be panned: a lack of subtlety. Though Leone spoke little English—'Watch me!' was known to be his directing method—he and Wise became friends during the Rome shoot of *Helen of Troy* in 1955. Leone was production company Cinecitta's hottest assistant director and—were it not for the slew of titles for which they already had him contracted, including William Wyler's *Ben Hur* (1959) and Fred Zinnemann's *The Nun's Story* (1959)—the Italian might have accepted Wise's roving invitation to assist on his next films. By 1989 Leone had travelled far, and after a long day working towards his next planned film epic based on the Siege of Leningrad, of all of the shit that might have been on TV, here was a film with meaning and feeling and entertainment too, by a friend. *I Want to Live!* opens to a basement jazz club. In the same building a few floors up a neon-lit Hayward's Graham withdraws happily from her client. As she

does, she glimpses a family photograph in his wallet. Police bust
in the door, attempt to arrest him. She knows her way around
the law and takes the wrap for their liaison. Saves the john.
'Gee, life's a funny thing,' he mutters as Graham is escorted out.
'Compared to what?!' She hurls back.

¶ Leone's funeral took place on Wednesday 3 May at 11:30am in the Basilica Papale San Paolo fuori le Mura, Rome.

Beforehand, his body was returned to his home's private screening room, 'facing the wide screen on the wall, in front of the five rows of green padded benches with lattice backs where friends used to be invited to watch his movies.' Visitors included Federico Fellini, Bernardo Bertolucci, Michelangelo Antonioni, Tonino Delli Colli and Ennio Morricone. Morricone was at the organ when the coffin arrived at the basilica, playing an extremely slowed version of the main theme from *Once Upon a Time in the West*. The attendant crowd of mourners stood up to applaud the arrival of Leone's body: Francis Ford Coppola, Dario Argento, Ettore Scola and all of the aforementioned. (Robert De Niro sent a weird telegram: 'To work with Leone was almost child's play. We were both perfectionists.') The crowd raised again and clapped and cheered to see the coffin out, Morricone reprising 'Once Upon a Time...'

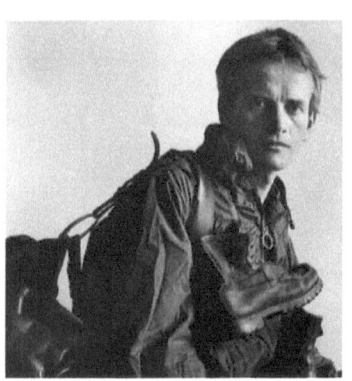

Bruce Chatwin (d. 1989)
Herdsmen of the Sun (Werner Herzog, 1989), 50m

¶ In the last week of Bruce Chatwin's life 'a face' would visit him each night.

He was unable to describe the face, but found it so terrifying he insisted every light be left on. The fear of what darkness brought grew so intense that his last day of wakefulness, though ravaged by disease, was spent outside, appealing to the sunnyside of Janus' month on the south-east coast of France.

Werner Herzog had just left Chatwin, called on by the writer for his 'healing powers.' In 1974, Herzog had taken a journey by foot from Munich to Paris, believing that this offering could stop the imminent death of his mentor, Lotte Eisner. Chatwin implored Herzog to click his heels for a second-time-lucky. The two had met six years earlier and bonded immediately over the filmmaker's position on tourism as a 'mortal sin' and walking on foot, a 'virtue.' 'Whatever went wrong and makes our civilisation something doomed is the departure from the nomadic life,' reiterates Herzog recalling his attendance to Chatwin's deathbed. He had brought the fresh rushes from his ethnographic film-study of the Wodaabe, a nomadic tribe in central Africa. Herzog describes the Wodaabe people's belief that no part of the earth belongs to any person; that it only possibly could if we earth-dwellers were 'herdsmen of the sun.'

The Wodaabe's resistance to the folly of land-ownership inoculates possession of people too. At the centre of *Herdsmen of the Sun* is the annual festival of salt and love, the Gerewol, when Wodaabe's congregate in one place for about a week. This is essentially a time outside of time, and the restrictions and responsibilities governing the nomads. Men lather themselves in garish make-up (primarily yellow, the colour of magic), and bob up and down arm-in-arm in an outward-facing circle, rolling their eyes wildly and sustaining smiles all teeth. Women are invited to select the tallest, leanest, and most beautiful man. His desirability is judged on the whiteness of his teeth, the wideness of his eyes, and the pointedness of his nose, but also on his fuckability, for which they have a specific word wholly distinct from 'beauty.' The woman makes her selection and the hours or days that follow are spent having extramarital fun in the bush. The man has the right to refuse his picker, but this right is 'seldom exercised.' In Sandrine Loncke's more recent film on the Wodaabe, it is said that this matriarchal slant on the wife-swap was conceived as a 'ritualisation of conflict,' meaning to remove the possibility of men's warring over women and sustaining peace and togetherness for the wider community. What need for violence when battle can be had through dance and song.

Herzog describes his images of this ritual as the last scene known to Chatwin as, during their meeting, he drifted off and failed to return to any cogent state. The music of the Wodaabe's is present in the film, but this particular sequence is overdubbed with Alessandro Moreschi's rendition of 'Ave Maria.' The only known recording of a castrato voice, Moreschi's strangled opera is the sand's dialogue with the jungle gramophone of Herzog's earlier film, *Fitzcarraldo* (1982; a tribute to the same kind of hero in Chatwin's work).* Why bother struggling to raise in the ranks of a well-trodden London—you probably can't really anyway, considering the entrenchment of class—when one can become a God where no Londoner has gone before? 'Ave Maria' may be self-reflexive, considering the filmmaker's presence at this ancient, sacred happening (everyone's heard of the football jersey doing the rounds on the backs of the 'uncontacted' tribespeople). Likewise, it may be random, a superficial decision for cinematic effect. But knowing its provenance inevitably gives pause to the comparison of societal conventions: one of the Wodaabe's endless moving across the landscape of their mysterious, unspeakable Goddess, and their giggles and grace; their free, equitable love-making. And the other, of the Catholic's settling to build their monument to God, revealed as he has been, be it Chatres or be it Wulstan, lobbing the balls off pre-pubic boys to keep their voices girly enough for the celestial choirs of the Church ('let women keep silent in the churches,' went the crazed Pauline dictum).

In an Africa dogged by a sedentary Islam (Chatwin's funeral was overwhelmed by the announcement only hours earlier of the fatwa against his friend, Salman Rushdie), the Wodaabe are scorned as 'Herdsmen in tatters,' criticised for their continued observance of a roving, pre-literate way of life. They are said to be broadly Islamic in their beliefs, but this may be a matter of self-preservation as their conventions obviously bely it. As Kafka suggested, literacy is a mixed blessing (the writer's day-job, as administrator, would surely agree with the nomads that book-keeping is the end of all beauty). The Wodaabe remember. When Herzog asks where they are going at the end of his film, and the end of the festival of salt and love, they respond that

---

* See *Cobra Verde*, Herzog's 1987 film based on Chatwin's 1980 novel, *The Viceroy of Ouidah*.

they do not know (deceiving, perhaps, as they practice trans-humance, but isn't the landscape a different place with each crossing?), only that they'll follow the cattle.

The particular type of cow the Wodaabe keep, the long-horned Zebu, is the subject of some of the oldest known figurative paintings by humans (the cow's mantle was recently rocked by a pig scrawled in a cave in Indonesia). By extension, these cows make for some of the earliest cinema-stars, moved as it is believed they were by the artist's invocation of fire. Chatwin was present quite by accident at the discovery of man's earliest known experimentation with fire. Though it was speculated at the time in 1984, he would never know this for sure. Confirmation by radiocarbon dating narrowly failed to reach him before he passed over. His biographer, Nicholas Shakespeare, quotes a letter Chatwin sent to a friend in the days that followed the discovery:

When visiting the excavation at Swartkrans with Bob Brain, one of the questions uppermost in my mind was man's use of fire: the myth of Prometheus is absolutely crucial, to my mind, in understanding the condition of the First Man—since it is with fire that Man could adequately protect himself at night from the predators.

Brain describes fire as a 'social facilitator,' explaining that daylight hours were extended by it and encouraged communal reflection on the day's events: it made stories happen; stories to remember, stories to protect.

To stray from the light was probably to die.

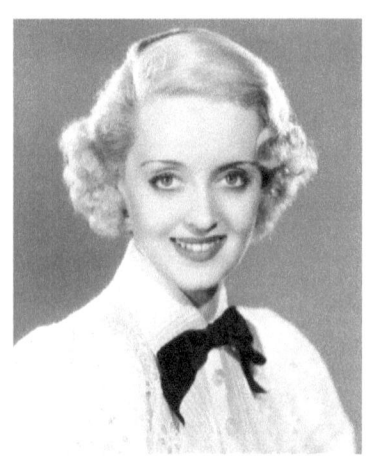

Bette Davis (d.1989)
Waterloo Bridge (James Whale, 1931), 81m

All it takes is one bad day to reduce the sanest man alive to lunacy.
 —Joker, *The Killing Joke*

¶ Funny man to The End, James Whale drowned himself.

It isn't known what he last saw, nor can it be said with certainty that Bette Davis watched his *Waterloo Bridge*, but at the San Sebastián film festival that year she was deliberate and reflective. She dazzled and defied; she watched the water. She knew she was on her way out. Even a glimpse of 1931's *Waterloo Bridge* might have provided antidote to the emergent cinema of 1989, a reservoir (or cesspit, as Davis might have had it) to the sea of the medium fifty years prior—of water both, but utterly distinct.

The prevailing image of Davis in her final days is that of a chain-smoking time-traveller; an exhalation locked up in the cavernous luxury of room 451 at San Sebastián's premier port hotel, the Maria Cristina. The Maria Cristina which, since hosting в's near-last sleep, does booming business with a re-named 'Bette Davis Suite' at the balcony of which a black flag flaps, and where one can stay for €1565 per night, with a surcharge of €24 for the privilege of breakfast. Outside, white voiles are bellowed by the sea wind, as в attempts to block out the blank stare of Michael Keaton's Cerne Abbas-sized cardboard Batman, an ad tethered to the building facing hers. 'A costume, not an actor,' в complained; 'aggressive.' She might have moved rooms, but by now her assistant, Kathryn, had mapped out the hotel as panopticon, with 451 as its watchtower. Using polaroid photographs, к produced police procedural-style diagrams for в, revealing every corner and crevice; the way down; the number of stairs; entries, exits. Frail as she was, this undertaking was ostensibly to manage her appearances—but I posit another motivation. Independence; escape; a *slipping out*...

Officially Davis left her room just twice: once for a press conference, and once to accept the Donostia Award.

Though she had been invited under the auspices of Whale's retrospective (because everyone else who had worked with him was dead)—and by all accounts the festival never expected she'd accept their invitation—the focus shifted rapidly (and wholly) to her.

A special lifetime achievement award, the Donostia had been dreamt up three years prior in 1986. The festival had been on the brink of collapse, and its general secretary was hot for Gregory Peck—so sod it—a breathless invitation was made: *but why should I come?* Asked Peck. *Uh... Donostia!?* Put on the spot, the general secretary blurted the accolade into creation, using the Basque name for the port city. Thereafter, the award stuck, and Davis was enticed by the victory of being the first woman to receive it.

Her conditions for attendance were relatively modest:

1 Travel with stopovers in New York, Paris and Biarritz;
2 No one could tell her when she had to leave the festival;
3 A television set in her room;
4 $100 per day pocket money;
5 An English-speaking driver. (Whom would carry some seventeen pieces of luggage at lowest estimation, fifty at most.)

Her arrival in San Sebastián, and residency for the festival's duration, was a carnival and a storm (it is notable that rain was her good luck charm; the storm a part of her origin myth: Lowell, Massachusetts, 1908: 'I happened between a clap of thunder and a streak of lightning. It almost hit the house and destroyed a tree out front. As a child, I fancied that the Finger of God was directing the attention of the world to me. Further and divine proof—from the stump of that tree—that one should never point.'), marked by the kind of fanfare and adulation she'd once known and still reasonably expected, but often failed to garner, abandoned as she had been by Hollywood's insolent inheritors to senile, exploitative TV roles. By the time she was picked up by Lindsay Anderson for *The Whales of August* in 1987, it was almost (*almost*) too late...

At 5 foot 2, she rarely sat; carrying strike-anywhere matches everywhere she went, and leaving a plume of smoke behind her. She was highly superstitious and needed a 'three-minute egg' to get her up in the morning. She was sustained by constant, casual bitchiness; criticising everything with a kind of life-affirming (and conquering) joy. Old Hollywood had called her 'the little brown wren,' to her eternal grump. The Spaniards called her 'La Lupe.' She-wolf. This she liked.

As per her second condition of festival attendance: she did stay on after its end, and neither press nor public had a clue. In the days following The End she went to dinner with the festival staff and city officials, whispering to the mayor: 'how incredible San Sebastián looks viewed from Mount Igueldo.' Cynics write this off to her third condition: a television set in the hotel room. But when she eventually left the Maria Cristina —via the luggage door—*nobody* knew about it. Nobody. And so why shouldn't she have visited Igueldo, disguised by the contents of one of her seventeen (or fifty) pieces of luggage? Why shouldn't she have visited the cinema too? *Waterloo Bridge* had been her moment of make or break. It offered, appropriately enough, a vantage point not unlike Igueldo, from which to look back on the great unknowable city of life, and the glimmer of ocean beyond.

Davis' part in *Waterloo Bridge* is minimal, as the feel-good sister of lead Mae Clarke's love-interest. It is a film about the simplicity of what makes life sacred: the fish & chips shared by strangers who are meant to be together, and won't be. In the face of war, and in any case, judgement and elitism are a choice, illusions to overcome. For its empathetic portrayal of a woman working the streets—and for the deepest-ever-love understanding of her, Clarke's Myra's fiancé, Douglass Montgomery's Roy, and his well-to-do family—it was banned internationally through the Hay's Code of 1934, though many local authorities banned it before it even reached their screens in 1931. Universal Pictures summarily dumped Davis for her efforts on the bridge, the last of three movies playing three sisters she'd make for the studio. Were it not for the cavalry George Arliss *finally* casting her as a love interest in a Warner Brothers picture, *The Silent Voice*, she was by her own admission prepared to abandon the dream of cinema forever. This film marked in earnest the onset of her ascent—credit in no small part to her many collaborations with Michael Curtiz, of whom she said little but likened to the 'Marquis de Sade.' George Cukor, who had given Davis her first ever acting job (and according to her, her first ever firing too) she likened to 'Judas.' Clark Gable? 'I can't stand a man who has fake store teeth and doesn't keep his uncircumcised cock clean under the foreskin ... I hear he shoots too soon and messes himself all the time. Great Lover? Great Fake!' And on the death of her arch rival, Joan Crawford, newspapers reported her comment thus: 'You should never say bad things about the dead, only good... Joan Crawford is dead? Good.'

When *Waterloo Bridge* was remade in 1940, a shift in the protagonist's class was inferred; Mae Clarke's chorus girl became Vivien Leigh's ballerina, and the production's judgement for this woman turning to sex work? Suicide. In Whale's version, loyal to Robert E. Sherwood's stage original, and based on his own experiences in World War I, she is killed in a German air raid.[*]

---

[*] Davis also acted in Sherwood's *The Petrified Forest* (1936); see John Dillinger, pp. 50–62.

Staring out over the Bay of Biscay, Davis finished her expanded autobiography, titled *The Lonely Life*. She ends it with a riff on her final lines in *Now, Voyager* (1942), her famed forbidden love story: *why ask for the moon, when we have the stars?*

Three days later, up she went.

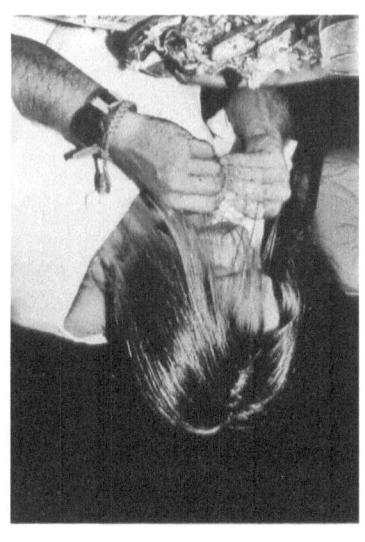

A search for an unlicensed image of Cobain drums up a litany of options, all alternative talismans for his persona, including this anonymous portrait simply captioned 'MAN CHOWS DOWN ON CRABS.' This stand-in, this automated false-likeness, serves as a symbolic pareidolia; we look to the cloud, see a near-Kurt —an 'ur' Kurt—which is no Kurt at all. As such, 'MAN' appears in this volume as testimony to the contradiction of our times. Ours is an age defined by the apparent availability of culture, and yet haunted by its costs, its theories of ownership, its exclusivity, and the kind of 'lock and key' that separates research matter from a reader.

Kurt Cobain (d.1994)
The Piano (Jane Campion, 1993), 121m

¶ 'I guess I secretly want to be a doctor,' Cobain offers in one of his final recorded interviews, when asked about the recurrence of baby vomit and bodily function in his lyrics. 'That or in a cremation factory.' The juvenility makes his suicide all the more depressing. Though self-inflicted, Cobain came to realise it was preposterous to be a 'rock star' (whereas former bandmate Dave Grohl evidently still does not know). He liked the rockumentary, *This is Spinal Tap*, and the masterpiece of coprophagia, John Waters' *Pink Flamingos*. He loved *Over the Edge*, Jonathan Kaplan's Bacchanalian revenge epic against parents and police. His favourite film of all time was Wim Wenders' *Paris, Texas*, which might be said to share the unlikely privilege of being both writer Sam Shepard's and actor Harry Dean Stanton's major career dud.

Cobain also hinted at going into movies as an alternative career path, and was afforded his own 'loose' portrait by Gus Van Sant in *Last Days*. Supposedly inspired by the films of Béla Tarr, and in turn inspiring the Robert Pattinson bat-vehicle (see Bette Davis, pp.218–224) of 2022, *Last Days* grew out of the impossibility of Sant's original wish to create a faithful biopic of the musician in his last days. Widow Courtney Love wouldn't have it, despite issuing some questionable licenses for Kurt's likeness elsewhere (an Action-Man ['not suitable for children under 3 years'] 'Smells Like Teen Spirit' themed figurine, for example; the 'smelly song' being one of a handful of Nirvana's with something like substance, critics visit 'More Than a Feeling' by Boston, and 'Eighties' by Killing Joke).

Cobain and Sant shared a common collaborator in William S. Burroughs, the filmmaker famously recording in the early 1980s Bill's 'Thanksgiving Prayer.' 'Thanks for the wild turkey and the passenger pigeons, destined to be shit out through wholesome American guts.' It is dedicated to John Dillinger 'in the hope he is still alive' (see Dillinger, pp.50–62). Both would have been shocked, or would have feigned shock, at the writer's appearance in a commercial for sportswear brand Nike, which first aired in 1994, shortly before Cobain's death (see Heaven's Gate, pp.240–251, the Nike-footed group who would die in the same year as Burroughs, 1997, the year which they, as prophesied by William Blake, believed to be *the last*).

'Punk,' as honoured and pursued by early Nirvana and their Seattle cohorts, was dedicated to anti-capitalism. To 'sell-out' was sacrilege, the worst thing you could possibly do. And this wasn't limited to punk: it was what it meant to be young and principled. In the late noughties it was still unthinkable to wear branded clothing, especially trainers. That the tables have turned so completely, with the present ambition being to sell-out; to be the individual to represent the sweatshop, proves what the real, religious punks knew: capitalism is the holocaust of all things sacred.

'The purpose of technology is not to confuse the brain, but to serve the body. To make life easier—to make anything possible,' smirks Bill Burroughs on Nike's dollar, in his apparent catch-all endorsement of Silicon Death Valley. This might feel naive considering what's come to pass (see Steve Jobs, pp. 258–263), but Bill is just the messenger, and Bill was *a junkie*. Only every junkie knows there's nothing better and nothing other than junk. It *is* the bounce in your trainer; the higher jump; the ball in the hoop; the swoosh *eternal*; the original, all-seeing technology. The religion. The UFO. Warm light. Fire hum. Sea lap. Distant applause. The master and the servant. Alpha, Omega. Eden. Every loser wins! Kurt knew it too but, between injections, he was nifty and he grifted and he pushed hard at the sober dystopia—spending hours on the phone to MTV, for example, demanding they play his 'goddamned smelly song.' Rarely is it delirious artistry that delivers the result, but the razor-sharp determination of business and PR. The big guys all have it: Warhol, Dylan. Kanye. And without pusher-man Allen Ginsberg, the beats simply wouldn't have been a *thing*. How else to explain Nirvana's international pop stardom, while supposedly embodying the anti-establishment outsider? And without songs?! And *look* at them?! A deal with the you-know-who? As Mark Fisher reflected, Kurt knew better than anyone that nothing sells on MTV like a protest against MTV. The revolution then was sold as and with the record; the project now is so complete it's sold before the recording even happens, never mind production and distribution of it. 'Get to three million dollars and then become a junkie, that was his plan,' says One-Love Courtney. Even in his previous life as a derelict, the clever boy in need of shelter would return to the waiting room of the hospital in which he was born, because who disturbs the sleeper waiting on a sick loved one? Nirvana squeezed most opportunities, appreciating the stark reality of a life without some measure of success, but stopped short of licensing songs for ads or movies. That this masque of integrity seems to have been so determinedly defiled by the in-testate heirs of Kurt may be ruthless greed, compounded by a failure to understand what he claimed to stand for. It could also just be payback for him leaving.

Kurt met Bill in 1993, following their mail-based correspondence and collaboration on *The "Priest" They Called Him*, a scruffy Christmas record that was meant to set precedent for an album of readings by the writer, with underscore shred by Kurt. What the band really wanted was an appearance in their music video for 'Heart Shaped Box' (directed by Anton Corbijn; see Ian Curtis, pp.162–172) by ever-emaciated Bill, wearing nothing but a loin-cloth and a Santa hat at the foot of his death-cross. In any case, the musician obviously relished the collaboration that did happen, and credited it on a par with his wife and newborn daughter as reason to live. Bill complained that Kurt frowned 'for no good reason,' and on news of his suicide, remarked: 'The thing I remember about him is the deathly grey complexion of his cheeks. It wasn't an act of will for Kurt to kill himself. As far as I was concerned, he was dead already.' And this on the authority of the original ghost.

There is no empirical evidence of Kurt's last days. He was effectively on the run, alone, and left no account. On April 1 he 'escaped' from rehab in Los Angeles (escaped inasmuch as he scaled a fence, though there was no kind of security or even surveillance cameras at the venue: he could have left by the front door without hassle—April fool's gag?), and travelled to Seattle (where it rains an average of 155 days per year; in Manchester, England, by contrast rains 205 days per year, see Ian Curtis, pp.162–172), also to escape Courtney. On April 3 he was seen at the Cactus restaurant in Madison Park eating with some friends. They began with dessert: Kurt had Bananas Dulce (which is still on the menu—banana pudding sautéed in brown sugar and rum), according to Brett Chatalas, co-owner of the restaurant, from whom they asked for the local movie listings. The diners agreed on Jane Campion's *The Piano*, and Kurt went to pay. His credit card bounced (Courtney had cancelled it to try to prevent him from scoring heroin), so he wrote a cheque. He was last seen later that night at Linda's Tavern (707 E Pine St, WA 98122).

At some point over the next day Kurt pens a letter to 'Boddah,' the imaginary friend of his childhood. He describes the ghoul as the only appropriate addressee, given the infantilism of his rambling tantrum; the cutting off of his head to spite his nose. Ultimately, this is a man who got exactly what he wanted, but everything everything was meant to solve, didn't. It's the

old story. He acknowledges this; his self-indulgence. He had in
a way forewarned the outcome, earlier boasting to interviewers
that for him a successful career in music was no more likely
than his gunning down of everyone at his high school, an activity he'd relish—though he said he'd probably pussy out and
shoot himself first. It wasn't until 1999 that the Columbine High
School massacre would mark the beginning of the school-shoot-
ing 'trend' in American kultur. Gus Van Sant would base his 2003
film *Elephant* on the Columbine massacre (in a so-called 'Death
trilogy' of works that includes *Last Days*), which Roger Ebert
(who last saw Terrence Mallick's *To the Wonder*) celebrated for
its refusal to glamourise killing in the way cinema often does,
writing 'I doubt that *Elephant* will ever inspire anyone to copy
what they see on the screen.' Alas, the loser-killer responsible
for the Red Lake High School shootings of 2005 is known to have
obsessed over his DVD-copy of *Elephant* in the weeks before he
took the lives of his grandfather and friend, and seven fellow
students.* Kurt writes about his unwavering dedication to his
wife and child, but offsets this with a quote from the song 'My
My Hey Hey' by Neil Young, writing 'It's better to burn out than
to fade away.' This so horrifies Young that he thereafter replaces
this line in live renditions of the song. No reference in the
letter is made to *The Piano*.

Bloated by dessert and eager to dive into the bags of junk
he'd just bought, Kurt might not have given *The Piano* his all,
but movies find a way in regardless—especially when seen at the
cinema. 'I don't think myself silent, because of my piano,' whispers the internal monologue of Ada (played by Holly Hunter),
our mute, widowed pianist at the sea-cold heart of Campion's
film. On the verge of sleep, Ada's daughter, Flora, a little girl of
six or seven years, pleads with her mother to sign the story once
again: of the jungle storm through which mummy and daddy
sang their song, and 'when their voices rose for the final bar of
the duet,' dad was struck by lightning and killed. Mummy hadn't
spoken since. 'Killed himself,' Kurt might have shivered, visual-
ising through his rum and brown sugar stupor a flicker of future,
with Courtney forced to sign an equivalent lightning bolt riddle
to Francis Bean. The piano that is Ada's tonic, her only means
of expression and lift to experience, is removed from her by the
man to whom she's blind-date married (Sam Neill). All the way

---

* In the movie, from one of the classrooms sifts the unintelligible drawl
of Bill Burroughs.

from Scotland to New Zealand the hunk of ivory and mahogany travels, only to be abandoned on the beach by the impotent, colonialist Sam, who insists she'll find her expression through him instead. He is, after all, her access to sustenance and security, in a world designed to be impossible for independent women. So, play that tune, girl... sing your supper!

Kurt's interest in playing had waned at this time, if not altogether sailed. A failed janitor, he felt that he too had necessarily traded in something sacred for something safe. The world demanded it. His response to the towering success of his album *Nevermind* was to hide in a closet with his buckets and broom for six months, injecting heroin and painting goblins. But just as Ada had no Scotland to return to, Kurt in the closet could only ever be a temporary analeptic. The world demanded him. An adoring public queued for his howl; commercial interests indentured it.

Baines (played by Harvey Keitel) is a whaler who inexplicably lives alone among the indigenous Māori. He hears Ada playing her piano on the beach one day. He loves it. He must have it. And by having *it*, by jove he'll be having her. Baines convinces Sam to swap the instrument for some stolen land, warning that he'll also be needing lessons. Under lock and key, he announces to Ada that he'll be learning 'by watching,' hyperventilating into her never-washed shawl and unbuttoning his chaps. Here's the pitch: she can reclaim her property but only a key at a time, traded out for tantalising violation after violation, one for the sniff of an armpit; one for the fingering of a mothhole in her tights. Two keys for a dry hump. Three or four or five or six for the handling of her breast. And so on. In time, they'll make some kind of love and she'll fall for him heels over head. In summary: you will learn to love your rapist. *The Piano*, so the true cliché goes, 'is a film that would never be made today,' with public and commercial interests alike unable to cope with the ambiguities of Campion's vision: too fatigued, coddled and prescription drug-addled to look beyond the surface and think. But Kurt evidently thought, and couldn't not have drawn a parallel between Ada's trap and his own. Baines' demands of Ada are the public and commercial demands of Kurt: to play for their pleasure, without any consideration for him. The alternative is not to play at all, and still to be possessed.

Long story short: the affair is revealed and Sam chops a finger from Ada in revenge. This weirdly 'frees' Ada and Flora

from Sam, who join Baines on his long-planned longboat-exit
to a better place. At a comfortable distance from the land,
middle fingers held unanimously aloft at lonesome Sam, Ada
pleads with Baines and the chanting rowers to chuck the piano
overboard. She has secretly twisted the rope securing the piano
around her ankle, and so as it plunges into the water, so does
she. Down, down she's pulled. Her face is emotionless, if
serene. Silence. The End.

Except that isn't The End. Bubbles! Splashes! Emotive
Michael Nyman music! (*The Piano*'s theme would later be licensed to Lloyds bank for one of their black horse commercials.)
Ada emerges into her unconvincing epilogue: sunshine and daf-
fodils and a whitewashed country house to correct the dreadful
melancholy of the island's midnight blue. George has made her
a metal finger with which she's able to play again. She teaches
music. She rhymes too, in the vain of the riddle told to Flora
about how and where her father went, of the silent deep-water
resting place of the piano, to which she 'dreams' herself still
tethered. The difference between Kurt and Ada is that her passion never really went away. The disaster is that neither epilogue
nor dreams are found in death or even in cinema, but in life.
The coda is 'unconvincing' precisely because it conjures all
of the inevitable unbelievability of living: chance, redemption,
reinvention. Cinema is the trap of the past, the holy domain
of death. Life is what we've got. Kurt could have had his metal
finger—however fucked up its beloved benefactor—and Kurt
could have taught his own high-school harem—however fucked
up any and all work—the young idealists to strum and scream,
The sun we see is the same as that which Heraclitus saw... 'A luta
continua!' And so it is and so it does.

Gary Smith is the unfortunate electrician appointed by
Cobain to install a new security system at his house in Denny
Blaine, an affluent suburb of Seattle (the Starbucks CEO was
Kurt's next-door neighbour). On arrival at the property on the
morning of April 8, he knocks at the front door of the house;
nobody answers. No surprise, rocker. And no problem: he
locates the wiring he needs externally, and follows it from the
house to the garage. Atop the garage is the room the Cobain's
call 'the greenhouse.' In the greenhouse there's a single piece
of furniture: a stool, its seat engraved with the words 'now
you have many legs to stand on.' There is drug paraphernalia
scattered about, and a few American Spirit cigarette butts on

the floor. There's a figure too, also on the floor, with a shotgun laid across their chest. At first, he thinks it's a mannequin.

Boddah's Dream #1 (*The Screenwriter's Lament*)

'Message from the North to the South. The man is in shape.
He's alive and well living at the edge of nowhere...' Boddah
watches over the land of make-believe (1994), where publications
and TV commissioners alike would fly the filmmaker (Chris
Petit) from the Thames to the Hudson for the sake of profiling
the last icon of a lost Hollywood (Rudy Wurlitzer). The screenwriter's lament. 'I peeked into Sam's room [Peckinpah's] and
he was standing in front of a full-length mirror, looking at himself completely naked—he had a bottle of tequila in one hand
a revolver in the other, and he was shooting at the mirror... at
this image of himself. And he turned around and said, "Hi boys,
how you doing?" And I said, "Sam, uh, this is Bob Dylan." And
he said, "Yeah, I heard of you: I heard you're coming down here
to take over my film." Dylan said "No."' On he goes, 'Buddhists
say you should avoid at all costs hope and fear.' And on. Boddah
paraphrases: Hollywood doesn't allow writers to make their own
mistakes. Everything is passed on to another. The artist must
be able to make their own mistakes. That's how you learn, become, develop muscle. And then it's over. With the night drawing in, Petit and Wurlitzer decide to take a drive: half an hour
to the cinema, where they'll watch *The Piano*. Queuing in line
to pay for their tickets they look at each other. 'Nah,' they agree,
turn around and drive home.

Boddah's Dream #2 (*Leaving Las Vegas*)

Five days after Kurt suicided, so did John O'Brien. For $2000, he'd sold the rights to his long out-of-print and only novel (a 189-page suicide note, effectively), *Leaving Las Vegas*, which a first-time producer had happened upon in a secondhand bookstore. In the book and the film, the protagonist travels from LA to Vegas to drink himself to death. With the money from the advance, a skeptical and regretful and principled anti-capitalist, O'Brien did more or less that, long before the film was made and he'd have an opportunity to see it. But he saw it, as the producer recalled: 'he was afraid that we'd put on a happy ending.'

Boddah's Dream #3 (*The Pub* & *The Apartment*)

Much later. Boddah dreams of England. A woman in a pub
bends around a pillar to catch the eye of a man. The man offers
her a drink. Many drinks are taken. The conversation is fine at
first. The man zones out at Ministry of Sound. She's a singer
apparently, and she's featured on a compilation. She may be
a reincarnation of Amy Winehouse, she suggests. At a certain
point in the conversation, she throws her hand out to one side,
and between the palm and the ground a frost of the air takes
hold, the abstract shape and size of a child. The conversation
changes; she has his attention again. 'You saw him, didn't you?
He was the first thing I saw when you came in here. He goes
with you wherever you go. He first came in through your window,
which opened from the top and was often left open several inches in the nighttime. That's when he first came in.' Boddah. With
this, things pick up. He continues to the home of the woman.
It's a large flat-block, just behind where they've been drinking.
First floor. The hallway is long, and down each side, stacked
from floor to ceiling, are magazines, all spines against the wall.
Her room is at the end of the hallway. In it there is nothing but
an enormous poster of Amy Winehouse above her bed. She
takes his hand and guides it to her chest, over scar tissue where
breasts once were. 'You don't mind, do you?' He takes her in his
arms and holds her hard. Cut. The door to the room is thrown
open. Her mother, presumably. 'What are *you* doing here?!'
She points at him, drawing closer, and screams again: 'What
are you doing here?!' He rushes past her, back down the hall
of magazines, past a darkened room in which he thinks he sees
an empty cradle. Boddah follows.

Boddah's Dream #4 (*The Last Words*)*

What are you going to do now? *Oh, I don't know. Try again, maybe
at something else.* May I try with you? We have you surrounded,
Joe Grant. Do not move. Put your hands in the air. We have you
surrounded, Joe Grant. Do not move. Put your hands in the air.
We have you surrounded, Joe Grant. Happy the man and happy
he alone, he who can call today his own, he who secure within
can say, tomorrow do thy worst for I have lived today. May the
light that I couldn't see anymore, and which once was mine,
illuminate me now for the last time. I have arrived. God told me
to. I'm not going without you, Mac. I wouldn't leave you here
this way. You're coming with me. Let's go. You're a long way
from home. We both are, commander. Until we meet again. Yes.
Until we meet again. Utterly baffled and beaten, what was the
lonely and broken-hearted man to do? He took the annuity and
returned to Ireland with his mother to complete his recovery.
Sometime later he travelled to the continent. His life there, we
have not the means to follow accurately. But he appears to have
resumed his former profession of a gambler, without his former
success. He never saw Lady Lyndon again. *Bond, what do you
think you're doing?* Keeping the British end up, Sir. Your words.
Do you remember? Well, I do. Oh, no. We're gonna take good
care of you. We're gonna nurse you back to health. And you're
strong, Cady. You're gonna live a long life, in a cage! That's
where you belong and that's where you're going. And this time,
for life! Bang your head against the walls. Count the years, the
months, the hours, until the day you rot. Well, I'm gonna miss
this old town. *It's gonna miss you. I'm not sure what my old dad
said about you Yanks.* You mean that part about being overpaid?
No, being over here. Jenny, it's been great. *It has.* So long. I'll tell
you what you can do for me, you can give me a light. It's too late.
Not for me! Without silence you can't experience music. There
isn't much I can say with words, they always fail me when most
needed. But please know that with all my heart I appreciate
everything you've done for me. Sincerely, Barbara. We wanted
to know where they were going, but nobody would tell us. We
follow the cattle, they said. We simply follow the cattle. *Goodbye,
goodbye darling. I'll think of you always. Every minute. Cheerio,
darling!* (*laughter*) Down there everything is so silent that it lulls

---

* The last lines from each of the Last Movies included in this book,
in order of their appearance.

me to sleep. It is a weird lullaby, and so it is. It is mine. 'There is a silence, where hath been no sound. There is a silence where no sound may be, in the cold grey, under the deep, deep sea.' Tea's ready. Want a biscuit? Who'd have thought it, eh. Look at you two sitting there like a couple of garden gnomes. Oh, this is the life, ain't it? *Forever.* Forever? *Forever.* Let's not use that word. You know? It frightens me. But I do love you... and you know... there is something that we need to do as soon as possible. *What's that?* Fuck. A man tells his stories so many times that he becomes his stories. They live on after him. And in that way, he becomes immortal. People say that it can't work, black and white. Well, here we make it work every day. We have our problems of course, but before we reach for hate we remember always the Titans. When you were a little girl, I imagined there was nothing that could ever come between us. You were everything to me. You were everything to me. When you were a little girl, I dreamt of a kingdom I would build for you. Where all you would see and all you would know would be yours. Then you were taken to a place so far away, so dark, so remote, so empty, I fear what you've become. I fear what was made of you. What was removed from you. What is left of you. How could there be anything left of you? I resolved to remember you as only a fantasy. A sorrow. A ghost. A ghost. A ghost that I secretly prayed would haunt me once more in this life. Aware I could not possibly survive the experience.

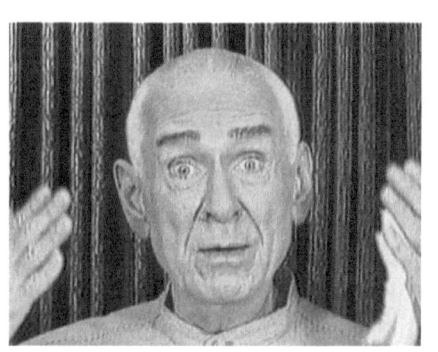

Heaven's Gate
(39 crew-members of the 'Angelish-Alien' sect, d. 1997)
Secrets & Lies (Mike Leigh, 1996), 142m

¶ Houston, 1970: Marshall Applewhite, the son of a preacher, is performing the role of a reverend and rapist, as bass baritone in the opera, *Susannah*. Meltdown! Something causes him to have a psychotic episode so severe he is hospitalised. Something may be the explosive double whammy of a musical career in the doldrums, and a marriage crushed by allegations of a homosexual affair. But *something* could also be the psychic and emotional contractions of *destiny*, for it is there and then he is believed to have first met the benevolent nurse, Bonnie Nettles. Bonnie, a midwife, might have delivered Marshall's second (or second millionth) birth: she offers to read his horoscope, and in doing so confirms that they've known each other FOREVER and 'share a purpose.' Nettles had been expecting Applewhite, alerted to his coming by a long-dead Franciscan monk (see Pier Paolo Pasolini, pp.112–121), whom she would sometimes consult for guidance in dreams. Without any means or destination, Bonnie and Marshall left all they knew and hit the road together (platonically), in search of that as yet unknown shared purpose. A year later, in 1971 (see Steve Jobs, pp.258–263), camping out by a lake in Oregon they witness the passing of a comet. And suddenly they get it.

Bonnie becomes 'Ti' and Marshall 'Do,' names adopted from *The Sound of Music*, Ti's favourite film, which their crew (yet to be assembled) would watch often (Ti and Do were also known as Bo and Peep [once they had a crew, 'sheep'], and Guinea and Pig [when the sheep fell out of line], and often simply 'He' and 'She', but for clarity we'll stick with *The Sound of Music*). Ti and Do would follow a simple seminary lifestyle of abstinence, awareness and contemplation, which sought to 'repair' their humanness. How cinema and junk food escaped these strictures is unclear, but we'll presume they thought of projection and television alike as divine light; and certainly, along with pizza, God's gift.

Heaven's Gate were not a literary bunch, and while Do might have snuck Robert Heinlein's *The Moon is a Harsh Mistress* into his horsehair four-poster, watching triumphed over reading as the consummate collective activity that it is.* *Something* has to happen in the evenings, and Goddess knows without pyres and poppers and coit and liquor it's a movie. Evenings were seen out with the stimulant *Star Trek*, and mornings were ushered in with the stimulant stargazing. One of the long-term 'crew' members shared a special relationship with both: Thomas Nichols believed he was an angelic alien fated to return to the stars from whence he came, and he was also the real-life brother of Nichelle Nichols, who played Lieutenant Nyota Uhura in the original series of *Star Trek*. For the Gate's publicity campaigns this was a real boon, with the mission of the show's characters analogous to their own (and afrofuturism already a hot ticket). Uhura's prominence in *Star Trek*, as a person of colour in a leading role, was so unusual for its time of sky-high racial tensions and capital's fear of colour that she was actively pursued by Martin Luther King—another big fan of the show—who persuaded her to extend her contract at the point she had wished to leave (her heart, like Do's, was really with the stage).

Ti and Do in their denomination as 'The Two' identified as the witnesses referenced in the Book of Revelation. As foretold by John of Patmos, it was their 'Demonstration' of ascending into a cloud, following trial and persecution by the people, that would begin the Day of Judgement; the End of the World. 'The Two' (with a little help from then-bestseller, *Chariots of the Gods?* —proponent of the 'ancient astronaut' theory—attributing all religions of the human world to alien visitations) realised that the cloud of Revelation was in fact a spaceship; so too had been the 'chariots' carrying 'angels,' with our ancestors lacking the sufficient language to describe them for what they truly were. Ti and Do set about 'repairing' themselves for 'the next level,' borrowing theories and practices from science fiction as much as Christianity and the New Age. Reparation was about a physical transformation to board a physical craft, to be jetted off for eternal life in a physical utopia. Do likened it to the metamorphosis of the caterpillar becoming the butterfly, and referenced Jesus' resurrection as a practical blueprint. Members joined on the basis of circulars and presentations alluding to these beliefs, but initially expressed metaphorically.

Heaven's Gate forbade certain activities: sex, for example. Desire too (and, hm, 'private thoughts' once Do alone took

---

* He'd later introduce the crew to something like the 'line marriage' concept pioneered in Heinlein's fiction and adopted by certain anarchist circles, corrupted by Do after Jesus to wed all 38 ascendant Gate-Crashers to be (*definition*: essentially a consensual group marriage, beginning with husband and wife: but the husband marries another wife and the wife another husband, and so it continues through the generations—financial and social burdens shared, children cared for by the whole group. The advantage is stability, to say nothing of excitement. A death won't tear apart a family or orphan children; since new partners marry into the line marriage, there are always partners in their prime).

control of the craft). One of the longest-standing members of twenty-years upwards ended up leaving the crew of his own volition, because he simply could not stop masturbating. But even those who abandoned the craft deny the use of coercion, control and manipulation by Ti and Do (some to this day). There was an open-door policy and nobody was blacklisted. You could leave anytime and return anytime. Each was their own agent, following an individual path to the ascendant cloud, supported (if policed) by the crew. No manual, no instructions. Former members have even cited the lack of direction in the beginning as a source of fatigue and frustration. This extended to what was watched. After a long and effectively nomadic period, they settled in a rented San Diego mansion (on Colina Norte in the wealthy suburb of Rancho; the building was later demolished and the street's name changed to Paseo Victoria to dissuade pilgrimage). Here there were six televisions, and viewing rules only obviously applied to what could be seen on 'the big set,' a whopping 72-inch television at the beating heart of 'the craft.' Bad faith judgement has it that Do was sole programmer, censoring what the group could and couldn't see, but come: in a good-natured environment with social time spent collectively in front of the TV, you want to make sure everyone is entertained. There's nothing like bad programming to destroy faith in the leadership.

The surviving screening schedules for 'the big set' don't suggest any obvious censorship model: *Chain Reaction* by Andrew Davis (18% Rotten Tomatoes); *The Frighteners* by Peter Jackson (67%); *Eddie* by Steve Rash (17%) were all chosen for group screenings. Rejects included *GoldenEye* by Martin Campbell (80%); *The Island of Dr. Moreau* by Richard Stanley (after H.G. Wells—23%), and *Multiplicity* by Harold Ramis (45%), but it isn't clear that these films are forbidden. On the approved list for 'the big set' was also the CBS general affairs dispatch, *60 Minutes*, and a documentary about the US space program (complete with sarcastic comment pencilled into the schedule, 'should be worth some laughs!'). The group also subscribed to the *San Diego Union-Tribune* newspaper. Nearing the end, though they may have formally renounced the outside world, they keenly and freely kept up with its goings-on.

The years that led to 1997 were tough. As if the 70s following the 60s wasn't bad enough, the 80s followed the 70s. The Gate launched an enormous recruitment campaign costing tens of thousands of dollars, attempting to bring in much-needed 'young blood.' But the world had changed. Just like the last living evidence of the French Revolution in France today is the systematic ill-treatment of the consumer by the worker, in America and Britain, companies like Apple and stores like Whole Foods have contaminated the roots of the Revolution's burnt-out tree, that once fruit-bearing shelter facilitating the utopian thinking of The Gate and their like.* Why drop out when you can swipe right? The Gate were early adopters of the Internet, defenders of 'tuning in,' eagerly experimenting with God's new toys. The development and design of web pages for clients primarily in the entertainment business became a source of income. They even started a company to this end: 'Higher Source.'

Although only in its infancy, the pirate utopia promised by the World Wide Web had already failed. Regulations ever intensified, and the model of the standard 'user' was established with a uniform of aggression, critique and abuse denied the person behind the user expression of in 'real life.' And masturbation, of course. Plenty of that. But for The Gate, ever the optimists, this communications interface seemed to offer an unprecedented platform for their invitation to salvation. They would alert the users to the End as nigh, offering the proverbial olive branch. The response? A kind of proto-cyberbullying: ridicule and persecution on a whole new level. Do and co quickly realised this was Revelation's 'Demonstration,' and had been all along. The trial and punishment of 'The Two' was in fact metaphor, which meant the ascension could also be symbolic, and the body, or 'vehicle,' a thing to overcome. The snake sheds the skin that no longer fits. The science-fiction-sanctity of the physical that had forever underpinned the group's programme was replaced by a position altogether more patently Christian. This was necessary: Ti, in her supposedly 'advanced' post-human state, had fallen ill and died. Do, in crisis, had to re-conceptualise how 'the next level' was arrived at, and only by moving away from the preoccupation with bodily ascendance, could it be said that Ti had 'gone before them,' and would be waiting, or better still: post-manning the starship that would pick them up. This would ultimately facilitate the black-sky thinking behind the group's big exit. If the 'Demonstration' had happened, and Ti had gone, the End really had arrived.

The long-persecuted people of the ancient Kurdish Yezidi religion think God is too important, too busy, and just too far away to concern himself with what's going on on earth. They also believe he might be seen up there, providing the stargazer's belief is strong enough, or their telescope advanced enough. Heaven's Gate had a similar idea: their stargazing was less meditation and more expectation. For years and years they kept it up, without any luck. And then: Hale-Bopp, that funnest-ever sounding comet, which for millenarian groups world-over harkened the end of mankind. This was bigger and brighter even than the star that'd set the course for Ti and Do, as they sat, feckless (and probably loaded) on that Oregon riverbank in 1971. Do's grief-stricken body-hating mania found dialogue with the cosmos, in this ball of fire and ice visible even by naked eye. Conspiracy theories raged: 'look a little further, and you will see the spaceship hiding in the comet's tail...' The Gate rushed out and bought a state-of-the-art telescope, only to return it with the complaint that 'it didn't work' (unable to see the spaceship!). Still, the idea was enough. Ti was coming to get them. Do hurried, as you would, to secure a decent wholesale price on handsome matching trainers (*Just Do It!* The unfortunate motto of Nike-sponsored suicide, who cancelled the iconic 'Decade' model immediately after the group's ascension, and so made these some of the most valuable trainers in this world and the next), and 'Away Team' embroidered patches to be sewn to the sleeves of their *Star Trek*-inspired uniforms.

March 19 was a big day. 'Exit-tape' day. These final recordings were later found on VHS stacked back-to-back with the crew's favourite movies. They're all smiles, filled with excitement for 'beaming up,' in testaments insisting that they're neither brainwashed nor mad. And then, with the last words spoken: the last movie taken. The Gate would spend a whopping $417.27 at a pizza parlour, before visiting the cinema to see Mike Leigh's *Secrets & Lies*. How and why this film was selected as their last? Perhaps they'd liked the director's previous work. *Naked*, the drunk-driven Dalston epic of David Thewlis as gadabout preacher-rapist, was the most recent. Perhaps they were none the wiser, attracted by the synopsis: 'Following the death of her adoptive parents, a successful young black optometrist establishes contact with her biological mother—a lonely white factory worker living in poverty in East London.' It is unlikely they'd anticipated the redemptive and moral heart of this Hackney-homecoming, instead expecting the exit vindication of a film expressly dealing with rape, racism, poverty, loneliness, underage pregnancy and

London's East End: those human horrors they were so relieved
to be escaping. The most likely clue to what guided their final
choice is the movie's promotional poster, headed as it is by an
excerpt from critic Roger Ebert's positive review: 'Two thumbs
up,' he wrote. 'Way up!'

Another film the terminal cinephiles might have chosen
was *Gray's Anatomy* by Steven Soderbergh, released in American
cinemas that same day. Both *Secrets & Lies* and *Gray's Anatomy*
have sight and unseeing as their central hypotheses: named
after Henry Gray's anatomy textbook of 1858, Soderbergh's film
follows a monologue by tall-tale-teller Spalding Gray, who,
diagnosed with a rare ocular condition called macular pucker
—producing distortions; blurring, bowing and doubling of vision
(see Spalding Gray, pp.252–256)—goes on a journey around the
world in search of a cure, eventually refusing surgery through
an emergent religious conviction. Nostradamus is believed to
have stared at the sun with eyes closed, dancing his fingers over
his eyelids, stimulating hallucination to invoke God. However
unlikely a technique applied in the calming dark of the optom-
etrist's surgery, it may be that Hortense, our expert in testing
sight, and focus of *Secrets & Lies*, is pushed to attempt such
an operation on her biological mother, Cynthia. Tricky, dippy,
errant and alcoholic, 'real' mom is tracked down to a terraced
house on Quilter Street, Shoreditch. A single mother, Cynthia
has been demolished by a factory life of packing boxes—'but
you gotta laugh, ain't ya, else you'd cry!' she says, and cries
throughout the entire film—and is broadly disdained by an
aspirant family that can't understand what's holding her back.
Hortense has known she was adopted since she was a child,
but only with the death of her adoptive parents does she take
a punt on her birth mum. Over a glass of Chardonnay with a
nympho friend, she reflects: 'We choose our parents in this life,
so they can teach us something in the next.' With this, did one
Gate-Crasher nudge another, nodding solemnly in recognition
of Hortense's half-cut contemplation? The film opens with a
funeral. To nudge or not to nudge? All in attendance knew
they'd each be having their own soon, or at least their 'vehicles'
would. And they must have felt some sadness, however broken
any bio-fam relationship was, for the forebears they'd selected and would never see again. A tinge of embarrassment too,
and perhaps regret, pondering the soil the tossers would, with
reluctant and trembling hands, be tossing on to their wooden

tops. The work of it all (and who would pay, with all their readies invested in the spaceship?). The crew saw Ti and Do as their great adopters, mobilising the transition from the factory world of ugly parents, to the sky-garden of Godly leisure, and tenuous connection makers as they were, *might* have viewed Hortense's adoptive parents as symbolic of something similar: notching her up a class, from working to middle. Certainly, it wouldn't be considered a coincidence that Hortense's adoptive mother, like Ti, was a midwife. Nudge, nudge. $76 on soda, but no popcorn. Fine cinema company. Gurgle. 'Secrets and lies...' spits the bloated angel, Timothy Spall: 'We're all in pain. Why can't we share our pain?' Nudge, nudge, nudge. Sob. They did.

There was much to do in the few days that followed the last movie. Loose ends to tie up. Groceries to collect. Rent to pay ($10,000 per month), a library fine to clear ($2.50). Dressed in black from head to toe, the crew were clean and shaven, with their Nike's kept fresh for blast-off. Several members kept pages of paper instructions / directions on their bodies, along with ID, and each had exactly $5.75 in a trouser pocket. This amount follows an account given by Mark Twain on the fee to ride the tail of a comet. (Twain was an *example*, saying in 1909: 'I came in with Halley's Comet. It is coming again next year. The Almighty has said, no doubt, "Now there are these two unaccountable freaks; they came in together, they must go out together."' He died on April 21, 1910—one day after the comet had once again visited its perihelion.) Laid out on freshly ironed, white cotton sheets, wrapped around the prison-mattresses of their black steel-framed bunk beds; with their hands at their sides, and feet set a foot apart, their upper torsos and faces were covered with purple shrouds.

Exit began March 21 / 22. Divided into three groups, each followed the other, comforting and cleaning up as they went. Vodka was taken to speed up the effectiveness of the barbiturates, which were laced into a sponge-pudding with 'Marshall' applesauce. To ensure a speedier, certain, and more comfortable exit, plastic bags secured by plastic bands were used to suffocate the traveller. The scene was clean, meticulously planned. There was no indication of violence or struggle. Do died early on. And though two sheriff department officials were reportedly hospitalised after being 'overcome by the odour of decomposition,' a medical examiner was interviewed by a sensationalist media on the scene inside the mansion. 'Peaceful,' he reflected. 'It's just very peaceful.' A neighbour, when questioned about the events, said: 'We left LA because it was getting gnarly up there. We thought we were moving to a safe utopia ... The only exciting thing around here is the ditch they are digging out front to put in a pipe...' (Until now.)

In Rainer Werner Fassbinder's *In a Year of Thirteen Moons* (1997 was one such year), a lovelorn woman—a new woman, having transitioned for the love of a man, in the hope this would dissolve the guilt and shame he felt for his homosexuality, and make their relationship possible—dejected, ascends to the attic of the office block in which he works. There she encounters the building's janitor, standing on a stool and looping a noose around his neck. 'No!' She appeals, stunned. He is calm, focused. 'You don't understand,' he responds: 'Suicide is not for those who want to die, but for those who want to live.' With this response she quietly withdraws, pushing herself back against a wall as he kicks the stool beneath him. Do, had he seen this (dangerous stuff), might have found an important cultural context for the narrative that'd lose the Gate-Crashers their earthly bodies—it may have helped stop or stall the conclusion. For the rest of the crew too, *Thirteen Moons* might have proved useful in reminding them that the problem isn't the body, but the system that governs and exerts control over it.

Genesis and Lady Jane Breyer P-Orridge's 'Pandrogyny' project—as another radical offshoot of 1960s thinking on breaking control, outing the ego and accelerating evolution—is loaded with the desire the Gate-Crashers sought to undo. But they effectively share the same impatient agreement, describing the body as 'container' and 'trap,' refusing the fiction of gender identity in pursuit of the divine hermaphrodite. P-Orridge lamented a surgical procedure advanced enough to install the individual with a working penis *and* a working vagina, all in the ambition of undoing division; of 'repairing.' The erstwhile androgynous futurism of the Gate-Crashers, had Do not lost his way in homophobic self-hatred and ceded to the superstitions of the Old Testament, might have looked more like this—as what P-Orridge describes is surely Godlier, or at least more impressively *alien* than castration (yes, some of them had their balls snipped before they offed; there are no coincidences, et cetera). By admission of their Exit tapes, the Gate-Crashers were each as individuals the janitor in the attic, whereas together they were the inheritors of Thirteen Moons, the team at the helm of the Eternal Spaceship.

Outcasts, these were highly intelligent and emotional people dedicated to life but unsure where or how to locate it. With the wrong guidance, this can easily give way to castration or mass-suicide, just as it might—with the right—give way to the installation of a vagina to go along with your penis (and horns and gills and webbed feet and wings). The Pandrogynes and the Gate-Crashers speak as strange harbingers to the hyper-religiosity of the body-centric present: both shaped and unshaped by an extremism forewarned by Hegel, and parroted by Zizek; the death of God does not mean the loss of God, but rather the integration of him as omnipotent agent. *He* is no longer elsewhere; no longer visible with a strong enough telescope, nor even in need of our belief, but subjective... Deep within this shallow skin.

The invitation of Heaven's Gate remained gentle however apocalyptic the message got. It could be accepted and rescinded at any time, right until the end. In the months leading up to the Collective Act, group members were encouraged to spend time with their biological families, if they wanted to (one member decided to stay there, while the rest all returned to the craft). Do even offered crew members $1000 each to leave (in '97 it cost about $10 for a crate of beers; back in '70 it cost just $1). The overtures he made to his own uncertainty were open and raw. Were the crew manipulated? Probably, but not so much until Do leant so singularly on the Bible. Christianity, with its doctrine of apocalyptic posturing, should perhaps be viewed as the *real* death cult here. But that Americans found their peace-loving, monkish existence so abhorrent, says more about their own fundamental contradictions. If Do lost his marbles and exacted increasing control over members, it was in desperation, grief, and a fear of losing more, all compounded by the trial of the American public, themselves servants to the establishment media narrative (cult!), which entrenched the memory of separateness and disassociation felt by crew members before they found the Gate. By the end, without Ti to keep Do in check, Heaven's Gate were really just a barnacle on the side of establishment Evangelicalism, with some science fiction chucked in to keep it exciting. Almost 10% of the American public then classed themselves as practicing Christians: a belief system without any empirical evidence, founded on a book of dubious origin, filled with stories that are almost all appropriated or lifted from others, about the son (sun) of a virgin (Goddess) who dies, is re-born (Alpha, Omega) and flies away, and will, if you speak to this gaunt, bloodied 2023-year old socialist hippy ghost *in your head*, repressing your deepest desires and apologising, endlessly, for things like being gay; sex out of wedlock; swearing; you may, *may*, if you feel bad enough about it all, be granted a place in eternal paradise. Meanwhile, to get by in life, you also had to be an adherent of capitalism: an insipid and individualistic regime of accumulating excess that cannot honestly co-exist with Christianity, but does, because without sin there can't be redemption. Such are the people who laughed at the crew, even and especially in death.

Of those laughing, did any feel genuinely connected to and have purpose within their family and community? And who of those laughing died or will die, and indeed live, believing profoundly in anything at all? Maybe it doesn't matter, and it's irresponsible to compare against the Collective Act, but 'normal' in life and death seems no less strange and no more irresponsible, if we live following rules that we know to be arbitrary and very often wrong, spending exhausting and uninspired lives in jobs we don't want to do, with shame, confusion, secrets and lies... dying alone and going nowhere. Do may have been mad, and this may have been murder. But it may be instead that the 'ascendants' all believed strongly enough to actually get to where they thought they were going. Either way, as an expertly handled artistic and cinematic monument to faith, the Exit should be viewed in the context of the history of religious art. We do not have to agree with or believe in the parable, fable, fantasy, to be moved by a hellish impressive depiction of it. And the Gate's is a rendering of Revelation to rival any other.

In the weeks following the Exit of the thirty-nine, Chuck Humphrey, a former member who would chase the crew in early '98, responded to the ship-of-fools media response by parading around a t-shirt that read: '*Heaven's Gate: What if They were Right?*' And what if they were, at least inasmuch as the world ended in 1997? Fear not and hold tight, as the world has ended and is ending often.

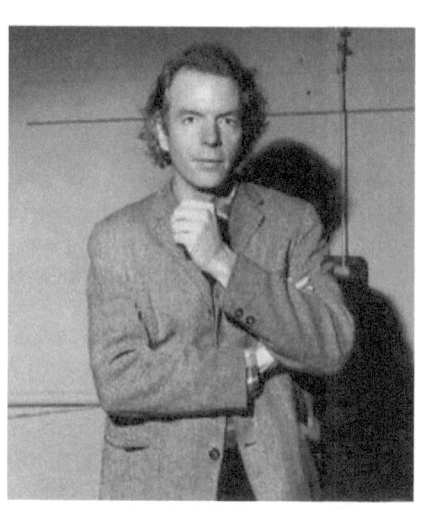

Spalding Gray (d. 2004)
Big Fish (Tim Burton, 2003), 125m

The biggest fish in the river gets that way by never getting caught.
—Jenny the Witch

¶ In Tim Burton's *Big Fish*, a common-sense son appeals for the deathbed truth of a fabulist father, after a lifetime of tall-tale-telling. The father counters with his own appeal: too weak to exercise his imagination, the son must use his own to deliver dad a last hurrah. *This* is the truth; the big gift dad had been trying to give his son all along. And so he does, summoning a summer day in his father's native Alabama, with a riverbank to wander and a lifetime's worth of friends to see him off. The son wades into the water and lowers the father he carries who, morphing into the titular fish, swims away. 'A man tells a story over and over so many times he becomes the story. In that way, he is immortal.' The End.

Spalding Gray's family last saw him at the cinema. He'd taken his two sons to see *Big Fish* at the Loews Village on Third Avenue and 11th Street, New York, in the afternoon of January 10, 2004. Afterwards, the kids were collected by their evening babysitter and Gray set out across the city, calling home from a payphone at the Staten Island Ferry terminal around 10:30pm. 'Checking in.' He told his eldest son he'd be back soon, and quietly ended 'love you.' He was declared missing on January 11. His wife, Kathleen Russo, reflected in the days that followed... 'Some friends said I shouldn't see it, but I had to, I went last night.' In the absence of her husband, she retraces his known steps. First by going to the same cinema for the same movie. 'You know, Spalding cried after he saw that movie. I just think it gave him permission. I think it gave him permission to die.'

Gray had to visit free-flowing water daily in order to feel sane. He often rode the Staten Island Ferry for relaxation and—ever the flirt with death—he had spoken freely about the idea of throwing himself overboard. In the morning before he went to see *Big Fish*, he'd been escorted away from the port terminal railing by ferry staff, who had watched him first carefully place his stuffed wallet on a nearby bench.

Four different witnesses came forward to report seeing Gray on the ferry that night. Nobody saw him jump.

If the creative process is one of reduction Spalding had it down. He'd work for only an hour each day, and his performances were cheap to produce; his fee, a table and chair. Lights, and a little music at a push. Famed for his free-wheeling, wide-open, wild and exhaustive theatre monologues on the weird and sheer life-ness of all things, he shot to fame with *Swimming to Cambodia* (1987), a cheeky exploit of his bit-part act ('backtor') as a

United States Consul in Roland Joffé's film, *The Killing Fields*
(1984). Originally a two-night, four-hour stage show in New York
with a soundtrack by Laurie Anderson (imagine Larry David's
Curb Your Enthusiasm theme adapted to score mass murder),
director Jonathan Demme (mercifully) squeezed it down to
eighty-five minutes for film. Towards the end of his performance,
Gray describes explaining on-set to fellow actor Athol Fugard
his 'new anxiety displacement theory,' that 'if ever you lack the
courage to do something and you need that courage, just take
a big pile of money and leave it somewhere it can be stolen,
and go do that thing.' He describes swimming far away from
the shore in Phuket, Thailand—money on the beach—and the
paralysing fear of being in the ocean; the power of it; the danger
of the sharks and the stonefish beneath; and then, further and
further out, all of a sudden, *nothing*. 'Suddenly there is no fear...
there is no *me*. It's just the great, body-temperature-warm Indian
Ocean... and I'm sleeping like a kid again in Jerusalem, Rhode
Island, the entire bed rocking, wrapped in the arms of the sea.
Fantastic sleep.'

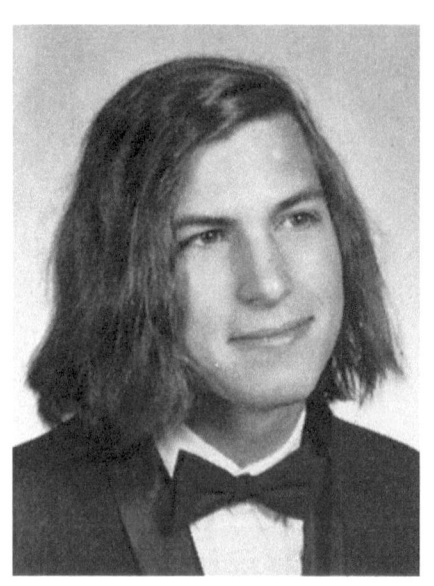

Steve Jobs (d.2011)
Remember the Titans (Boaz Yakin, 2000), 113m

¶ 'I was so surprised he wanted to watch that movie. I was like, Are you sure? Steve was not interested in sports at all. And we watched and we talked about a number of things and I left thinking that he was pretty happy. And all of a sudden, things went to hell that weekend.'

Tim Cook had been appointed CEO of Apple eight weeks earlier at Job's Palo Alto home, where he'd been invited once again, this time to watch *Remember the Titans*. A 'true' story about an American football underdog, it's the kind of film made passable by long distance air travel, or, indeed, sickness. Job's health permanently failed soon afterwards.

Set in 1971, *Remember the Titans* tells the 'true' story of Herman Boone (Denzel Washington), appointed head football coach at a recently desegregated Virginia high school. He's pitted against the former head coach, Bill Yoast (played by Will Patton), who has for some reason been relegated to an assistant position. Boone battles racial prejudice and wins the support of the community: the head and the assistant work together on a playing field evened, and they learn to love each other—all of the boys learn to love each other too. This produces an unbroken string of victories, winning the season and eventually ranking the team the nation's second best. Tough, smouldering, delirious. *America*.

Tim's dim reflection on Steve and sports suggests his instalment as CEO of one of the world's most innovative and successful businesses as mere puppetry or even parasitising—the 'true' boss would pull the shots from the sidelines. He can't have thought for a moment that this film would be his last. And the football, Tim, is a device: this is a movie about the capacity of a great leader to turn adversity into power. The team is nothing without their coach. Change is only possible in pursuit of greatness, and greatness is only possible collectively... but with a clear leader, *obviously*. And though winning is real, the 'true victory,' Boone reflects, is 'getting on with each other.' Training camp elevates the boys away from the contaminating prejudices of parents. They learn that love knows not borders, nor skin colours. Boone tells them they've already won.

1971 was a big year for Jobs. Commencing his senior year at high school, he met through an electronics class his *destiny* in Stephen Wozniak, a computer designer (and former football team quarterback), the Boone to his Yoast, the John to his Paul, and if he wasn't nicknamed Oz... he is now. Jobs describes a dark scene of fellow students gathering around a television set to watch *Star Trek* (see Heaven's Gate, pp.240–251). Oz was there, equipped with a self-made concealed pocket device emitting TV signals. With a simple press of its single button, Oz could turn the picture to static. As soon as anyone got up to bang the set to attempt to fix it, he'd release the button, only for them to sit down again and the static return. It's a model that Oz would be dismayed to see deployed with permanence in the suicidal guarantee of any Apple product. Jobs is in your laptop, laughing.

The revolution of the 1960s was real, and then the times a'changed. The boys must have known? The Manson murders had happened; Martin Luther King had been assassinated. The course was set, but it was yet to locate (or reveal) its alpha and omega in the logo bearing the bitten apple, that symbol of original sin.

Oz put Jobs on to Bob 'if you're not busy being born, you're busy dying' Dylan. When they weren't fiddling with wires and shooing away the most likely outcome of their labour—the lobotomisation of the whole wide world on a simulacrum of drug-addicted sex-slaves—they'd be out in Berkeley and San Jose searching for Bob bootlegs (or, Bob-legs as the Trekkers would have it). Nights were spent in fields and cars, with marijuana and LSD, decoding the master-magician's lyrics; hallucinating about how they'd accommodate any devil, if it meant getting Bob to star in a commercial promoting any one of the products they were yet to create (finally in 2006 for the iPod, in which the apocryphal cowboy looks fabulous and forever, and his company, the black silhouetted, white-wired iPodded drunken auntie grooving, looks like ancient history—Bob 'he's got the ... in his hands' Dylan also starred in a Victoria's Secret ad that same year, hobbling around an empty, Venetian hall, but for a winged angel in knickers—not bad work if you can ... after all, he had in 1965 warned a press conference that if he ever appeared in a commercial, it'd be for ladies undergarments). Jobs made constant overtures to the artists he admired, seeing no difference in their innovation and anti-authoritarian spirit, to the brand he was creating. This magical marketing coup was perhaps his single greatest achievement: convincing millions of people that they're different, innovative, anti-authoritarian, freedom-loving individuals, each by possessing precisely the same gratuitously expensive, slave-made consumer device.

Oz flew too close to the sun in a flying device he was ill-equipped to pilot, and the shock of the fall would ultimately trigger his exit from Apple (an exit from any position of input and management, but to this day he still receives a weekly $50 cheque for the seed; meanwhile teaching high school kids). The departure, however, was a long time coming: he and Jobs were practically black and white in their positions on the ethos and direction of their collaboration. Oz wanted to open the technology, liberating the person through the machine, even selling it to the public at cost price; but while he played the Native fun-boy counting coup, Jobs craved fields of gold: closed, barbed, the Selfish Giant. The two deny any prior knowledge of the religious connotations in their machine's first asking price, which feels like a hell of a dance. It was $666.66.

¶ Apple Macintosh announced the release of its first personal computer in 1983, with an infamous advert directed by Ridley Scott (fresh from *Blade Runner*). A neo-luddite athlete launches a mallet at a massive screen, so opening the screen to the assembled masses. Apple promised that 'on January 24... you'll see why 1984 won't be like *1984*.' What they failed to add is that all subsequent years would be. Oz and Jobs made it through '84, but no further, both leaving the company they founded (the latter due to a bitter falling out with Apple chief executive, John Sculley). Jobs then bought George Lucas' ailing animation studio Pixar for a pittance and delivered his masterpiece of coaching, and finest work: *Toy Story* (the fourth film in the franchise, which Jobs had nothing to do with, is the only genuinely accessible and elegant critique of capitalism made in film-form in the first twenty years of this century). He would ultimately return to 'save Apple from bankruptcy' as interim CEO in 1997 (see Heaven's Gate, pp.240–251). For a moment, drunk on power, Jobs had changed the name of the company to 'Bicycle,' before retracting his bid and remembering the 'Beatles concept' (and channeling *Remember the Titans*), an idea discussed by Dim Tim as forming the Apple core: any negative qualities of the individual would be removed by the performance of the perfectly functioning collective. When the family works, keep it in the family. Jobs' model throughout his life for the process of creative work, from conception to delivery, is located in the Bob-legged tapes he kept of 'Strawberry Fields Forever' by The Beatles. These studio recordings that he regularly listened to track the first tinkling of the song, through to the eventual manicure of mellotron. In these, he figured, were the fount and apex; absolute perfection. This is a notion shared by Bill Drummond, who locates his origin and trajectory through the song, and believes that all recorded music has now 'run its course.' No more consumption, only participation. It doesn't take a mallet to open up an iPhone. Alpha, omega. Living is easy with eyes closed... *nothing is real*... et cetera.

(Surrounded by his family, Jobs took a good look at each of them, and then his gaze rose, as though to the sky, and he spoke his last words: 'Oh wow. Oh wow. Oh wow.')

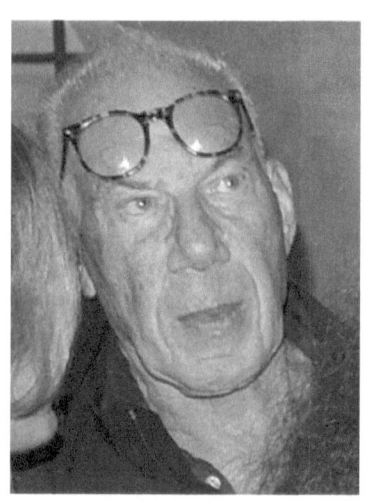

Bob Rafelson (d. 2022)
The Old Man (Jonathan E. Steinberg, 2022), 47–64m, *Episodic*

¶ In *The Guardian*'s online obituary of Rafelson, published one day after his passing on 24 July in 2022, the article closed 'Rafelson died at his home in Aspen on Saturday night surrounded by his family after watching the film *Joker*.' This detail wasn't included in any other coverage of Rafelson's death, and is no longer present on the newspaper's archived page. In the following months I return to focus on Rafelson for the *Last Movies* project, and hesitate, check myself... was this the closure I desired and unwittingly made up? And then Godard passed. The End.

14.08.23

Dear Rafelson Media,

I am a huge admirer of Bob Rafelson's work, currently preparing to write a tribute to him. I appreciate the strangeness of this enquiry, and assure you it is made with the sensitivity and respect due: at the time of Rafelson's passing, it was reported that he watched Todd Philip's *Joker* on his last night. Is this true? Or was I dreaming?!

Thank you for your patience and attention.

Stanley Schtinter

*

15.08.23

Stan—

This is Peter, Bob's first son.

I cannot confirm nor deny this but I can tell you that a few weeks prior to his passing I visited and climbed into bed with Bob, where we watched and shared our love and appreciation for a close friend, who he referred to as his favourite actor, Jeff Bridges in *The Old Man*.

Let me know if I may be of further help,

Peter

*

16.08.23

Dear Peter,

I am moved by your message and grateful for your openness.
I watched the first three episodes of *The Old Man* last night, and
I'll return to watch Bridges in *Stay Hungry* once it's done (and
then, appropriately, *The Last Picture Show*). Did Bob share any
thoughts on *The Old Man*?

If I did indeed dream of his last viewing experience as *Joker*,
I don't think it speaks to that film, but rather of his own body
of work infiltrating my dreamscape as only the most potent
cinema can. Another 'character' in this project is F.W. Murnau,
whose last stop was at the gas station chosen by Bob for *Postman*,
and which I understand he alone stayed at for a night and a
day to understand how the sunbeams and the moonbeams hit?
(I guess he knew about this connection with Murnau.)

To best demonstrate my project—'a parallel history of the first
century of cinema according to what a selection of its key cultural icons saw just before they crossed over'—I am attaching
various examples of the cast and their movie(s). Can you consent
to my featuring Bob and *The Old Man* as part of the project?
I am forever indebted—in art and life—to the example of Bob
Rafelson, and thank you once again for your engagement.

Stanley

*

¶ In *The Old Man*, a television series made by Disney, Jeff Bridges stars as a dog-loving ex-secret services guy who can and will destroy any one and thing that gets in his way or threatens his daughter, with whom he strictly maintains only telephone contact. After many years of living in hiding under an assumed name, Bridges' location is uncovered, and he becomes the target of the FBI in league with some shady Middle Eastern warlord. He takes a new name, adjusts his wardrobe, and, with the help of his killer dogs, moves across the country to avoid capture. He regularly hallucinates his deceased wife, 'Abbey,' who we learn he smuggled to America a long time ago, her safety endangered by the very same Middle Eastern warlord.

In *Joker*, Todd Philips of *The Hangover* fame channels the New Hollywood movement birthed by Rafelson through contemporary kultur's endless re-hash of comic-book characters, lifting superficially from Alan Moore's *Killing Joke* to produce a glitzy, nihilistic paint-by-numbers befitting lonely and mentally-ill (end) times. We get the pictures we deserve. Joaquin Phoenix plays the Frank Sinatra-loving, Fred Astaire-dancing, girlfriend-hallucinating villain as a fragile and deeply unfunny man. Jack Nicholson was quiet on Phoenix's performance, but railed against the notion of Heath Ledger in the role in Christopher Nolan's earlier Batman film, *The Dark Knight* (2008). By the time Nicholson played Joker in Tim Burton's *Batman* (1989)—the self-proclaimed 'avant-garde of the new aesthetic,' scarification-crazed acid creep binge-listening Prince—and shaped contemporary kultur's view of the character, it was really Nicholson playing Nicholson. In Rafelson's films (*Five Easy Pieces*, *The King of Marvin Gardens*, *The Postman Always Rings Twice*), Nicholson is Nicholson before Nicholson. Their collaborations evidence the range and brilliance of Jack, who, having long been ignored, was content to play himself forever-after where Bob wasn't. The director withdrew to Aspen, Colorado, to stick to his principles and raise his children. He'd practice shooting prints of Richard Nixon's face with neighbour Hunter S. Thompson, collect 'exotic totems' to decorate his mountain lair, and return briefly to movie-making around the millennium with *Porn.com* ('cause why not). 'I may have thought I started his career,' Nicholson told *Esquire* magazine in a 2019 article titled 'The Last Rhino,' 'but I think he started my career.'

Rafelson's wilful obscurity resulted in declarations of death long before the fact. In 2017, *Sight and Sound* magazine published a long feature on Martin Scorsese, and listed Bob Rafelson alongside Robert Altman, Hal Ashby, Michael Cimino, and Dennis Hopper as 'gone.' Rafelson contacted the editor in response, requesting five copies of the issue and a free subscription to *Sight and Sound*, however 'I do not want a retraction,' he explained: 'There are several people who have heard the rumours of my death that I owed money to so I suppose I should be grateful.' In fact, he was out so long, as the 'aloof stranger' to Hollywood, that an Italian extra managed to secure $400,000.00 to produce a film as Bob Rafelson, with Marcello Mastroianni, Catherine Deneuve, Patrick Bouchat and Franco Nero all set to star. In advance of meetings between the actors and the director, they were each told they must not look at Bob Rafelson. He would enter a hotel room behind them and the whole conversation was undertaken back-to-back. The director later regretted that the financiers foiled the plot of Rafelson's impersonator, who had secured more money than he was customarily paid. 'Let him take the money, and if it's a good movie I will take the credit. If it's bad... I won't... do what you want, throw him in jail, but let him make the movie.' Rafelson began to prepare a documentary on the story, which he likened to Abbas Kiarostami's *Close-Up*, but, overwhelmed by work on *The King of Marvin Gardens*, it never happened. Years later, the actor Patrick Bouchat said the imposter's script was better than anything Rafelson ever did.

Rafelson's first job in cinema came while stationed in Japan, subtitling films by the likes of Yasujirō Ozu (whose grave bears no name, just 'mu,' meaning nothingness), who Rafelson considered his biggest influence in film, and whose late international recognition he speculated was due to what a horrible translation job he'd done. 'I singlehandedly destroyed the reputation of Ozu.' To make amends, Rafelson later took on his responsibility as a filmmaker with an extraordinary obsession and precision: during *Five Easy Pieces* he became 'consumed' with finding the right sound for the ashtray in Nicholson's car. He recorded four hundred different rattling ashtrays in order to find the right one. Making movies 'comes easier to some than it does to others,' Rafelson said, 'Because most people don't give a shit about the sound of an ashtray.'

*

26.08.23

Hi James,

During your research for the *Last Movies* project, you wrote
to me highlighting a passage in *The Guardian*'s obituary of
Rafelson, stating that he watched *Joker* on the night of his passing. Since that date I've listed it as one of the 'last movies,' but
I'm now not sure I actually factchecked your factchecking at the
time. Did this come from the actual article or were you taking
the piss? I've been in touch with his family who 'neither confirm
nor deny' but say that Jeff Bridges in *The Old Man* was a shared
experience between he and son Peter not long before Bob's
crossing...

s

*

26.08.23

Stanley—

Not terribly ashamed that you took it so far but still surprised
that the most sussed person I know even fell for the less subtle
claim that Simone de Beauvoir watched *Confessions of a Pop
Performer* shortly before she expired. At the risk of the boy who
cried wolf this is genuine: when does your book go to print?
I have the new biography of Ian Fleming on double secret
embargo till Oct 3 with a ton of great stuff on JFK and indeed
Lee Harvey Oswald and *From Russia with Love*, although it
doesn't actually alter the last movie date.

James

*

26.08.23

Joker—

Given the engagement of Peter and my ultimate wish to honour
Bob in the book, I can only think to print your admission and
go from there.
　　Glad to bring *Confessions* back in to the fold, but you
needn't think you're going to score a hattrick with this rubbish
about an embargoed Fleming bio.

Any last words?

S

*

¶ *Five Easy Pieces* was written with Carol Eastman and directed by Rafelson, inspired by the proverbial black sheep; specifically, Teddy, of the Kennedy political dynasty. Nicholson plays an accomplished middle-class musician from a family of accomplished middle-class musicians, who throws it all away to go faraway and work on an oilfield. The film struck at the heart of America's broken dream, and formed an all-seeing pyramid of heavy-hitters with Dennis Hopper's *Easy Rider* and Peter Bogdanovich's *The Last Picture Show*, each produced by Rafelson's company, BBS. The founding concept of BBS was simple: America had all of the talent good to go, but nobody with the talent to identify it. In came Bob and business partner Bert Schneider (who'd eventually abandon the project for radical politics). He re-mortgaged his house (bought on the back of his success founding the first openly manufactured pop group, The Monkees, whose suicide he would stage in *Head*, their movie-biopic, as 'revenge') to make *Easy Rider*, stating 'I'd known Hopper as an artist, an actor... an out of work actor, a very difficult person. I didn't think the movie he would make would be like any other bike movie, I thought it would be exceptional. I thought he deserved the chance to make the kind of film that philosophically I believed should happen in America.' The world-beating success of *Easy Rider* surprised everyone, and studios were chomping at the bit for golden bunny Hopper's next big picture. 'It'll be a movie where you don't know what's real and what's not real, what's illusion and what's reality.' Lofty, Pagan, South American. *The Last Movie*. 'Dennis had begun to believe his own myth.' Rafelson rejected the picture for BBS and it proved just the kind of financial disaster the cynics at the commissioning studio deserved. 'The studio boss called me on the first day [of shooting] and asked: how do you talk to Dennis Hopper? BBS had brought about a certain kind of movement, that when they latched onto it as their own, the only thing missing was that these people in the studios had no way of talking to those people [Hopper, *et al*]. They had no dialogue.' Rafelson continues, describing an incident of Hopper pulling a gun on him. Into his mouth he took the chamber and encouraged him to shoot.

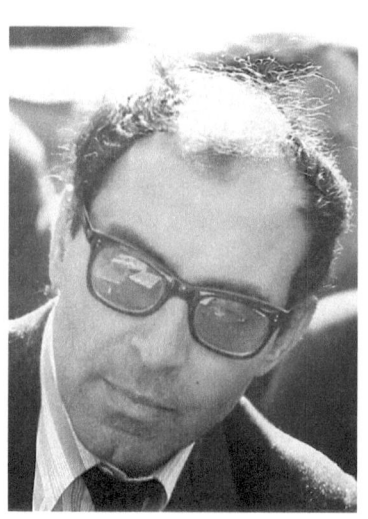

Jean-Luc Godard (d. 2022)
Film annonce du film Drôles de Guerres (1er tournage) /
Announcement of the Film 'Phony Wars' (1st shoot)

* We have elected to translate the English language iteration of Godard's title more explicitly than has Saint Laurent Productions owing to the importance of the word 'annonce' to Godard, *vis-à-vis* the Biblical *L'annonce faite à Marie* (1991).

¶ Godard finished *Film annonce du film Drôles de Guerres* (1er tournage) / *Announcement of the Film 'Phony Wars'* (1st shoot) and returned to his desk.* There, he smoked his final cigar, and booked a taxi to take him to the assisted suicide facility. He asked his publicist to make it very clear that he wasn't ill, and he wasn't depressed, but simply 'exhausted.'

Nicole Brenez, Last Instants / Drôles de Guerres

Translated from the French by
Clodagh Kinsella

Tous ces tableaux sont sublimes, mais pas un seul n'est parfait.
*All these paintings are magnificent, but not a single one is perfect.**
      —Jean-Luc Godard, dernier instants /
      final moments

* Thomas Bernhard, *Maîtres anciens. Comédie* (1985), traduit de
l'allemand par Gilberte Lambrichs, (Paris: Gallimard, 1988), p.16. /
Thomas Bernhard, *Old Masters: A Comedy*, trans. Ewald Osers
(London: Penguin, 1989; 2010), p.6.

1er mars 2022

D'une voix fatiguée mais ferme et emplie de joie, Jean-Luc Godard déclare à Fabrice Aragno et Jean-Paul Battaggia qui l'enregistrent, à propos de *Film annonce du film Drôles de Guerres (1er tournage)*: «Je ne sais pas ce que vous en avez pensé quand je vous ai dit que c'était l'un de mes meilleurs films, ce que j'aime bien c'est que c'est très lent, très silencieux de temps en temps, et puis il y a autre chose, donc c'est la perfection.»

Pour qui s'est habitué à l'autocritique permanente grâce à laquelle évolue le travail de Godard, la surprise est de taille. Après Sisyphe, imaginer Godard heureux? Jean-Luc a pensé la durée de chaque plan sur le modèle physique des quelques secondes dévolues par les visiteurs d'un musée de peinture à la perception de chaque tableau, avec à l'horizon la figure antagoniste radicale de Reger, ce personnage de Thomas Bernhard qui, pendant trente ans, vient s'asseoir tous les deux jours devant *L'homme à la barbe blanche* du Tintoret (*Maîtres anciens*, 1985).

Donc :

- la lenteur, version cinétique d'un résidu contemporain d'expérience contemplative, oui ;
- le silence, la page blanche, oui.

1st March, 2022

In an interview about *Announcement of the Film 'Phony Wars'*
(1st shoot), recorded by Fabrice Aragno and Jean-Paul Battaggia,
Jean-Luc Godard declares in a fatigued but firm and joyful voice:
'I don't know what you thought when I told you it was one of
my best films. What I like is that it's very slow, sometimes very
silent, and then there's something else, so it's perfect.'

For anyone accustomed to the permanent autocritique
propelling Godard's work, it's a surprise. To imagine Godard, in
the wake of Sisyphus, happy?* Jean-Luc conceived of the duration of each shot along the same lines as the few seconds visitors
accord to looking at a painting in an art museum; looming in
the backdrop, the radically antagonistic figure of Reger, that
character from Thomas Bernhard's *Old Masters* who, for thirty
years, sits down every other day in front of Tintoretto's *Portrait
of a White-Bearded Man*. A model, then, of—

- slowness: a kinetic take on a modern surplus of
  contemplative experience... yes.
- silence, the blank page... yes.

---

* TRANSLATOR'S NOTE: a reference to Camus' *The Myth of Sisyphus* (1942),
in which he claims—as per the absurdist stance—that, once Sisyphus
acknowledges the futility of his task, he is free to reach a state of
contentment.

Mais alors, en quoi consisterait cette «autre chose» qui permet d'accéder à une perfection même ironique ?

Premières hypothèses, tirées du film lui-même :

- des êtres engagés dans leur cause jusqu'à la mort;
- l'irruption d'un plan en mouvement dans l'histoire millénaire des images immobiles, dont parfois un film ravive le caractère miraculeux;
- un dense écheveau de relations ouvertes entre les mots, les images et les sons;
- les derniers éclats d'une recherche infinie sur le négatif;
- beaucoup de souffrances, de tortures, de batailles perdues, d'idéaux bafoués, sur un papier qui porte un nom d'arme («Canon»);
- diverses phases du travail, parfois très anciennes, mises à nu et ajointées;
- bouches d'ombre, chutes, vertiges;
- le chemin vers un texte où l'on peut lire: «Si elle est morte, n'oublie pas. Si elle est morte, un simple faire-part. Un simple faire-part.»
- le chemin vers un livre qui annonce: «Souvenirs d'un agitateur.»
- le chemin vers une œuvre qui commence par une première question: «Pourquoi, suis-je venu ce soir, penser devant ces feuilles blanches?»

But what might this 'something else' ushering in perfection, albeit of an ironic kind, look like?

First hypotheses, drawn from the film itself—
- beings committed to their cause until death.
- the irruption of a moving shot in the ancient history of still images, whose miraculous nature a film can sometimes revive.
- a dense web of open-ended connections between words, images and sounds.
- the final flaring of an infinite investigation into the negative.
- a lot of suffering and torture, many battles lost, and ideals flouted, on a piece of paper bearing a weapon's name (the 'Canon').
- various phases of the work, sometimes very old, stripped back and joined together.
- shadowy mouths, falls, faintness.
- the path to a text that reads:
'If she is dead, don't forget. If she is dead, a simple announcement. A simple announcement.'*
- the path to a book that announces: 'Memoires of an agitator.'**
- the path to a work that begins with an initial question: 'Why have I come here tonight to think in front of these blank pages?'***

---

* Charles Plisnier, *Faux-passeports* (Paris: Éditions Corréa, 1937), p.150. TRANSLATOR'S NOTE: Godard wanted to adapt Plisnier's text for *Phony Wars*. For the official English translation, see Charles Plisnier, tr. Geoffrey Dunlop, *Memoires of a Secret Revolutionary* (London: Boriswood, 1938). All translations my own unless otherwise stated.
** TRANSLATOR'S NOTE: The subtitle of Plisnier's novel.
*** Plisnier, *Faux-passeports*, p.15.

4 juillet 2022

En raturant son contexte, Jean-Luc Godard met en valeur une phrase tirée du *Henri IV* de Luigi Pirandello: «ce plaisir d'un nouveau genre : celui de vivre—en toute lucidité.»

4 July, 2022

Erasing its source, Jean-Luc Godard foregrounds a line
from Luigi Pirandello's *Henri IV*: 'this new kind of pleasure:
living—in total lucidity.' *

* A line drawn from an annotated photograph, Jean-Luc Godard,
  excerpted from an email correspondence with Nicole Brenez, Fabrice
  Aragno, Jean-Paul Battaggia and Elias Sanbar (4 July, 2022). Illustration
  courtesy of the Fondation Jean-Luc Godard, © 2023.

12 septembre 2022

Sept jours plus tôt, rendez-vous avait été pris avec l'association Exit pour assister Jean-Luc Godard dans sa disparition. Fabrice Aragno et Jean-Paul Battaggia se rendent une dernière fois auprès de Jean-Luc, afin de convenir des derniers détails quant au montage de *Film annonce du film Drôles de Guerres (1er tournage)* et aux suites du grand projet qui l'occupe depuis déjà quatre ans, *Scénario*. Sur papier blanc, à l'encre bleue, Jean-Luc trace encore quelques esquisses explicatives.

13 septembre 2022

10h. Via le quotidien *Libération* dont il était proche, le monde entier apprend le suicide de Jean-Luc Godard.

10h, c'est l'heure du rendez-vous, pas celle de l'absorption de la potion toxique. De sorte que, au moment où le monde se fige ou fond en larmes, Jean-Luc Godard est toujours en vie.

Toujours en vie.

L'essentiel, c'est de ne jamais être synchrone.

Toujours en vie.

Un dernier film plein de silence pour mieux faire entendre le bruit et la fureur, hurlant des conflits des xxe et xxie siècles, qui s'achève en plein vol sur l'un des plus douloureux, longs, irrésolus de tous, le conflit entre Israël et Palestine.

Toujours en vie.

Bande-son de *Film annonce du film Drôles de Guerres (1er tournage).*
Judith Lerner crie : « Lyon, 1943, La Gestapo ! »

12 September, 2022

Seven days earlier, to assist Jean-Luc Godard with his disappearance, a meeting had been convened with the group Exit. Fabrice Aragno and Jean-Paul Battaggia visit Jean-Luc one last time to agree on the final edits of *Announcement of the Film 'Phony Wars' (1st shoot)*, and on the next steps for *Scenario*, a big project he's been working on for the past four years. On a blank page, in blue ink, Jean-Luc does several sketches by way of explanation.

13 September, 2022

10am. Via the daily newspaper *Libération*, to which he was close, the world at large reads about Jean-Luc Godard's suicide.

10am, the time of the appointment, but not when he took the toxic substance. Meaning that, at the instant when everyone is rooted to the spot or bursting into tears, Jean-Luc Godard is still alive.

Still alive.

The main thing is to never be synchronous.

Still alive.

A final film full of silence to further amplify the sound and fury, howling out the conflicts of the twentieth and twenty-first centuries, and ending in full flight with one of the most painful, prolonged and unresolved conflicts of all, that between Israel and Palestine.

Still alive.

The soundtrack of *Announcement of the Film 'Phony Wars' (1st shoot)*.
Judith Lerner shouts: 'Lyon, 1943, the Gestapo!'

9 février 1943: rafle de la rue Sainte-Catherine à Lyon. Quatre-vingt-six Juifs arrêtés par la Gestapo sur ordre de Klaus Barbie. Parmi les victimes, Simon Badinter, le père de Robert Badinter, futur Ministre de la Justice d'un gouvernement socialiste qui, en 1981, supprimera la peine de mort en dépit de l'opposition de l'opinion publique française.

Toujours en vie.

Le dernier plan, le dernier son : nous les laisser en l'état d'une plaie à jamais ouverte.

Toujours en vie.

Un dernier film non pour se dégager du monde, au contraire pour l'affronter encore dans ce qu'il contient de plus terrifiant.

Toujours en vie.

Un dernier film qui trouve encore de nouveaux moyens pour hurler face au caractère interminable de l'horreur humaine.

Toujours en vie.

Sa sagesse moderne.

Toujours en vie.

Un dernier film gros de tous les films qui équivalent à leurs ébauches, si souvent plus puissantes que les films terminés.

Toujours en vie.

Un dernier film gros de tous les films non-faits qui révèlent une idée, un désir, une nécessité, souvent tellement plus parfaits que les films achevés.

Toujours en vie.

Le cinéma.

9 February, 1943: a raid on Rue Sainte-Catherine in Lyon. Eighty-six Jews are arrested by the Gestapo, on Klaus Barbie's orders. Among the victims: Simon Badinter, the father of Robert Badinter, future Minister of Justice in a socialist government which, in 1981, would abolish the death penalty despite opposition from French public opinion.

Still alive.

The last shot, the last sound: leaving them to us as a forever open wound.

Still alive.

A final film not to free himself from the world, but on the contrary to confront the world once again in its most terrifying aspect.

Still alive.

A final film again finding new ways to howl in the face of the interminable nature of human horror.

Still alive.

His modern wisdom.

Still alive.

A final film fortified by all the films which are equal to their drafts, and so often more powerful than the finished films.

Still alive.

A final film fortified by all the unrealised films which reveal an idea, a desire, a necessity, and are often far more perfect than previous achievements.

Still alive.

The cinema.

(An iterative index of sources and works cited.)

Agamben, Giorgio, *A che punto siamo? L'epidemia come politica* / tr. Dani, Valeria, *Where are We Now? The Epidemic as Politics* (Lanham, MD: Rowman & Littlefield, 2021)

Agamben, Giorgio, *Quando la casa brucia* / tr. Attell, Kevin, *When the House Burns Down* (Calcutta: Seagull Books, 2022)

Adler, David, *Eating the Elvis Presley Way* (London: John Blake Publishing, 2001)

(p.223) Adolfi, John G., *The Silent Voice / The Man who Played God* (1932), 80m

Allen, Lewis, *Suddenly* (1954), 77m

(p.128) Allison, Jerry; Holly, Buddy; & Petty, Norman, 'That'll be the day,' Buddy Holly & the Three Tunes, *That'll Be the Day* (Decca, 1956), 2m16

(p.222) Anderson, Lindsay, *The Whales of August* (1987), 90m

(p.45) Anger, Kenneth, *Hollywood Babylone / Hollywood Babylon* (Paris: J.J. Pauvert, 1959; Phoenix, AZ: Associated Professional Services, 1965)

(p.189) Anka, Paul, (A) 'You Are My Destiny' / (B) 'When I Stop Loving You, That'll Be the Day' (ABC-Paramount, 1957), 2m42 / 1m51

(p.70) Archer, Jeffrey, *Kane & Abel* (London: Hodder & Stoughton, 1979)

(p.44) Armstrong, Samuel; Elliotte, John; Ferguson, Norm; Jackson, Wilfred; & Kinney, Jack, *Dumbo* (1941), 64m

(p.170) Arnold, Danny & Flicker, Theodore J., *Barney Miller* (ABC, 1975–1982), 25m, *Episodic*

Aronson, Marc, *Master of Deceit: J. Edgar Hoover & America in the Age of Lies* (Somerville, MA: Candlewick Press, 2012)

(p.191) Ashley, John, (A) 'The Hangman' / (B) 'The Net' (Dot Records, 1959), 2m30 / 2m20

(p.36) Avildsen, John G., *Rocky* (1976), 119m

Babbs, O.B. & Catoline, A.J., *Timothy Leary's Last Trip* (1997), 56m

(p.75) Bare, Richard L., *So This is Hollywood* (NBC, 1955), 30m, *Episodic*

(p.189) Bartholomew, Dave; King, Pearl; & Seinman, Anita (as performed by Presley, Elvis), 'One Night of Sin' (RCA Victor, 1958), 2m32 [released as 'One Night,' with the (A) side, Schroeder, Aaron & Hill, David, 'I Got Stung,' 1m51]

(p.204) Bartol, Vladimir, *Alamut* (1938), tr. Biggins, Michael (Scala House Press, 2004)

(p.152) Baum, Bernie; Giant, Bill; & Kaye, Florence (as performed by Presley, Elvis), 'Poison Ivy League,' *Roustabout* (RCA Victor, 1964), 2m04

(p.152) Baum, Bernie; Giant, Bill; & Kaye, Florence (as performed by Presley, Elvis), 'Wolf Call,' *Girl Happy* (RCA Victor, 1965), 1m28

(p.178) Baverstock, Donald, *Songs of Praise* (BBC, 1961 & on), 35m, *Episodic*

Beauchamp, Cari, *Joseph P. Kennedy's Hollywood Years* (London: Faber & Faber, 2009)

(p.82) Beauvoir, Simone de; Merleau-Ponty, Maurice; & Sartre, Jean-Paul, *Les Temps Modernes / Modern Times* (Gallimard, Bimonthly, 1945–2019)

Beineke, John, *Hoosier Public Enemy: A Life of John Dillinger* (Bloomington, IN: Indiana Historical Society, 2014)

(p.39) Ben-Dov, Ya'ackov, *Shivat Zion / Return to Zion* (1920), 45m

(p.147) Bennett, Roy C. (as performed by Presley, Elvis), 'A Cane & a High Starched Collar,' *Flaming Star* (RCA Victor, 1960), 1m47

(p.90) Bergman, Ingmar, *Djävulens öga / The Devil's Eye* (1960), 87m

(p.191) Bernstein, Elmer (& the City of Prague Philharmonic Orchestra), 'McBain / Main Titles,' 2m38 [see Curtiz, Michael, *The Comancheros* (1961), 107m]

(p.155)	Berry, Chuck (as performed by Presley, Elvis), 'Promised Land,' *Promised Land* (RCA, 1975), 2m58
(p.145)	Bilbrew, A.B. (as performed by The Ramparts), (A) 'The Death of Emmett Till' [Part I] / (B) 'The Death of Emmett Till' [Part II] (Dootone Records, 1956), 2m54 / 2m55
(p.150)	Blackwell, Otis & Scott, Winfield (as performed by Presley, Elvis), 'We're Coming in Loaded,' *Girls! Girls! Girls!* (RCA Victor, 1962), 1m20
(p.98)	Boetticher, Budd, *A Time for Dying* (1969), 73m
(p.273)	Bogdanovich, Peter, *The Last Picture Show* (1971), 118m
(p.57)	Boleslavsky, Richard; Dan, Allan; Goulding, Edmund; Reisner, Charles; Rowland, Roy; Mack, Russell; & Wood, Sam (but mostly Boleslavsky), *Hollywood Party / Working Title(s): The Hollywood Revue of 1933 & Star-Spangled Banquet* (1934), 68m
(p.193)	Bonaccorti, Enrica & Modugno, Domenico, 'Amara terra mia,' *Tutto modugno* (RCA, 1973), 3m25
(p.104)	Boulting, Roy, *Twisted Nerve* (1968), 118m
(p.102)	Bricusse, Leslie & Barry, John (as sung by Sinatra, Nancy), (A) 'You Only Live Twice' / (B) Wheeler, Billy Edd & Lieber, Jerry, 'Jackson' (Reprise, 1967), 2m55 / 3m08
(p.193)	Bruch, Max (as performed by Bell, Joshua & the Academy of St Martin in the Fields), 'Violin Concerto No. 1 in G Minor, Op. 26: 1. Vorspiel. Allegro moderato,' *Bruch, Mendelssohn, Mozart Violin Concertos* (Decca, 1988), 8m42
(p.89)	Buchan, John, *Pilgrim's Way: An Essay in Recollection* (Cambridge, MA: Houghton Mifflin, 1940)
(p.191)	Ein grosses Bundesblasorchester mit Männerchor, 'In einem Polenstädtchen,' *Marches Traditionnelles Allemandes* (Disques Vogue, 1972), 3m20
(p.228)	Burroughs, William S., 'A Thanksgiving Prayer,' *Dead City Radio* (Island Records, 1990), 3m22
(p.230)	Burroughs, William S., & Cobain, Kurt, 'The "Priest" They Called Him' (Tim / Kerr Records, 1993), 2m23
(p.269)	Burton, Tim, *Batman* (1989), 126m
(p.252–256)	Burton, Tim, *Big Fish* (2003), 125m
(p.151)	Byers, Joy (as performed by Presley, Elvis), 'Hard Knocks,' *Roustabout* (RCA Victor, 1964), 1m45
(p.143)	Calhoun, Claude (as performed by Presley, Elvis), (A) 'Shake, Rattle & Roll' / (B) Price, Lloyd, 'Lawdy, Miss Clawdy' (RCA Victor, 1956), 2m30 / 2m07
(p.244)	Campbell, Martin, *GoldenEye* (1995), 130m
(pp.226–239)	Campion, Jane, *The Piano* (1993), 121m
(p.139)	Capra, Frank, *It's a Wonderful Life* (1946), 131m
(p.103)	Capra, Frank, *Hole in the Head* (1959), 120m
(p.82)	Chandler, Raymond, *The Big Sleep* (New York, NY: Alfred A. Knopf, 1939)
(pp.30–41)	Chaplin, Charlie, *The Kid* (1921), 53m
(p.36)	Chaplin, Charlie, *Modern Times* (1936), 87m
	Chatwin, Bruce, *The Viceroy of Ouidah* (London: Jonathan Cape, 1980)
(p.215)	Chatwin, Bruce, *On the Black Hill* (London: Jonathan Cape, 1982)
	Chatwin, Bruce, *The Songlines* (London: Franklin Press, 1987)
	Chatwin, Bruce, *Utz* (London: Pan Macmillan, 1989)
(p.191)	Chevalier, Maurice & Cicognini, Alessandro, *A Breath of Scandal: Music from the Motion Picture Soundtrack* (Imperial, 1960)

(pp.64-70) St. Clair, Malcom, *The Lighthouse by the Sea* (1934), 70m
(p.230) Cobain, Kurt, 'Heart Shaped Box,' *In Utero* (David Geffen Company, 1993), 4.42m
(p.159) Coen, John & Coen, Ethan, *Inside Llewyn Davis* (2013), 105m
Cohen, David, *Phill Ochs: A Bio-Bibliography* (Westport, CT: Greenwood, 1999)
(pp.122-125) Cohen, Larry, *God Told Me To* (1976), 91m
(p.193) Cohen, Leonard, 'Sisters of Mercy,' *Songs of Leonard Cohen* (Columbia, 1967), 3m34
(p.189) Cohen, Leonard, 'So Long, Marianne,' *Songs of Leonard Cohen* (Columbia, 1967), 5m43
(p.193) Cohen, Leonard, 'Suzanne,' *Songs of Leonard Cohen* (Columbia, 1967), 3m51
(p.189) Cohen, Leonard, 'Teachers,' *Songs of Leonard Cohen* (Columbia, 1967), 3m04
(p.193) Cohen, Leonard, 'Winter Lady,' *Songs of Leonard Cohen* (Columbia, 1967), 2m17
(p.193) Cohen, Leonard, 'Bird on the Wire,' *Songs from a Room* (Columbia, 1969), 3m28
(p.193) Cohen, Leonard, 'Chelsea Hotel #2,' *New Songs for the Old Ceremony* (Columbia, 1974), 3m06
(p.189) Cohen, Leonard, 'Lover Lover Lover,' *New Skin for the Old Ceremony* (Columbia, 1974), 3m21
(p.189) Cohen, Leonard, 'Why Don't You Try,' *New Skin for the Old Ceremony* (Columbia, 1974), 3m50
(p.271) Cohen, Norman, *Confessions of a Pop Performer* (1975), 91m
(p.228) Coleman, Jaz; Ferguson, Paul; Raven, Paul; & Walker, Kevin (as performed by Killing Joke), (A) 'Eighties' / (B) 'Coming Mix' (E.G., 1984), 3m51 / 3m57
(p.189) Collins, Tommy (as performed by The Berlin Ramblers), 'High on a Hilltop,' *Bonnie & Clyde* (Tip, 1967), 2m39
(p.295) Columbus, Chris, *Home Alone* (1990), 103m
(p.191) Comedian Harmonists, (A) 'Veronika, der Lenz ist da' / (B) 'Wochenend Und Sonnenschein' (Electrola Gesellschaft, 1930), 3m48 / 3m11
(p.263) Cooley, Josh, *Toy Story 4* (2019), 100m
(p.99) Coppola, Francis Ford, *Apocalypse Now* (1979), 183m
(pp.165-166) Corbijn, Anton, *Control* (2007), 122m
(p.178) Cowgill, Bryan & Fox, Paul, *Olympic Grandstand* (BBC, 1958-2007), Various Running Time(s), *Episodic*
(p.149) Cukor, George, *Wild is the Wind* (1957), 114m
(p.276) Cuny, Alain, *L'annonce faite à Marie* / *The Annunciation of Marie* (1991), 91m
(p.67) Cummings, Irving, *The Man from Hell's River* (1922), [5 Reels]
(p.166) Curtis, Deborah, *Touching from a Distance* (London: Faber & Faber, 1995)
(p.185) Curtiz, Michael, *Die Sklavenkönigin* / *The Moon of Israel* (1924), 103m
(pp.180-195) Curtiz, Michael, *20,000 Years in Sing Sing* (1932), 99m
(p.186) Curtiz, Michael, *The Charge of the Light Brigade* (1936), 115m
(p.149) Curtiz, Michael, *Angels with Dirty Faces* (1938), 97m
(pp.55, 106, 186, & 149) Curtiz, Michael, *Casablanca* (1942), 102m
(p. 149) Curtiz, Michael, *Mildred Pierce* (1945), 111m
(pp.187-188) Curtiz, Michael, *Flamingo Road* (1949), 94m
(p.145-146) Curtiz, Michael, *King Creole* (1958), 116m
Cutler, Chris, *File Under Popular: Theoretical & Critical Writings on Music* (New York, NY: Autonomedia, 1985)

(p.170)   Dahl, Roald, *Tales of the Unexpected* (Anglia Television, 1979–1988), 25m, *Episodic*

(p.191)   Dalida, 'Am Tag als der Regen kam,' *Rendez-vous mit Dalida* (Sinetone AMR, 1961), 2m53

(pp.103–104) Damiano, Gerard, *Deep Throat* (1972), 61m

(p.243)   Däniken, Erich von, *Erinnerungen an die Zukunft: Ungelöste Rätsel der Vergangenheit / Chariots of the Gods? Unsolved Mysteries of the Past* (Berlin: Econ-Verlag, 1968; New York, NY: Putnam, 1968)

(p.244)   Davies, Andrew, *Chain Reaction* (1996), 107m

(p.224)   Davis, Bette, *The Lonely Life: An Autobiography* (New York, NY: Putnam's, 1962)

            Davis, Miles, *Ascenseur pour l'échafaud / Elevator to the Gallows* (Fontana, 1958)

(p.81)   Delannoy, Jean, *The Hunchback of Notre Dame* (1956), 115m

(p.81)   Delaunay, Charles & Panassié, Hugues, *Circulaire du Hot Club de France* (a short-lived bulletin periodical, 1921)

(p.100)   DeLillo, Don, *Libra* (New York, NY: Viking, 1988)

(p.101)   DeLillo, Don, *Underworld* (New York, NY: Scribner, 1997)

(p.255)   Demme, Jonathan, *Swimming to Cambodia* (1987), 85m

(p.168)   Demme, Jonathan, *The Silence of the Lambs* (1991), 118m

(p.189)   Dietrich, Marlene; Leip, Hans; & Schultze, Norbert (as performed by Dietrich, Marlene, (A) 'Lili Marleen' / (B) Alstone, Alex; Tabet, André Gaston Isaac, 'Symphonie' (Decca, 1945), 4m45 / 3m05

(pp.72–76) Dorsey Bros., *Stage Show* (1955), 30m

(p.74)   Dorsey, Tommy (as performed by Vaughan, Sarah), (A) 'You Taught Me to Love Again' / (B) Just Friends,' with Carpenter, Charles; Dorsey, Tommy; & Woode, Henri (Columbia, 1950), 3m18 / 3m24

(p.171)   Dostoyevsky, Fyodor, *Идиот / tr.* Whishaw, Frederick, *The Idiot* (Moscow: *The Russian Messenger* [Serialised, 1868–1869]; London: Henry Vizetelly, 1886)

            Doyle, Jonathan, 'Larry Cohen: The Last Interview,' *Little White Lies* (26 March, 2019)

            Draycott, Philip; Ferguson, Nicholas; Hanson, Valerie; Kemp-Welch, Joan; McBain, Kenny; Mills, Brian; & Moffatt, Peter, *Lady Killers* (Granada, 1980–1981), 60m, *Episodic*

(pp.50–62) Dyke, W.S., & Cukor, G, *Manhattan Melodrama* (1934), 99m

(p.88)   Dylan, Bob, 'Murder Most Foul,' *Rough & Rowdy Ways* (Columbia Records, 2020), 16m56

(p.74)   Eastwood, Clint, *Bird* (1988), 161m

(p.177)   Edwards, Blake, *The Pink Panther* (1963), 113m

            Eisner, Lotte H., *Murnau* (Berkeley, CA: University of California Press, 1973)

            Eliot, Marc, *Phil Ochs, Death of a Rebel* (London: Omnibus Press, 1990)

(p.149)   Enright, Ray, *The Angels Wash Their Faces* (1939), 86m

            Epstein, Jerry, *Remembering Charlie: A Pictorial Biography* (London: Bloomsbury, 1988)

(p.249)   Fassbinder, Rainer Werner, *In einem Jahr mit 13 Monden / In a Year with Thirteen Moons* (1978), 124m

(p.106, 187) Fassbinder, Rainer Werner, *Die Ehe der Maria Braun / The Marriage of Maria Braun* (1978), 120m

(p.182)   Fassbinder, Rainer Werner, *Berlin Alexanderplatz* (1980), *Episodic*, 894m

(p.187)   Fassbinder, Rainer Werner, *Lili Marleen* (1981), 120m

Fassbinder, Rainer Werner, (eds.) Lensing, Leo A. & Töteberg, Michael, (tr.) Winston, Krishna, *The Anarchy of the Imagination: Interviews, Essays, Notes* (Baltimore, MD: John Hopkins University Press, 1992)

Fassbinder, Rainer Werner, (ed.) Kardish, Laurence & Lorenz, Juliane, *Rainer Werner Fassbinder* (New York, NY: The Museum of Modern Art, 1997)

(p.90)   Fellini, Federico, *La Dolce Vita* (1960), 165m

Ferreri, Marco, *Dillinger is Dead* (1969), 90m

(p.189)   Ferry, Brian & Mackay, Andy (as performed by Roxy Music), 'A Song for Europe,' *Stranded* (Island, 1973)

Fielding, Henry, *The History of Tom Jones, a Foundling* (London: Andrew Millar, 1749)

(p.236)   Figgis, Mike, *Leaving Las Vegas* (1995), 111m

Fisher, Austin, *Radical Frontiers in the Spaghetti Western: Politics, Violence, and Popular Italian Cinema* (London: I.B. Tauris, 2011)

(p.45)   Flaherty, Robert, Van Dyke, W.S., *White Shadows in the South Seas* (1928), 88m

(p.83)   Flaubert, Gustave, *Madame Bovary* (Paris: Michel Lévy Frères, 1857; tr. Eleanor Marx, London: Vizetelly & Co., 1886)

(p.93)   Fleming, Ian, *Casino Royale* (London: Jonathan Cape, 1953)

(p.90)   Fleming, Ian, *Live & Let Die* (London: Jonathan Cape, 1954)

(p.89, 140)   Fleming, Ian, *Dr. No* (London: Jonathan Cape, 1957)

(pp.89, 93)   Fleming, Ian, *From Russia, with Love* (Jonathan Cape, 1957)

(p.89)   Fleming, Ian, *The Spy Who Loved Me* (London: Jonathan Cape, 1962)

(p.139)   Fleming, Victor, *The Way of All Flesh* (1927), Nine Reels

(pp.103, 105)   Fleming, Victor, *Gone with the Wind* (1939), 221m

(p.106)   Ford, John, *The Searchers* (1954), 119m

(pp.106, 126–134, 159)   Forman, Milos, *One Flew Over the Cuckoo's Nest* (1975), 113m

(p.66)   Frank, Anne, *Het Achterhuis* / tr. Mooyaart-Doubleday, Barbara, *The Annex* (New York, NY: Doubleday, 1952), published latterly as *Anne Frank: The Diary of a Young Girl* by Doubleday & Company (United States) and Vallentine Mitchell (United Kingdom), 1952.

(p.102)   Frankenheimer, John, *The Manchurian Candidate* (1962), 126m

(p.67)   Franklin, Chester M., *Where the North Begins* (1923), 60m

Frayling, Christopher, *Sergio Leone: Something to Do with Death* (London: Faber & Faber, 2000)

Frayling, Christopher, *Once Upon a Time in Italy: The Westerns of Sergio Leone* (New York, NY: Harry N. Abrams, 2005)

(p.129)   Freedman, Jerry, *Kansas City Bomber* (1972), 99m

(p.140)   Fukunaga, Cary Joji, *No Time to Die* (2021), 163m

Gage, Beverley, *G-Man: J. Edgar Hoover & the Making of the American Century* (New York, NY: Viking, 2022)

(pp.78–85)   Gast, M., *I Spit on Your Graves* (1959), 110m

Gerh, Herbert; Lorenz, Juliane; & Schmid, Marion, *Chaos as Usual: Conversations about Rainer Werner Fassbinder* (New York, NY: Applause, 1997)

(p.58)   Gilbert, Burt, *Three Little Pigs* (1933), 9m

(p.102)   Gilbert, Lewis, *You Only Live Twice* (1967), 117m

(pp.89, 90, 105, 136–156, 159, 176)   Gilbert, Lewis, *The Spy Who Loved Me* (1975), 125m

(p.189)   Gilkyson, Terry; Dear, Richard; & Miller, Frank (as performed by Martin, Dean), 'Memories Are Made of This' (Capitol, 1955), 2m15

Girardin, G. Russell & Helmer, William J., *Dillinger: The Untold Story*, Anniversary Ed. (Bloomington, IN: Indiana University Press, 2009)

(p.189)   Glick, Elmo (an occasional pseudonym for the work of Lieber, Jerry & Stoller, Mike) & King, Ben E. (as performed by King, Ben E.), (A) 'Stand by Me' / (B) 'On the Horizon' (Atco, 1961), 2m57 / 2m18

(pp.274–277, 279–291)   Godard, Jean-Luc, *Film annonce du film Drôles de Guerres (1er tournage)* / *Announcement of the Film 'Phony Wars' (1st shoot)* (2023), 20m

(p.170)   Goff, Ivan & Roberts, Ben, *Charlie's Angels* (ABC, 1976–1981), 50m, *Episodic*

(p.82)   Gondry, Michel, *L'écume des jours* / *Mood Indigo* (2013), 131m

(p.191)   Goodman, Benny (& his Orchestra), (A) 'Mission to Moscow' / (B) 'It's Always You' (Columbia, 1942), 2m38 / 3m08

(p.74)   Gordon, Max, *Life at the Village Vanguard* (New York: Bernard Geiss Associates, 1963)

Gordon, Max & Funke, Lewis, *Max Gordon Presents* (New York: Bernard Geiss Associates, 1963)

Gorn, Elliot J., *Dillinger's Wild Ride: The Year that Made America's Public Enemy Number One* (New York, NY: Oxford University Press, 2009)

(p.154)   Graham, William, *Change of Habit* (1969), 93m

(p.189)   Granata, Rocco, 'Buona Notte bambino,' German version (VM Records, 1988), 3m05

(p.191)   Grant, Gogi & The Ray Heindorf Orchestra, 'On the Sunnyside of the Street,' 2m09, *The Helen Morgan Story* (RCA Victor, 1957) [see Curtiz, Michael, *The Helen Morgan Story* (1957), 118m]

(p.191)   Grant, Gogi & The Ray Heindorf Orchestra, 'Speak to Me of Love,' 1m51, *The Helen Morgan Story* (RCA Victor, 1957) [see Curtiz, Michael, *The Helen Morgan Story* (1957), 118m]

(p.191)   Grant, Gogi & The Ray Heindorf Orchestra, 'Why Was I Born,' *The Helen Morgan Story* (RCA Victor, 1957), 2m28 [see Curtiz, Michael, *The Helen Morgan Story* (1957), 118m]

(p.189)   Green, Peter (as performed by Fleetwood Mac), 'Albatross' (CBS, 1968), 3m07

(p.103)   Griffith, D.W., *Birth of a Nation* (1915), 187m

Guralnick, Peter, *Last Train to Memphis: The Rise of Elvis Presley* (Boston, MA: Little, Brown, 1994)

Halberstam, David, *The Best & the Brightest* (New York, NY: Random House, 1972)

(p.204)   Hallström, Lasse, *Mitt liv som hund* / *My Life as a Dog* (1985), 101m

(p.105)   Hamilton, Guy, *Goldfinger* (1964), 110m

(p.105)   Hamilton, Guy, *Diamonds are Forever* (1971), 120m

(pp.104–105)   Hamilton, Guy, *The Man with the Golden Gun* (1974), 125m

Hammer, Les, *F.W. Murnau: For the Record* (Morgan Hill, CA: Bookstand Publishing, 2010)

(p.103)   Hand, David; Cottrell, William; Jackson, Wilfred; Morey, Larry; Pearce, Perce; & Sharpsteen, Ben, *Snow White & the Seven Dwarfs* (1937), 83m

(p.170)   Harding, Sarah; Richards, David; James, Pedr; Kitchen, Charles; Robinson, Matthew; Lawrence, Diarmuid, *The Practice* (Granada, 1985–1986), 60m, *Episodic*

(p.57)   Hart, Lorenz, & Rogers, Richard, 'Blue Moon' (Robins Music, 1934), 2m15

(p.93)   Hathaway, Henry, *Niagara* (1953), 92m

(p.149)   Hathaway, Henry, *True Grit* (1969), 128m
(p.191)   Hazlewood, Lee (as performed by Sanford Clark), (A) 'Run Boy Run' /
            (B) 'New Kind of Fool (London Records, 1959), 2m08 / 1m28
(p.202)   Hebborn, Eric, *Art Forger's Handbook* (London: Overlook, 1997,
            Posthumous)
(p.59)   Heisler, Stuart, *I Died a Thousand Times* (1955), 109m
(p.53)   Herodotus, tr. A.D. Godley, *The Persian Wars, Vol. II., Books III–IV*
            (Cambridge, MA: Harvard University Press / Loeb Classical
            Library, 1921)
(p.191)   Herrmann, Bernard, 'The Red Sea & Childhood,' 2m41 [see Curtiz,
            Michael, *The Egyptian* (1954), 140m]
(p.191)   Herrmann, Bernard, 'The Ruins,' 2m34 [see Curtiz, Michael, *The
            Egyptian* (1954), 140m]
(pp.162–172) Herzog, Werner, *Stroszek* (1977), 116m
            Herzog, Werner, *Nosferatu the Vampyre* (1979), 124m
(p.215)   Herzog, Werner, *Cobra Verde* (1987), 111m
(pp.212–216) Herzog, Werner, *Herdsman of the Sun* (1989), 50m
            Herzog, Werner, *Vom Gehen im Eis* / tr. Herzog, Martje & Greenberg,
            Allan (Minneapolis, MN: University of Minnesota Press, 2015)
            Herzog, Werner, *Nomad: In the Footsteps of Bruce Chatwin* (2019), 89m
(p.103)   Heusen, Jimmy Van & Cahn, Sammy (as sung by Sinatra, Frank),
            (A) 'High Hopes' / (B) ' All My Tomorrows' (Capitol, 1959),
            2m41 / 3m13
(p.244)   Hewitt, Don & Leonard, Bill, *60 Minutes* (CBS, 1968 & on), 60m [with
            commercials], *Episodic*
(pp.174–179) Hickox, Douglas, *Brannigan* (1975), 111m
(p.171)   Kiken, Nat, *The Phil Silvers Show* AKA *Sergeant Bilko* (CBS, 1955–1959),
            30m, *Episodic*
            Hill, Clint & McCubbin, Lisa, *Five Presidents: My Extraordinary
            Journey with Eisenhower, Kennedy, Johnson, Nixon, & Ford*
            (London: Simon & Schuster, 2016)
(p.89)   Hitchcock, Alfred, *The 39 Steps* (1935), 81m
(p.168)   Hitchcock, Alfred, *Psycho* (1960), 109m
            Hook, Peter, *Unknown Pleasures: Inside Joy Division* (London:
            Simon & Schuster, 2012)
(p.168)   Hooper, Tobe, *Texas Chainsaw Massacre* (1974), 83m
(pp.160, 273) Hopper, Dennis, *Easy Rider* (1969), 95m
(p.273)   Hopper, Dennis, *The Last Movie* (1971), 108m
(p.193)   Horowitz, Vladimir, 'Kinderszenen, from Foreign Lands & People
            (Kinderszenen, op. 15: Von fremden Ländern und Menschen),'
            Kinderszenen, op. 15: Von fremden Ländern und Menschen (Sony,
            1962), 1m33
            Horowitz, Vladimir, *Horowitz Plays Schumann* (RCA Gold Seal, 1989)
(p.191)   Horton, Johnny, (A) 'The Battle of New Orleans' [Traditional] /
            (B) 'All for the Love of a Girl' (Columbia, 1959), 2m33 / 2m46
(p.189)   Hosen, Athena & Gordon, Hall (as performed by Francis, Connie),
            'Schöner fremder Mann' (MGM Records, 1961), 2m42
(p.106)   Huston, John, *The Treasure of the Sierra Madre* (1925), 126m
(p.106)   Huston, John, *Maltese Falcon* (1941), 101m
(p.106)   Huston, John, *Key Largo* (1948), 101m
(p.106)   Huston, John, *The African Queen* (1951), 105m
(p.90)   Huston, John, *The Misfits* (1961), 124m
(pp.139, 176) Huston, John, *Casino Royale* (1967), 137m
(p.189)   Hütter, Ralf; Schneider, Florian; & Schult, Emil (as performed
            by Kraftwerk), 'Radio-Aktivität' / 'Radioactivity,' *Radioactivity*
            (EMI, 1975), 6m42

(p.38)   Isaak, Chris, 'Baby Did a Bad, Bad Thing,' *Forever Blue* (Reprise
              Records, 1995), 2m53
              Isenberg, Noah, *We'll Always Have Casablanca: The Life, Legend
              & Afterlife of Hollywood's Most Beloved Movie* (London: Faber &
              Faber, 2017)
(p.244)   Jackson, Peter, *The Frighteners* (1996), 123m
(p.189)   Jagger, Mick & Richards, Keith (as performed by The Rolling Stones),
              'We Love You,' *The Rolling Stones* (Decca, 1967), 4m38
(p.89)   James, Marquis, *The Raven: A Biography of Sam Houston* (Indiana-
              polis, IA: Bobbs-Merrill, 1929)
(p.256)   Joffé, Roland, *The Killing Fields* (1984), 141m
(p.35)   Kafka, Franz, *Der Process* / tr. Willa & Edwin Muir, *The Trial* (Berlin:
              Verlag die Schmiede, 1925; London: Victor Gollancz, 1937)
(p.34)   Kafka, Franz, 'Forschungen eines Hunde' / 'Investigations of a Dog'
              (1922), published posthumously in *Beim Bau der Chinesischen
              Mauer* (Berlin, 1931); see Kafka, Franz, *The Complete Stories*
              (New York, NY: The Schocken Kafka Library; Penguin Random
              House, 1995)
              Kafka, Franz, (ed.) Brod, Max, tr. Benjamin, Ross, *Diaries* (New York,
              NY: The Schocken Kafka Library; Penguin Random House, 2023)
(pp. 143, 144) Kanter, Hal, *Loving You* (1957), 102m
(p.228)   Kaplan, Jonathan, *Over the Edge* (1979), 95m
(p.191)   Karas, Anton, (A) 'The Harry Lime Theme' / (B) 'The Café Mozart
              Waltz' (Decca, 1949), 2m58 / 2m16
(p.191)   Karl-Heinz-Steinfeld-Chor, 'Horch, was kommt von draussen rein,'
              Schwarzwald-Souvenir (Maritim, Unknown), 2m17
              Katz, Robert & Berling, Peter, *Love is Colder than Death: The Life &
              Times of Rainer Werner Fassbinder* (London: Jonathan Cape, 1987)
(p.104)   Kelly, James, *What the Peeper Saw* (1972), 95m
              Kennedy, John F., *Why England Slept* (Montclair, NJ: Wilfred Funk,
              1940)
              Kennedy, John F. & Sorenson, Ted, *Profiles in Courage* (New York, NY:
              Harper & Brothers, 1956)
              Kennedy, John F., *Prelude to Leadership: The European Diary of John
              F. Kennedy, Summer 1945* (Washington DC: Regnery, 1995)
              Kennedy, John F., (ed.) Fensch, Thomas, T*he Kennedy-Krushchev
              Letters* (New Delhi: New Century Books, 2002)
              Kennedy, John F., *A Nation of Immigrants, Reprint* (New York, NY:
              Harper Perennial, 2018)
(p.159)   Kerouac, Jack, *On the Road* (New York, NY: Viking, 1957)
(p.189)   Kern, Jerome & Harbach, Otto A. (as performed by The Platters),
              (A) 'Smoke Gets in Your Eyes' / (B) Ram, Buck, 'No Matter What
              You Are' (Mercury, 1958), 2m39
(pp.131, 132, 159)   Kesey, Ken, *One Flew Over the Cuckoo's Nest* (New York, NY:
              Viking, 1962)
(p.270)   Kiarostami, Abbas, *Klūzāp, nemā-ye nazdīk / Close-Up* (1990), 98m
(p.139)   King, Louis, *The Way of All Flesh* (1940), 86m
(p.94)   Kirkbride, Ronald, *The Short Night* (London: Pan Books, 1971)
(p.179)   Kosinski, Jerzy, *Being There* (San Diego, CA: Harcourt Brace, 1971)
(p.178)   Kotcheff, Ted, *Billy Two Hats* (1974), 100m
(p.189)   Kristofferson, Kris, 'Me & Bobby McGee,' *Kristofferson* (Monument,
              1970), 4m23
(p.35)   Kropotkin, Peter, *Memoirs of a Revolutionist* (Boston, MA: Houghton,
              Mifflin & Co., Riverside, 1899)
(p.131)   Kubrick, Stanley, *Spartacus* (1960), 197m

(p.102)	Kubrick, Stanley, *Dr. Strangelove* (1964), 95m
(p.106)	Kubrick, Stanley, *2001: A Space Odyssey* (1968), 139m
	Kubrick, Stanley, *The Moon Landing* (1969)
(p.104)	Kubrick, Stanley, *A Clockwork Orange* (1971), 136m
(pp.30–41)	Kubrick, Stanley, *Barry Lyndon* (1975), 203m
(p. 38)	Kubrick, Stanley, *The Shining* (1980), 146m
(pp.30–41)	Kubrick, Stanley, *Eyes Wide Shut*, Trailer (1999), .59s
(p.49)	Lang, Fritz, *M* (1931), 117m
(p.49)	Lang, Fritz, *The Testament of Dr. Marbuse* (1933), 124m
(p.263)	Lasseter, John, *Toy Story* (1995), 81m
(p.106)	Lee, Harper, *To Kill a Mockingbird* (Philadelphia, PA: J.B. Lippincott & Co., 1960)
(p.144)	Leiber, Jerry & Stoller, Mike (as performed by Presley, Elvis) 'Hot Dog,' *Loving You* (RCA Victor, 1957), 1m15
(p.191)	Leiber, Jerry & Stoller, Mike (as performed by Presley, Elvis) 'Trouble,' *King Creole* (RCA Victor, 1958), 2m16
(pp.240–251)	Leigh, Mike, *Secrets & Lies* (1996), 136m
(p.263)	Lennon, John & McCartney, Paul, (A) 'Strawberry Fields Forever' / (B) 'Penny Lane' (Parlophone, 1967), 4m07 / 3m03
(pp.105–106)	Leone, Sergio, *Per un pugno di dollari* / *A Fistful of Dollars* (1964, 1965), 99m
(pp.105–106)	Leone, Sergio, *Per qualche dollaro in più* / *For a Few Dollars More* (1965), 132m
	Lubin, David M., *Shooting Kennedy: JFK & the Culture of Hollywood* (Berkeley, CA: University of California Press, 2003)
	Lebensztejn, Jean-Claude, *Figures pissantes, 1280–2014* / tr. Nagy, Jeff, *Pissing Figures, 1280–2014*
(pp.99–101)	Lerner, Irving, *Cry of Battle* (1963), 99m
(p.149)	LeRoy, Mervyn, *I am a Fugitive from a Chain Gang* (1932), 93m
	Lewin, Albert, *The Picture of Dorian Gray* (1945), 110m
(p.177)	Lewis, Roger, *The Life & Death of Peter Sellers* (London: Century, 1994)
(p.149)	Litvak, Anatole, *The Amazing Dr. Clitterhouse* (1938), 87m
	Logevall, Frederik, *JFK: Coming of Age in the American Century* (New York, NY: Random House, 2020)
(p.214)	Loncke, Sandrine, *Dance with the Woddaabes* (2010), 90m
(p.75)	Lord, Del, *Sneezing Beezers* (1925), [2 Reels]
(p.115)	Loy, Nanni, *Il padre di famiglia* / *The Head of the Family* (1968), 110m
	Louderback, Lew, *Pretty Boy, Baby Face—I Love You: The Gangsters of the '30s & their Molls* (Hodder & Stoughton, 1969)
(pp.90, 138)	Lucas, George, *Star Wars* (1977), 121m
(p.149)	Lupino, Ida, *The Hitchhiker* (1953), 71m
(p.172)	Macdonald, John D., *The Executioners* (New York, NY: Simon & Schuster, 1957)
	Mackendrick, Alexander, *The Ladykillers* (1955), 91m
(p.191)	Malando, Arie & his Orchestra, (A) 'Guapita' / (B) 'Olé Guapa' (Philips, 1956), 3m / 2m50
(p.85)	Malle, Louis, *Ascenseur pour l'échafaud* / *Elevator to the Gallows* (1958), 91m
(p.231)	Mallick, Terrence, *To the Wonder* (2012), 112m
	Manchester, William, *Death of a President* (New York, NY: Harper & Row, 1967)
	Mancini, Michele & Perrella, Guiseppe (ed.) Reichenbach, Benedikt, *Pasolini's Bodies & Places* (Zürich: Patrick Frey, 2017)
(p.193)	Mahler, Gustav (as performed by Boulez, Pierre & the Wiener Philharmoniker), 'Symphony No. 5 In C Sharp Minor: IV.

Adagietto. Sehr langsam,' *Mahler: Symphony No.5* (Deutsche
Grammophon, 1997), 10m59

(pp.59, 61)   Mann, Michael, *Public Enemies* (2009), 140m

(p. 170)   Mann, Michael, *Vegas* (ABC, 1978–1981), 55m, *Episodic*

(p.178)   Manone, Wingy; Razaf, Andy; & Garland, Joe (as performed by Miller,
Glen and his Orchestra), (A) 'In the Mood' / (B) 'I Want to Be
Happy' (Bluebird, 1939), 3m40 / 3m11

Martin, Lerone A., *The Gospel of J. Edgar Hoover: How the FBI Aided
& Abetted the Rise of White Christian Nationalism* (Princeton,
NJ: Princeton University Press, 2023)

Marsh, James, *The Burger & the King* (1996), 60m

Matera, Dary, *John Dillinger: The Life & Death of America's First
Celebrity Criminal* (Boston, MA: Da Capo, 1995)

(pp.52, 58, 59, 106, 223)   Mayo, Archie, *The Petrified Forest* (1936), 82m

McGilligan, Patrick, *George Cukor: A Double Life, a Biography of the
Gentlemen Director* (New York, NY: St Martin's Press, 1991)

Meslay, Oliver; Barker, Scott Grant; Lubin, David M.; Nemerov,
Alexander; Longford, Nicola, *Hotel Texas: An Art Exhibition
for the President & Mrs. John F. Kennedy* (Dallas, TX: The Dallas
Museum of Art, 2013)

Milius, John, *Dillinger* (1973), 109m

(p.189)   Miller, Glenn (and his Orchestra), (A) 'Moonlight Serenade' /
(B) 'Sunrise Serenade (Bluebird, 1939), 3m22 / 3m27

(p.178)   Miller, George T. & Wincer, Simon, *Against the Wind* (Seven Network,
1978), 50m, *Episodic*

(pp.220, 269)   Moore, Alan (illustrated by Bolland, Brian & Higgins, John); ed.
O'Neil, Dennis, *Batman: The Killing Joke* (DC Comics, 1988)

(p.75)   Moore, William G & Burt, Robert M., *Captain Midnight* (CBS,
1954–1956), 30m, *Episodic*

Morley, Paul, *Joy Division: Piece by Piece, Writing about Joy Division,
1977–2007* (London: Plexus, 2008)

(p.191)   Moustaki, Georges, 'Le métèque,' *Le métèque* (Polydor, 1969), 2m23

(p.193)   Moustaki, Georges, 'Rue des Fosses Saint-Jacques,' *Le métèque*
(Polydor, 1969), 1m27

(p.193)   Mozart, Wolfgang Amadeus (as performed by Brown, Iona & the
Academy of St Martins in the Fields), 'Symphony No.33 In B-Flat
Major, K. 319: 1. Allegro assai,' *Symphony No.33 KV 319 / Serenade
No. 9 "Posthorn," KV 320* (Haenssler Classic, 2000), 5m51

(p.106)   Mulligan, Robert, *To Kill a Mockingbird* (1962), 129m

Mulvey, Laura, *Death 24x a Second* (London: Reaktion, 2006)

(p.44)   Murnau, F.W., *Nosferatu* (1922), 94m

(p.44)   Murnau, F.W., *The Last Laugh* (1924), 101m

(p.44)   Murnau, F.W. *Sunrise* (1927), 95m

(pp.42–49)   Murnau, F.W., *Tabu: A Story of the Sea* (1931), 86m

(p.191)   Nascimbene, Mario & The Minor Friars of San Damanio & Porzi-
uncola Assisi Choir (& the 20th Century Fox Studio Orchestra),
'Death of Francis,' 1m47 [see Curtiz, Michael, *Francis of Assisi*
(1961), 105m]

(p.191)   Nascimbene, Mario & The Minor Friars of San Damanio & Porzi-
uncola Assisi Choir (& the 20th Century Fox Studio Orchestra),
'Clara's Theme—Dressing of Clara,' 3m22 [see Curtiz, Michael,
Francis of Assisi (1961), 105m]

(p.191)   Nascimbene, Mario & The Minor Friars of San Damanio & Porzi-
uncola Assisi Choir (& the 20th Century Fox Studio Orchestra),
'Theme & Main Title,' 3m14 [see Curtiz, Michael, *Francis of
Assisi* (1961), 105m]

(pp.34–35)   Neilan, Marshall, *Daddy-Long-Legs* (1919), 85m
                Neroth, Pelle, *The Life & Death of Olof Palme: A Biography* (Independently Published, 2017)
(pp.196–199)   Nichols, Mike, *The Graduate* (1967), 106m
(p.170)   Nimmo, Stuart; Kay, Christopher; & McLeish, Graham, *The Electric Theatre Show* (LWT / Grampian, 1981), 30m, *Episodic*
(p.269)   Nolan, Christopher, *The Dark Knight* (2008), 152m
(p.171)   Norton, Roy, *Saturday Night at the Mill* (BBC, 1976–1981), 60m, *Episodic*
(p.129)   Ochs, Phil, *Rehearsals for Retirement* (A&M, 1969)
(p.129, 133)   Ochs, Phil, *Greatest Hits* (A&M, 1970)
(p.129)   Ochs, Phil, *Gunfight at Carnegie Hall* (A&M, 1970)
                Ochs, Phil, (ed.) Cohen, David, *I'm Gonna Say it Now: The Writings of Phil Ochs* (London: Backbeat Books, 2020)
(p.49)   Odar, Baran bo, Friese, Jantje, *Dark* (Netflix, 2017–2020), 1h, *Episodic*
(pp.200–205)   Osten, Suzanne, *Bröderna Mozart / The Mozart Brothers* (1986), 109m
(p.205)   Osten, Suzanne, *Skyddsängeln / The Guardian Angel* (1990), 108m
(p.166, 171)   Osterberg, James 'Iggy Pop' Newell, *The Idiot* (RCA, 1977)
                De Palma, Brian, *Carrie* (1977), 98m
                Parker, Chan, *My Life in E-Flat* (Columbia, SC: University of South Carolina Press, 2021)
(p.114)   Pasolini, Pier Paolo, *Le ceneri di Gramsci / Gramsci's Ashes* (Milan: Garzanti, 1957)
                Pasolini, Pier Paolo, *Mamma Roma* (1962), 106m
                Pasolini, Pier Paolo, *Il vangelo secondo Matteo / The Gospel According to St. Matthew* (1964), 137m
(pp.114–115)   Pasolini, Pier Paolo, *Uccellacci e uccellini / Hawks & Sparrows* (1966), 88m
(pp.112–121, 205)   Pasolini, Pier Paolo, *Edipo re / Oedipus Rex* (1967), 104m
(pp.115,116,120–121)   Pasolini, Pier Paolo, *Salò o le 120 giornate di Sodoma / Salò, or the 120 Days of Sodom* (1975), 116m
                Pasolini, Pier Paolo, *Una vita violenta* (1959) / tr. Weaver, William, *A Violent Life* (Manchester, Carcanet, 2007)
                Pasolini, Pier Paolo, *Ragazza di vita* (1955) / tr. Goldstein, Ann, *The Street Kids* (New York, NY: Europa, 2016)
                Pawel, Ernst, *The Nightmare of Reason: A Life of Franz Kafka* (New York, NY: Farrar, Straus & Giroux, 1984)
(p.75)   Pelletier, Louis & Spier, William, *Willy* (CBS, 1954–1955), 22m, *Episodic*
(p.143)   Penniman, 'Little' Richard Wayne & Dorthy LaBostrie (as performed by Presley, Elvis), 'Tutti Frutti,' *Elvis Presley* (RCA Victor, 1956), 2m01
(p.260)   Petit, Chris, *Chinese Boxes* (1984), 87m
(p.269)   Philips, Todd, *The Hangover* (2009), 100m
(pp.266–267, 269)   Philips, Todd, *Joker* (2019), 122m
                Poulsen, Ellen, & Hyde, Lori, *Chasing Dillinger: Police Captain Matt Leach, J. Edgar Hoover & the Rivalry to Capture Public Enemy No.1* (Jefferson, NC: Exposit, 2018)
(p.189)   Prieto, Joaquin; Vance, Paul; & Pockriss, Lee (as performed by The Walker Brothers, 'In My Room', *Portrait* (Phillips, 1966), 2m34
                Presley, Priscilla, *Elvis & Me* (New York, NY: Putnam, 1985)
(p.75)   Pritchett, Harry (Sr,); Wyckoff, Ed, *Winky Dink & You* (CBS, 1953–1957), 30m, *Episodic*
(p.156)   Putman, Curly (as performed by Presley, Elvis), 'Green Green Grass of Home,' *Today* (RCA, 1975)

(p.191)   Quinn, Freddy, 'Unter fremden Sternen,' *Freddy e seus maiores sucessos* (Polydor, 1958), 2m47

(p.191)   Raben, Peer & Wilde, Oscar (A) 'Each Man Kills the Things He Loves,' as performed by Moreau, Jeanne / (B) Raven, Peer & Moreau, Jeanne, 'Young and Joyful Bandit,' as performed by Kaufmann, Günther, *Querelle* (Carosello, 1983), 2m50 [see Fassbinder, Rainer Werner, *Querelle* (1982), 108m]

(p.191)   Raben, Peer & Ambach, David, (as performed by Moreau, Jeanne), 'Men are at Peace,' 3m20 [see Fassbinder, Rainer Werner, *Querelle* (1982), 108m]

(p.191)   Raben, Peer & Ambach, David, 'Sailor's Accordion,' 2m12 [see Fassbinder, Rainer Werner, *Querelle* (1982), 108m]

(p.193)   Raben, Peer & Ambach, David, 'The Tears of the Lady,' 2m17 [see Fassbinder, Rainer Werner, *Querelle* (1982), 108m]

(p.171)   Radosh, Steven, *Catchphrase* (ITV, 1986 & on), 30 / 45 / 60m

(p.273)   Rafelson, Bob, *Head* (1968), 86m

(pp.269–270, 273)   Rafelson, Bob, *Five Easy Pieces* (1970), 98m

(pp.269–270)   Rafelson, Bob, *The King of Marvin Gardens* (1972), 104m

(p.268)   Rafelson, Bob, *Stay Hungry* (1976), 102m

(pp.46, 268, 269)   Rafelson, Bob, *The Postman Always Rings Twice* (1981), 122m

(p. 269)   Rafelson, Bob, *Porn.com* (2002), 28m

(p. 244)   Ramis, Harold, *Multiplicity* (1996), 117m

(p. 189)   Ram, Buck (as performed by The Platters), (A) 'The Great Pretender' / (B) Gottlieb, Seymour, 'I'm Just a Dancing Partner' (Mercury, 1955), 2m36 / 2m15

(p. 189)   Rapp, Tom (as performed by Pearls Before Swine), 'Morning Song,' *One Nation Underground* (ESP-Disk, 1967), 4m10

(p. 224)   Rapper, Irving, *Now, Voyager* (1942), 117m

(p. 91)   Ray, Nicholas, *55 Days at Peking* (1963), 154m

(p. 244)   Rash, Steve, *Eddie* (1996), 100m

(p. 203)   Reed, Carol, *The Third Man* (1949), 104m

(p. 228)   Reiner, Rob, *This is Spinal Tap* (1984), 82m

(p. 194)   Renoir, Jean, *The Woman on the Beach* (1947), 71m

(p. 90)   Resnais, Alain, *L'Année dernière à Marienbad / Last Year at Marienbad* (1961), 94m

(pp.151, 152)   Rich, John, *Roustabout* (1964), 101m

            Rich, Nathaniel, 'The Passion of Pasolini,' *The New York Review of Books* (September 27, 2007)

(pp.93–94)   Richardson, Tony, *Tom Jones* (1963), 128m

(p.90)   Rieber, Alfred & Nelson, Robert, *A Study of the USSR & Communism* (Chicago, IL: Scott, Foresman, 1962)

(p.145)   Robbins, Harold, *A Stone for Danny Fisher* (Alfred A. Knopf, 1952)

            Robertson, James C., *The Casablanca Man: The Cinema of Michael Curtiz* (London: Psychology Press, 1993)

            Rode, Allan K., *Michael Curtiz: A Life in Film* (Lexington, KY: University Press of Kentucky, 2017)

(p.96)   Robins, Jerome & Wise, Robert, *West Side Story* (1961), 153m

(p.144)   Robinson, Timothy J. (as performed by Presley, Elvis), 'Let's Have a Party,' *Loving You* (RCA Victor, 1957), 1m31

(p.150)   Roberts, Bob & Batchelor, Ruth (as performed by Presley, Elvis), 'Because of Love,' *Girls! Girls! Girls!* (RCA Victor, 1962), 2m32

(p.149)   Roberts, Bob & Batchelor, Ruth (as performed by Presley, Elvis), 'Thanks to the Rolling Sea,' *Girls! Girls! Girls!* (RCA Victor, 1962), 1m29

(p.75)   Rogers, Richard & Hart, Lorenz, *A Connecticut Yankee* (Televised Performance, NBC, 1955) (pp.138, 242, 246, 261) Roddenbury, Gene, *Star Trek* (NBC, 1966–1969), 30m, *Episodic*

(p.159) Ronk, Dave Van, 'Hang Me, Oh Hang Me,' *Folksinger* (Prestige International, 1962), 3m02

(p.193) Rosas, Juventino (as performed by Nazarov, Nikolai & the First Separate Exemplary Orchestra of USSR Defence Ministry), 'Over the Waves,' *Old Waltzes Performed by a Soviet Army Brass Band* (RCD, 1998), 6m55

(p.143) Rose, Vincent (as performed by Presley, Elvis), 'Blueberry Hill,' *Loving You* (RCA Victor, 1957), 2m39

(p.191) Rota, Nino, 'Amarcord,' 13m17, *Amarcord* (RCA Red Seal, 1974) [see Felini, Federico, *Amarcord* (1973), 127m]

(p.91) Rowland, Roy, *The 5000 Fingers of Dr. T* (1953), 92m

(pp.152, 153) Sagal, Boris, *Girl Happy* (1965), 96m

Sarris, Andrew, 'The Man in The Glass Closet,' *The New York Times* (December 15, 1991), Sect.7, p.1

Schlesinger, Jr., Arthur M., *A Thousand Days: John F. Kennedy in the White House* (Boston, MA: Houghton Mifflin Harcourt, 2002)

(p.193) Schubert, Franz (as performed by Heino), 'Am Brunnen vor dem Tore,' *Die schönsten deutschen Volkslieder* (Electrola, 1972), 2m58

(p.193) Schuricke, Rudi (as performed by Hain, Magda), 'Capri-Fischer, Serenade' (Odeon, 1943), 3m16

(p.231) Van Sant, Gus, *Elephant* (2003), 81m

(p.228) Van Sant, Gus, *Last Days* (2005), 97m

(pp.106) Schaffner, Franklin J., *Patton* (1970), 172m

(pp.38–39) Schnitzler, Arthur, *Das weite Land / The Distant Land* (1908, published 1911); see *The Vast Country: A Tragicomedy in Five Acts*, in (ed.) Heinz Ludwig Arnold, *Arthur Schnitzler: Comedy of Seduction, Timepieces 1909–1924* (Frankfurt: S. Fischer Verlag, 1961), pp.7–124.

(p.39) Schnitzler, Arthur, *Der Weg ins Freie / The Road to the Open* (Berlin: S. Fischer, 1908)

(p.38) Schnitzler, Arthur, *Traumnovelle / Dream Story* (Berlin: S. Fischer Verlag, 1908)

(p.228) Scholz, Tom (as performed by Boston), (A) 'More Than a Feeling' / (B) 'Smokin'' (Epic, 1976), 3m25 / 4m45

(p.148) Schroeder, Aaron & McFarland, J. Leslie (as performed by Presley, Elvis), 'Stuck on You,' *Elvis is Back!* (RCA Victor, 1960), 2m20

Schumacher, Michael, *There but for the Fortune: The Life of Phil Ochs* (Westport, CT: Hyperion, 1996)

(p.119) Schwartz, Barth David, *Pasolini Requiem* (Ann Arbor, MI: University of Michigan Press, 1992)

(pp.104, 125) Scorsese, Martin, *Taxi Driver* (1976), 114m

(p.139) Seaton, George, *Miracle on 34th Street* (1947), 96m

(p.105) Seiler, Lewis, *Murder in the Air* (1940), 55m

(p.91) Sellers, Peter, *Mr. Topaze* (1961), 97m

Sermak, Kathryn, *Miss D & Me: Life with the Invincible Bette Davis* (New York, NY: Hachette Book, 2017)

Shakespeare, Nicholas, *Bruce Chatwin* (New York, NY: Anchor Books, 2001)

Siciliano, Enzo, tr. Shepley, John, *Pasolini: A Biography* (New York, NY: Random House, 1982)

Siegel, Don, *The Lineup* (1958), 87m

(p.147) Siegel, Don, *Flaming Star* (1960), 92m

(p.147) Siegel, Don, *Dirty Harry* (1971), 102m

(p.147) Siegel, Don, *Escape from Alcatraz* (1979), 112m

Sikov, Ed, *Mr Strangelove: A Biography of Peter Sellers* (London: Pan Macmillan, 2003)

(p.187) Sirk, Douglas, *Written on the Wind* (1956), 99m

(p.38) Smith, John, *Blight* (1996), 15m

Smith, Steven C., *A Fire at Heart's Centre: The Life & Music of Bernard Herrmann* (Berkeley, CA: University of California Press, 2002)

(p.247) Soderbergh, Steven, *Gray's Anatomy* (1997), 80m

Sorenson, Ted, *Counsellor: A Life at the Edge of History* (New York, NY: Harper, 2008)

(p.193) Spohr, Louis (as performed by Baker, Margaret; Schumacher, Rainer; & Reutter, Hermann, '6 Deutsche Lieder, Op.103: No.4, Wiegenlied,' *Spohr: 6 Deutsche Lieder, Op.103* (SWR Classic Archive, 2019), 3m30

Stanley, Billy, *The Faith of Elvis* (Edinburgh: Thomas Nelson, 2022)

(p.244) Stanley, Richard, & Frankenheimer, John, *The Island of Dr. Moreau* (1996), 96m

(p.153) Star, Randy (as performed by Presley, Elvis), 'Old MacDonald,' *Double Trouble* (RCA Victor, 1967)

(pp.64–273) Steinberg, Jonathan E., Levine, Robert, *The Old Man* (Disney, One Season to Date, 2022), 47–64m, *Episodic*

(p.191) Steiner, Max (& the National Philharmonic Orchestra), 'Four Wives —Symphonie Moderne,' 8m17 [see Curtiz, Michael, *Four Wives* (1939), 110m]

(p.191) Steiner, Max (& The Warner Bros. Studio Orchestra), 'As Time Goes By,' *Casablanca* (Turner Classic Movies & Rhino Records, 1997), 4m57 [see Curtiz, Michael, *Casablanca* (1942), 102m]

(p.191) Steiner, Max (& The Warner Bros. Studio Orchestra), 'Play It Sam... Play "As Time Goes By",' *Casablanca* (Turner Classic Movies & Rhino Records, 1997), 4m57 [see Curtiz, Michael, *Casablanca* (1942), 102m]

(p.68) Stephanitz, Max von, *Der deutsche Schäferhund in Wort und Bild / tr. Rev. C. Charke, The German Shepherd Dog in Word & Picture* (Augsburg: Vereins für deutsche Schäferhunde, 1901, 1921; Jena: Anton Kämpfe, 1923)

Stewart, Tony, *Dillinger, the Hidden Truth: A Tribute to Gangsters & G-Men of the Great Depression Era* (Independently Published, 2015)

Stocklassa, Jan, tr. Chase, Tara F., *The Man Who Played with Fire: Stieg Larsson's Lost Files & the Hunt for an Assassin* (Seattle, WA: Amazon Crossing, 2019)

Stone, Oliver, *JFK* (1991), 206m

(p.189) Strauss II, Johann, Berliner Philharmoniker, 'An der schönen blauen Donau,' *An der schönen blauen Donau* (Deutsche Grammophon, 1982), 11m47

(p.193) Suicide, 'Frankie Teardrop,' *Suicide* (Red Star, 1977), 10m24

(p.75) Tanner, Jerome, *Funny Boners* (NBC, 1954–1955), 30m, *Episodic*

(p.104) Tarantino, Quentin, *Kill Bill (Vol.1, 2003; Vol.11, 2004)* 111m, 137m

(p.205) Tarkovsky, Andrei, *Offret / The Sacrifice* (1986), 142m

(pp.149–150) Taurog, Norman, *Girls! Girls! Girls!* (1962), 106m

(p.153) Taurog, Norman, *Double Trouble* (1967), 92m

(p.154) Taurog, Norman, *Speedway* (1968), 94m

(p.148) Tepper, Sid & Bennett, Roy C. (as performed by Presley, Elvis), 'Ito Eats,' *Blue Hawaii* (RCA Victor, 1961), 1m29

(p.149) Tepper, Sid & Bennett, Roy C. (as performed by Presley, Elvis), 'Song of the Shrimp,' *Girls! Girls! Girls!* (RCA Victor, 1962), 2m20 (p.150) Tepper, Sid & Bennett, Roy C. (as performed by Presley, Elvis), 'Vino Dinero Y Amor,' *Fun in Acapulco* (RCA Victor, 1963), 1m55

(p.152) Tepper, Sid & Bennett, Roy C. (as performed by Presley, Elvis), 'It's a Wonderful World,' *Roustabout* (RCA Victor, 1964), 1m50

(p.189) Tillis, Mel (as performed by Rogers, Kenny & The First Edition), 'Ruby, Don't Take Your Gun to Town,' *Ruby, Don't Take Your Gun to Town* (Reprise, 1969), 2m58

(pp.98–101) Topper, Burt, *War is Hell* (1961), 81m

(p.96) Thompson, J. Lee, *Guns of Navarone* (1961)

(pp.162–172) Thompson, J. Lee, *Cape Fear* (1962), 106m

(p.150) Thorpe, Richard, *Fun in Acapulco* (1963), 97m

Toland, John, *The Dillinger Days* (New York, NY: Random House, 1963)

(p.70) Tolstoy, Leo, *Война и миръ* / tr. Clara Bell, *War & Peace* (Moscow: The Russian Messenger, [Serialised, 1865–1867]; New York: Gottsberger, 1886)

(p.90) Truffaut, Francois, *Jules et Jim* / *Jules & Jim* (1962), 105m

(p.90) Vajda, Ladislao, *It Happened in Broad Daylight* (1958), 100m

(p.193) Verdi, Guiseppe (as performed by Pavarotti, Luciano, The London Opera Chorus, National Philharmonic Orchestra), 'La traviata / Act 1: Un dì felice, eterea,' *Verdi: La Traviata* (Decca, 1981), 6m09

(p.82) Vian, Boris, *L'Écume des jours* / tr. Chapman, Stanley, *Froth on the Daydream* (Paris: Gallimard, 1947; London: Rapp & Carroll, 1967)

(p.84) Vian, Boris, 'Le Déserteur' / 'The Deserter' (as performed by Mouloudji, Marcel in concert, May 7, 1954)

(pp.83–85) Vian, Boris, (under pseudonym, Sullivan, Vernon), *J'irai cracher sur vos tombes* / tr. Rosenthal, Milton, *I Spit on your Graves* (Paris: Éditions du Scorpion, 1946; New York, NY: Audubon Books, 1971)

Vian, Boris, see (eds.) Rolls, Alistair; West-Sooby, John; & Fornasiero, Jean, (tr.) Freij, Maria, Hodges, Peter, *If I Say If: The Poems & Short Stories of Boris Vian* (Adelaide: The University of Adelaide Press, 2014)

Vian, Boris, tr. Older, Julia, *Boris Vian Invents Boris Vian* (Boston, MA: Black Widow Press, 2015)

Vian, Boris & Dudognon, Georges, tr. Knobloch, Paul, *Boris Vian's Manual of Saint Germain des Pres* (New York, NY: Rizzoli, 2004)

Viertel, Salka, *The Kindness of Strangers* (New York, NY: Holt, Rinehart, & Winston, 1969)

Viertel, Salka, tr. Bradford, Terry, *Vercoquin et le plankton* / *Vercoquin & the Plankton* (Cambridge, MA: Wakefield Press, 2022)

Virilio, Paul, *Guerre et Cinéma: Logistique de la perception* / tr. Camiler, Patrick, *War & Cinema: The Logistics of Perception* (London: Verso, 1989)

(p.117) Visconti, Luchino, *Bellissima* (1951), 114m

(p.61) Vukelich, George, *The Last Menominee* (1966), 29m

Wainwright, Rupert, *Dillinger* (1991), 90m

(pp.59, 149) Walsh, Raoul, *High Sierra* (1941), 95m

(p.149) Walsh, Raoul, *They Drive by Night* (1940), 93m

(p.59) Walsh, Raoul, *Colorado Territory* (1949), 94m

(p.82) Walters, Jennifer, 'Death and Boris Vian,' *Papers on Language and Literature*, 8 (1972)

(p.228) Waters, John, *Pink Flamingos* (1972), 92m

(p.121) Waters, John, *Prayer to Pasolini* (Sub Pop, 2021), 17m04

(p.170) Warren, Tony, *Coronation Street* (Granada, 1960 & on), 30 / 60m, *Episodic*

(p.151)	Weisman, Ben & Wayne, Sid (as performed by Presley, Elvis), 'It's Carnival Time,' *Roustabout* (RCA Victor, 1964), 1m34
(p.153)	Weisman, Ben; Fuller, Dolores; & Wayne, Sid (as performed by Presley, Elvis), 'Do the Clam,' *Girl Happy* (RCA Victor, 1965), 3m16
(p.154)	Weisman, Ben & Wayne, Sid (as performed by Presley, Elvis), 'He's Your Uncle, Not Your Dad,' *Speedway* (RCA Victor, 1968), 2m28
(p.154)	Weisman, Ben-; Kaye, Buddy; & Fuller, Daniel (as performed by Presley, Elvis), 'Have a Happy,' *Change of Habit* (RCA Victor, 1969)
(p.92)	Weill, Kurt & Anderson, Maxwell (as performed by Huston, Walter), (A) 'September Song' / (B) 'The Scars' (Columbia Records, 1938), 2m51 / 2m42
(p.187)	Welles, Orson, *Touch of Evil* (1958), 111m
	Welles, Orson, *The Trial* (1962), 118m
(p.202)	Welles, Orson, *F for Fake* (1973), 88m
(p.47)	Wellman, William A., *A Star is Born* (1937), 111m
(p.228)	Wenders, Wim, *Paris, Texas* (1984), 147m
(pp.218–224)	Whale, James, *Waterloo Bridge* (1931), 81m
(pp.155, 159)	White, Tony Joe (as performed by Presley, Elvis), 'Polk Salad Annie,' *On Stage* (RCA, 1970), 4m50
(p.92)	Wilder, Billy, *Sunset Boulevard* (1950), 115m
(p.187–188)	Wilder, Robert, *Flamingo Road* (New York: G.P. Putnam's Sons, 1942)
(p.156)	Williams Sr., Hank (as performed by Presley, Elvis), 'Jambalaya,' *Evening Show* (Civic Centre, Lake Charles, LA); *Southern Nights* (1975, RCA Victor, 2006)
(p.166)	Wilson, Tony, *24 Hour Party People* (London: Pan Macmillan, 2003)
(pp.165–166)	Winterbottom, Michael, *24 Hour Party People* (2002), 117m
(pp.145–146)	Wise, Fred & Weisman, Ben (as performed by Presley, Elvis & White, Kitty), 'Crawfish,' *King Creole* (RCA Victor, 1958)
(p.208)	Wise, Robert, *Helen of Troy* (1956), 118m
(pp.206–210)	Wise, Robert, *I Want to Live!* (1958), 120m
(p.242)	Wise, Robert, *The Sound of Music* (1965), 174m
	Wolfe, Tom, *The Electric Kool Aid Acid Test* (New York, NY: Farrar, Straus & Giroux, 1968)
(p.147)	Wyche, Sidney & Schroeder, Aaron H. (as performed by Presley, Elvis), 'A Big Hunk O' Love,' *50,000,000 Elvis Fans Can't Be Wrong: Elvis' Gold Records, Vol.2* (RCA Victor, 1959)
(p.208)	Wyler, William, *Ben Hur* (1959), 212m
(p.104)	Wyler, William, *The Collector* (1965), 119m
(pp.258–263)	Yakin, Boaz, *Remember the Titans* (2000), 113m
(pp.89, 140)	Young, Terrence, *Dr. No* (1962), 110m
(pp.86–110, 140, 176)	Young, Terrence, *From Russia with Love* (1963), 115m
(p.105)	Young, Terrence, *Thunderball* (1965), 130m
(p.231)	Young, Neil, 'My My, Hey Hey (Out of the Blue),' *Rust Never Sleeps* (Reprise, 1979), 3m45
(pp.44, 91)	Zinnemann, Fred, *High Noon* (1952), 85m
(p.178)	Zinnemann, Fred, *Oklahoma!* (1955), 145m
(p.208)	Zinnemann, Fred, *The Nun's Story* (1959), 152m
	Zischler, Hanns, *Kafka Goes to the Movies* (Chicago, IL: University of Chicago Press, 2003)
(p.193)	Von Zuccalmaglio, Anton Wilhelm (as performed by Heino), 'Kein Schöner Land,' *Kein schöner Land in dieser Zeit* (Columbia, 1967), 2m14
(p.177)	Various, *Best Sellers* (NBC, 1976), Various Running Time(s), *Episodic*
(p.170)	Various, *Match of the Day* (BBC, 51 Seasons to Date, 1964 & on), *Episodic*

Various, tr. Marešova, Soňa, *The Prague Golem: Jewish Stories of the Ghetto* (Vitalis, 2000)

Various, 'Nigers Wodaabe People of the Taboo,' *National Geographic*, Vol.164, No.4 (The National Geographic Society, October 1983)

(p.189)   Traditional (arranged & performed by Presley, Elvis), 'Santa Lucia,' *Elvis for Everyone!* (RCA Victor, 1965), 1m11

(Endless.)

LIBERATION (*grol*) THROUGH HEARING (*thos*)
IN THE INTERMEDIATE STATE (*bardo*)

The author and editor invite you to contribute further entries
for prospective inclusion in future, multimedia iterations of this
project. Please send notes on the disappeared and the deceased,
with proof of their last movie, to editors@tenementpress.com /
(cc) mail@purge.xxx with the subject heading 'Bardo Thodol.'
These uncollected 'Last Movies' and honourable mentions will
be maintained in a (digital) safe deposit box, and published
in due course.

(Acknowledgments & dedications.)

For the gift of life and the promise of death I thank my parents. For their engagement and encouragement I thank Dominic Jaeckle, Erika Balsom, Iain Sinclair, Nicole Brenez, Bill Drummond, Chris Petit, Ian Greaves, Ben Rivers, Eleni Gioti, Matthew Stuart, Andrew Walsh-Lister, Gabriela Soares, Clodagh Kinsella; as ever, Gareth Evans, and especially Matilda Munro. For his assistance researching the films and their dead I thank James Norton. For support in developing this project as a durational public programme I thank Guilherme Blanc, Lidia Quierós, and Ana David, along with Hugo Ramos, Joana Galhardas, and the audience of 101 (who stayed from the start to the end) at Batalha Centro de Cinema. *Sin fin.* I also thank CM von Hausswolff, Laura Mulvey, Sukhdev Sandhu, Ehsan Khoshbakht, Thomas Beard, Ed Halter, and all those who have assisted the project in some way, and all those from whose passionate and strange work I've drawn: the writers, researchers, filmmakers, stars, *ad infinitum.*
    Schtinter, MMXXIII

Stanley Schtinter has been described as an 'artist' by the *Daily Mail* and as an 'exorcist' by the *Daily Star*.

Erika Balsom is a Reader in Film Studies at King's College London, and the author of four books, including TEN SKIES (Fireflies Press, 2021).

Bill Drummond's personal three word strap line is still 'Best Before Death.' He is the co-creator of the People's Pyramid, and responsible for *The 25 Paintings* twelve-year world tour.

Nicole Brenez is Professor of Film Studies at the University of Sorbonne nouvelle, curator of the Cinémathèque française's avant-garde film series and Director of the Analysis & Culture Department at the Femis (Paris).

Clodagh Kinsella is a travel writer and French-to-English translator who embodies the continental drift. Her translations include Michèle Bernstein's *The Night* (Book Works, 2013, 2021), and Nicole Brenez's *We Support Everything since the Dawn of Time That Has Struggled and Still Struggles* (Sternberg Press, 2015).

Last Movies
Stanley Schtinter

Stanley Schtinter, © 2023.

Last Movies was first published in the United Kingdom
by Tenement Press, 2023, edited by Dominic J. Jaeckle, and
designed and typeset by Traven T. Croves (Matthew Stuart
& Andrew Walsh-Lister).

All 'character' portraits (pp.30, 37, 40, 42, 50, 64, 72, 78, 86, 97,
112, 122, 126, 136, 162, 174, 180, 196, 200, 206, 212, 218, 226, 240, 252,
258, 264, 274) are public domain, care of Wikipedia; p.17 carries
a photograph of a re-enactment of the death of John Dillinger,
a creative collaboration (or fabrication) between Warner Bros.
and the Federal Bureau of Investigation (date unknown, National Archives and Records Administration), © Tallandier / courtesy
of Bridgeman Images, 2023; p.25 carries a photograph of the
audience assembled outside the Biograph Theatre (Chicago, IL)
on July 22, 1934, shortly after the death of Dillinger. Associated
Press (public domain).

The rights of Stanley Schtinter to be identified as author of
this work have been asserted in accordance with Section 77
of the Copyright, Designs and Patents Act 1988. All efforts to
identify copyright and secure permissions have been pursued
where necessary and possible; fair dealing of works is listed
in Section 30A, Schedule 2 (2A) of the Copyright, Designs
and Patents Act 1988.

Erika Balsom's programme notes, 'Killing Time,' were first
commissioned by Schtinter to accompany a screening held at
the Batalha Centro de Cinema (Porto, Portugal), April 29 to
April 30, 2023 (Erika Balsom, © 2023), pp.19–23; Bill Drummond's
'INTERMISSION' is excerpted from a correspondence with
Schtinter, Summer 2023 (Bill Drummond, © 2023), pp.157–160;
Nicole Brenez's afterword, 'Last Instants,' was translated from
the French by Clodagh Kinsella and commissioned for this
publication (Nicole Brenez, © 2023; English language copyright, Brenez & Kinsella, © 2023), pp.279–291. Drummond and
Brenez's works appear in this volume for the first time.

Libera me, Domine, de morte æterna, in die illa tremenda / Quando cœli movendi sunt et terra / Dum veneris iudicare sæculum per ignem. / Tremens factus sum ego, et timeo, dum discussio venerit, atque ventura ira / Quando cœli movendi sunt et terra. / Dies illa, dies iræ, calamitatis et miseriæ, dies magna et amara valde / Dum veneris iudicare sæculum per ignem. / Requiem æternam dona eis, Domine: et lux perpetua luceat eis.

The entries on Rainer Werner Fassbinder and Olof Palme were first published (in variation) in Vol. IV of the annual *Prototype Anthology* (ed. Jess Chandler, 2023), pp.44–53, and issue 0.04 of the *Swedenborg Review* (ed. Gareth Evans, Autumn 2022), pp.18–19.

Stickered editions are adorned with a study of John Dillinger's death mask (forged following Dillinger's death in 1934) care of the Bureau's ongoing '#Artifactofthemonth' social media series. The creation of the 'mask' is attributed to one Harold May... 'Just 12 hours after Dillinger's death on July 22, 1934, Harold May of the Reliance Dental Manufacturing Co. created this death mask of Dillinger's face at the Cook County Morgue in Chicago to demonstrate the quality of [his] company's plaster.' A limited hardback edition of this title, co-published with purge.xxx, was published in the Autumn months of 2023 and carries a negative, 'glow-in-the-dark' iteration of May's 'fossil' Dillinger. Image care of the Federal Bureau of Investigation / Wikimedia Commons, 2023. As a work pertaining to the US federal government, the image is in the public domain.

A CIP record for this publication is available from the British Library.

Tenement Press 10, MMXXIII
ISBN 978-1-7393851-1-8

Printed and bound by Lulu.
Typeset in Arnhem Pro Blond.

Tenement Press is an occasional publisher of esoteric;
experimental;
accidental;
and interdisciplinary literatures.

www.tenementpress.com
editors@tenementpress.com

www.ingramcontent.com/pod-product-compliance
Lightning Source LLC
Chambersburg PA
CBHW031608210526
45464CB00004B/1482